£49·95

The Political Economy of the Minimal State

THE LOCKE INSTITUTE

Founded in 1989, The Locke Institute is an independent, non-partisan, educational and research organization. The Institute is named for John Locke (1632–1704), philosopher and political theorist, who based his theory of society on natural law which required that the ultimate source of political sovereignty was with the individual. Individuals are possessed of inalienable rights variously defined by Locke as 'life, health, liberty and possession', or, more directly, 'life, liberty and property'. It is the function of the state to uphold these rights since individuals would not enter into a political society unless they believed that it would protect their lives, liberties and properties.

The Locke Institute seeks to engender a greater understanding of the concept of natural rights, its implications for constitutional democracy and for economic organization in modern society. The Institute encourages high-quality research utilizing in particular modern theories of property rights, public choice, law and economics, and the new institutional economics as a basis for a more profound understanding of important and controversial issues in political economy. To this end, it commissions books, monographs, and shorter studies involving substantive scholarship written for a wider audience, organizes major conferences on fundamental topics in political economy, and supports independent research. The Institute maintains a publishing relationship with Edward Elgar, the international publisher in the social sciences.

In order to maintain independence, The Locke Institute accepts no government funding. Funding for the Institute is solicited from private foundations, corporations, and individuals. In addition, the Institute raises funds from the sale of publications and from conference fees. The Institute is incorporated in the State of Virginia, USA. The Institution is a non-profit educational organization recognized under Section 501(c)(3) of the US Internal Revenue Code.

Officers of the Institute are listed above. Please direct all enquiries to the address given below.

4084 University Drive, Suite 103 • Fairfax, Virginia 22030, US
(703) 934-6960

The Political Economy of the Minimal State

Edited by

Charles K. Rowley

General Director
The Locke Institute
and
Professor of Economics
George Mason University

The Shaftesbury Papers

Edward Elgar
Cheltenham, UK • Brookfield, US

Published by
Edward Elgar Publishing Limited
8 Lansdown Place
Cheltenham
Glos GL50 2HU
UK

Edward Elgar Publishing Company
Old Post Road
Brookfield
Vermont 05036
US

British Library Cataloguing in Publication Data
The political economy of the minimal state. – (The
 Shaftesbury papers)
 1. Economics
 I. Series   II. Rowley, Charles K. (Charles Kershaw), 1939–.
 Charles K.
 330. 1

Library of Congress Cataloguing in Publication Data
The Political economy of the minimal state / edited by Charles K.
 Rowley.
        — (The Shaftesbury papers)
        Combines the also separately published volumes 5–8 of The Locke
 Institute's series. The Shaftesbury papers, along with an
introductory chapter written for this volume.
        "Made possible by a colloquium ... on the theme of 'Ethics,
 Liberty and Markets' held ... in Boston, Massachusetts in June 1993" —
 Pref.
        Contents: Before resorting to politics / Anthony de Jasay —
 Classical liberalism in the age of post-communism / Norman Barry —
 Adam Smith into the twenty-first century / Edwin G. West — Economic
 policy in a liberal democracy / Richard E. Wagner.
        1. Free enterprise—Congresses.   2. Economic policy—Congresses.
 3. Liberalism—Congresses.   4. Individualism—Congresses.
 I. Rowley, Charles Kershaw.   II. Series.
 HB95.P593   1996
 338.9—dc20   95–40192
 ISBN 1 85898 199 9   CIP
 Typeset by Manton Typesetters, 5–7 Eastfield Road, Louth, Lincolnshire LN11 7AJ, UK.
Printed in Great Britain at the University Press, Cambridge

Contents

Contributors

NORMAN BARRY   Professor of Politics at the University of Buckingham.

ANTHONY DE JASAY   Independent scholar located in Paluel, France.

CHARLES K. ROWLEY   General Director of The Locke Institute and Professor of Economics at George Mason University. Co-Editor of *Public Choice*.

RICHARD E. WAGNER   Education Director of Center for Study of Public Choice and Holbert L. Harris Professor of Economics at George Mason University. Co-Editor of *Constitutional Political Economy*.

EDWIN G. WEST   Professor Emeritus of Economics at Carleton University.

Preface

This book brings together four papers published separately in paperback form by The Locke Institute in *The Shaftesbury Paper Series* coordinated by a substantive introductory chapter. The book was made possible by a colloquium generously funded by The Liberty Fund Inc. on the theme of 'Ethics, Liberty and Markets' held under my direction in Boston, Massachusetts in June 1993. The book would not have been completed without the financial support of the Lynde and Harry Bradley Foundation. The Locke Institute is grateful also to the Sunmark Foundation, and to two anonymous donors for invaluable financial support. I am personally grateful for the stimulating intellectual environment provided by The Atlas Economic Research Foundation and for the generous personal support provided by Dr Alejandro Chafuen and his colleagues.

For
Amanda and Sarah

Who will help to carry the torch of liberty on its next lap

What is Living and What is Dead in Classical Liberalism

Introduction

The momentous upheaval in Eastern Europe in 1989, followed by the complete disintegration of the USSR, did not usher in the 'end of history' as claimed by overly-enthusiastic Western commentators such as Fukuyama (1992) in the first wave of euphoria over the collapse of Marxist–Leninist dogma. However, as James Buchanan (1991) noted, it did end a vision of socioeconomic political reality based on collectivist-socialist ideas. It is now possible to analyse the complexities of social interaction among individuals without regard to the collectivist-socialist shadow that has been cast over such discussions for the better part of the 20th century.

It is especially important, in such circumstances, that those who place a high value on individual freedom do not become complacent about their cause. On the one hand, the collapse of the Soviet Empire has provided unequivocal evidence that socialism cannot create wealth and cannot tolerate liberty. If the proposition is accepted that ideas have consequences, then the failure of the socialist idea should open up opportunities for halting and reversing the drift towards collectivization in the advanced Western democracies. On the other hand, false complacency among pro-market scholars and advocates, based on unfounded notions that the philosophic and economic debate has ended in a decisive victory, may lower the vigilance that is continuously necessary to protect liberty against the forces of mercantilism.

As Buchanan (1991) has observed, the demise of socialism has discredited, perhaps forever, the appeal of 'politics in the large' in the sense of the centrally planned and controlled economy in which individuals must seek their own realization as integral components of a socialist community. However, the demise of socialism does not seem to have discredited the appeal of 'politics in the small' in the sense of piece-by-piece interference with market processes. The electorate in its majority has not come to any robust acceptance of the notion that, if politicization does not work when applied over all markets, then it will not work in the case of particular markets, taken one at a time.

In large part, this hesitancy is explained by pressures of public choice. In not inconsiderable measure, however, it is reinforced by a failure of conviction or of continuing resolve among classical liberal scholars including those who once were the intellectual giants of the classical liberal movement. It is the principal purpose of this book to review the determinants of this failure of resolve and to restate in clear and compelling terms the classical liberal case for the minimal state.

In Retreat from Utopia

In 1974, Robert Nozick challenged the most commonly held political and social positions of that time – liberal democrat, socialist and conservative – by reasserting that individuals have rights and that there are things that no person or group may do to them without violating their rights. So strong and far-reaching are these rights that they raise the question of what, if anything, the state and its officials may do.

His main conclusions were that a minimal state, limited to the narrow functions of protection against force, theft and fraud and concerned with the enforcement of contracts, is justified; that any more extensive state must violate individuals' rights to do certain things, and is unjustified; and that the minimal state is *inspiring* as well as right. Two noteworthy implications are that the state may not use its coercive apparatus for the purpose of requiring some citizens to aid others; or in order to prohibit individuals from certain activities for their own good or protection.

In 1989, Nozick categorically repudiated this concept of Utopia, denied the relevance of philosophy for matters of substantive policy and opted for the zigzag of politics rather than for the principled position of his earlier political philosophy. This retreat from classical liberalism was driven by a judgement that any focus on individual rights detracts from communitarian impulses and fails to embrace humane considerations and joint cooperative activities:

> There are some things we choose to do together through government in solemn marking of our human solidarity, served by the fact that we do them together in this official fashion and often also by the content of the action itself. (Nozick, 1989, p. 287)

In this view, democracy is a mechanism through which individuals seek symbolic self-expression as a means of intensifying the reality of social solidarity and humane concern for others. The libertarian view, by looking exclusively at the *purpose* of government, fails to take account of the *meaning* of government.

More than this, joint political action does not merely express our ties of concern, it also constitutes a relational tie itself. So important are these relational ties that individuals who do not feel such ties should be required to pay taxes to support the programs that such ties involve. If a democratic majority desires jointly and symbolically to express its most solemn ties of concern and solidarity, the minority who prefer differently will have to participate sufficiently to be spoken for.

Such bonds of concern may imply limitations on liberty concerning particular kinds of human action, for example justifying anti-discrimination laws in employment, public accommodations, rental or sale of dwelling units, etc. They may lead even to justified limits on the freedom of speech and assembly. No general principle draws the line on such limitations on liberty. All depends upon the extent and range of the general population's actual feelings of solidarity and concern, and their need to give these symbolic political expression.

Let us suppose that there are multiple competing values that can be fostered, encouraged and realized in the political realm. Further suppose that it is impossible to include all such goals in some consistent manner. Nevertheless, argues Nozick, many goals that cannot be pursued together at the same time can be reconciled over time by pursuing one for some years, then another some years later. This explains why the electorate zigzags between political parties over time. Given a choice between permanently institutionalizing the particular content of any group of political principles thus far articulated and the zigzag process of democratic politics, Nozick is clear which direction he will take: 'I'll vote for the zigzag every time' (Nozick, 1989, p. 296).

In the Bunkers of Civil Society

John Gray's early writings on the philosophies of John Stuart Mill, Friedrich von Hayek and Isaiah Berlin placed him forthrightly in the camp of classical liberal political philosophy. Surely, his writings never embraced the concept of the minimal or nightwatchman state in the sense of Robert Nozick (1974). Yet throughout the period 1976 to 1988 he embraced the notion that individual liberty represents an important and worthwhile ethical goal and that classical liberalism can be justi-fied by reference to extant political philosophy.

In his 1976 paper on John Stuart Mill, Gray acknowledges that '[i]f there is a consensus on the value of Mill's political writings, it is that we may turn to them for the sort of moral uplift that sustains the liberal hope' (Gray, 1989a, p. 1). He continues by noting that 'Mill's writings contain an argument for an open society which has not yet been deci-sively refuted, and of which every generation needs reminding' (Gray, 1989a, p. 1). He endorses the central argument of *On Liberty*, 'the claim that a liberal society is the only kind of society in which men confident of their own manifold possibilities but critical of their own powers and of each other, men who aspire to the status of autonomous agents and who cherish their own individuality, will consent to live' (Gray, 1989a, p. 2).

Following a detailed review of Mill's utilitarian-driven political phi-losophy, Gray concludes that '[t]hough we must not expect from Mill's writings a blueprint for the achievement of a liberal society in a world in many ways very different from Mill's, ... radicals will be unreason-able if they neglect Mill's thought on some of the principal dilemmas that perplex us today' (Gray, 1989a, p. 8).

In his 1980 paper on negative and positive liberty, Gray extols the analysis of Isaiah Berlin whose paper on 'Two Concepts of Liberty' (1968) argues that the concept of negative freedom (the absence of coercion of one individual by another) is to be favoured over all other concepts of freedom. Gray endorses Berlin's doctrine of value plural-ism and his preference for a liberal society in which a wide diversity of ends is promoted.

In his 1981 essay on Hayek, Gray criticizes Hayek for blurring the boundaries of individual freedom and for assimilating it to other goods such as the rule of law and social stability. For this reason, 'Hayek's account of law and liberty runs the risk of losing the peculiar impor-tance of individual freedom conceived as a virtue of political order' (Gray, 1989a, p. 97). Gray concludes that a conception of individual rights can be defended only as abstraction from political experience.

Yet, in 1989, Gray pronounced that his 12-year project to define classi-cal liberalism and to give it a foundation had been a failure and he condemned classical liberal ideology as an impossibility. The various projects of grounding liberalism as a set of universal principles in a comprehensive moral theory – rights-based, utilitarian, contractarian or whatever – had all turned out to be inadequate and essentially incoherent.

This failure was not to be lamented, he argued, 'since liberal political philosophy expresses a conception of the task and limits of theorizing that is hubristic and defective' (Gray, 1989a, p. vii). The ruin of classical liberal political philosophy 'is only the most spectacular instance of the debacle of the received tradition, modern as much as classical, of philosophy as a discipline' (Gray, 1989a, p. vii).

In 1993, in his book, *Post-liberalism*, Gray poked around among the rubble of classical liberal philosophy to determine what, if anything, was left. He concluded that none of the four constitutive elements of doctrinal liberalism – universalism, individualism, egalitarianism and meliorism (or human flourishing) – could survive the ordeal by value pluralism and that liberalism, as a political philosophy, therefore was dead. What is living in liberalism is the historic inheritance of a civil society whose institutions protect liberty and permit civil peace. This is so because such a civil society is the best one for all contemporary cultures, which harbour a diversity of incommensurable conceptions of the good.

If civil society is all that is left – the living kernel – of classical liberalism, what then is its nature? Gray's response to this question is expansive. If there is an ultimate diversity of forms of human flourishing, embodied in ways of life only some of which can be accommodated within a classical regime, then classical liberal orders have no general superiority over orders that are not classically liberal. In short, value-pluralism dictates pluralism in political regimes and undermines the claim that only classically liberal regimes are fully legitimate.

A civil society, for John Gray, is one which is tolerant of the diversity of views, religious and political, that it contains, one in which the state does not seek to impose on all any comprehensive doctrine. Thus Calvin's Geneva was not a civil society, and none of the 20th century species of totalitarianism encompassed civil societies.

A second feature of civil society is that both government and its subjects are restrained in their conduct by a rule of law. A state in which the will of the ruler is the law, and for whom, therefore, all things are permissible, cannot contain or shelter a civil society. One implication of this is that civil society presupposes a government that is not omnipotent, but limited.

A third feature of civil society is the institution of private or several property. Societies in which property is vested in tribes, or in which most assets are owned or controlled by governments, cannot be civil societies.

In Gray's view, civil societies thus defined need not have the political and economic institutions of liberal democracy; in historical terms, most do not. Nor need they contain the moral culture of individualism. In his view, Tzarist Russia was a civil society for the last 50 years of its existence, as was Bismarkian Prussia. The authoritarian societies of modern East Asia – South Korea, Taiwan and Hong Kong – are all civil societies .

Nor finally, for John Gray, is civil society to be identified with market capitalism. Several or private property may come in a variety of forms, each of them artefacts of law. The institution of the capitalist corporation is only one species of the private or several property institution on which a civil society rests.

Russia will go badly astray if it seeks to replicate the form of Western capitalism. What is needed in post-1991 Russia is a radical deconcentration of economic activity to municipal, village and cooperative levels in which the native Russian tradition of cooperation can be revived. In Japan, also, Westernization would only involve injury to valuable social forms with few, if any, corresponding advantages.

Evidently, civil societies come in many varieties. They may be democratic or authoritarian, capitalist or non-capitalist, individualist or non-individualist in nature. What they have in common is the practice of liberty, as evidenced in the rule of law, private or several property, and the civil liberties of voluntary association, conscience, travel and expression. They need not shelter democratic freedom.

This broad tent is put forward as the living kernel of classical liberalism – all that remains from several centuries of classical liberal philosophy. In my view, it is not a living kernel but an empty shell. In the remainder of this chapter, I search for an explanation of what has led leading scholars to abandon classical liberal philosophy and I attempt to set the record straight by outlining a consistent and coherent Lockeian justification for the minimal state.

Anarchy versus Order: The Political Philosophy of Thomas Hobbes

Two great dichotomies dominate the political thought of all times: oppression versus freedom, and anarchy versus order (Bobbio, 1993, p. 29). Thomas Hobbes (1588–1679) belongs in the company of those whose political thought has been inspired by the latter dichotomy. The ideal which he defends is not liberty against oppression, but order against anarchy. Hobbes is obsessed by the idea of the dissolution of authority, the disorder that results from the freedom to disagree about what is just and what is unjust, and with the disintegration of the unity of power, which he views as inevitable once individuals begin to contend that power must be limited. The ultimate goal that motivates individuals in his moral philosophy is pursuit of peace and not of liberty.

Fundamentally, Hobbes is obsessed by the threat of anarchy, which he considers to be the return of mankind to the state of nature. The evil which he most fears is not oppression, which derives from the excess of power, but insecurity, which derives from the lack of power. Hobbes feels called upon to erect a philosophical system as 'the supreme and insuperable defense against insecurity' (Bobbio, 1993, p. 29); insecurity, first of all, of one's life; second, of material goods; and last, of that small or great liberty which an individual may enjoy while living in society.

Hobbes's three main political works, *Elements* (1650), *De Cive* (1651) and *Leviathan* (1651), provide descriptions of the state of nature which substantively are identical and which are meant to play the same functional role. The principal objective condition is that human beings, *de facto*, are equal. Being equal by nature, they are capable of inflicting the greatest of evils on one another: death. To this is to be added the second objective condition, scarcity of goods, which causes individuals each to desire the same thing. The combination of equality and relative scarcity generates a permanent state of reciprocal lack of trust, which induces all to prepare for war, and to make war if necessary, rather than to seek peace.

Among the objective conditions, *Elements* and *De Cive* emphasize the *ius de omnia*, the right to all things which nature gives to anyone living outside civil society. *De facto* equality, together with the scarcity of resources and the right to all things, inevitably generates a situation of merciless competition, which always threatens to turn into a violent struggle. This situation is made worse by the fact that nature has placed in this predicament individuals who are dominated by passions which incline them to unsociability.

Hobbes does not have a flattering opinion of his fellow men. While discussing freedom and necessity with Bishop Bramhall, Hobbes asserts that 'human beings resist truth because they covet riches and privilege; they crave sensual pleasures, they cannot bear to mediate, and they mindlessly embrace erroneous principles' (Bobbio, 1993, p. 40).

In *Leviathan*, after dividing human beings into those devoted to covetousness and those devoted to sloth, he comments that these 'two sorts of man take up the greatest part of mankind' (1946, XXX, 224). In describing the state of nature, Hobbes stresses vainglory as the passion 'which deriveth from the imagination of our *own power* above the power of him that contendeth with us' (1928, I, pp. 9,1,28).

In *Leviathan*, Hobbes links together three causes of conflict: competition, which makes individuals fight for gain; diffidence, which makes them fight for security; and vainglory which makes them fight for reputation. In *Leviathan*, Hobbes clarifies, in two lines, the fundamental problem of political science, the problem of power: 'So that in the first place, I put forward a general inclination of all mankind, a perpetual and restless desire for power after power, that ceaseth only in death' (1946, XI, p. 24). The state of nature is terrifying because the desire for power generates a situation which is a state of war. This is an intolerable condition, which individuals sooner or later must abandon if they wish to save what is most precious to them: their lives.

Right reason suggests to human beings a set of rules in the form of laws of nature which aim at ensuring peaceful cohabitation. These rules are subordinated to a first rule which prescribes the seeking of peace. Individuals have no interest in observing a rule if they are not certain that others will do the same. There is but one way to make the laws of nature effective and to make human beings act according to their reason and not their passions: the institution of the irresistible power of the state. To exit the state of nature and to establish civil society reasoning individuals must enter into a universal and permanent *covenant of union*.

Since the state of nature is insecure, the principal aim of the agreement is to eliminate the causes of insecurity. The principal cause of insecurity is the lack of a shared power. The aim of the contract that founds the state is to constitute a shared power. The only way to do so is for all to consent to give up their own power and to transfer it to one person, be it natural or artificial, for example an assembly. This person will have as much power as is necessary to prevent each individual from harming others by the exercise of his own power.

Individuals acquire a fundamental obligation as a consequence of this *pactum subiectionis* (pact of subjection), namely the obligation to obey all commands of the holder of shared power. This agreement is the *covenant of union*, an agreement in which all parties agree to subject themselves to a third party *who does not participate in the contract.* This power combines the supreme economic power (dominium) and the supreme coercive power (imperium). 'There is no power on earth', says the verse from the book of Job which describes the sea monster *Leviathan*, 'which is equal to it' (Job 41:24).

By holding that the sovereign power is irrevocable, Hobbes opposes the theory of trust on which Locke later rested his social contract. By holding that the sovereign power is absolute, in the sense of *legibus salutus* (not bound by laws), he denies the various theories that favour limiting the power of the state. Since individuals give up the right to all things in the covenant, in order to preserve their lives, they retain only the right to their own lives. Thus, human beings must consider themselves released from the obligation to obedience only if the sovereign endangers their lives.

Hobbes's justification of absolutism runs counter to a long-held principle of English constitutional doctrine, according to Bracton's classical formulation: 'The king must not be under man, but under God and under the law, because law makes the king' (Bracton, 1968, p. 33). Hobbes easily rejects the thesis according to which the sovereign is subject to civil law (*thesis* in the terminology of Hayek), with the argument that no one can oblige himself. Since civil laws are issued by the sovereign, the sovereign would impose an obligation on himself, were he subject to them.

But a more serious question must be answered: If the sovereign power is unlimited, how is this to be reconciled with other laws, namely the common law (*nomos* in the terminology of Hayek) and natural law? Not surprisingly, Hobbes is a declared enemy of the supporters of the common law, most notably hostile to Sir Edward Coke, the great protagonist of the common law: 'Custom of itself maketh no law' (1946, XXVI, p. 176).

Hobbes, as a proponent of natural law, repeatedly affirms that the sovereign is subject to the laws of nature and of God. However, in his view, the laws of nature are rules of prudence, or technical norms, compliance with which depends on one's judgement about the feasibility of pursuing one's objectives in given circumstances. Only the sovereign can make this judgement in his relations with his subjects, towards whom he is not bound by any covenant. He has no *external* obligation to anyone to comply with the dictates of right reason.

Since the laws of nature oblige only in conscience, the dictates of right reason do not limit the sovereign's power. Once the state has been instituted, there exist for the subjects no criteria of just or unjust other than the civil laws. This view makes Hobbes's moral theory one of the most extreme expressions of ethical legalism: what is right is what the sovereign commands. Hobbes insists, for example, that 'though the law of nature forbid theft, adultery, etc. yet if the civil law commands us to invade anything, that invasion is not theft, adultery, etc.', and 'No civil law whatsoever, which tends not to a reproach of the Deity ... can possibly be against the law of nature' (1845, XIV, pp. 10, 190–91).

In this perspective, there can be no theory of the abuse of power, since abuse consists of going beyond established limits. On the contrary, what may prompt subjects to consider themselves released from the duty of obedience is not abuse, but defect of power. A sovereign who proves incapable of preventing his subjects from relapsing into the state of nature does not perform his task. Subjects then, and only then, have the right to look for another protector.

In this perspective, Thomas Hobbes's political philosophy conforms to only one version of modern natural law theory, namely that natural law constitutes the foundation of validity of the positive legal order, taken as a whole (Bobbio, 1993, p. 157). This version of natural law theory serves well his purpose of founding rationally the ideology of the absolute state. The specific feature of this version of natural law theory is its acknowledgement that, once the state has been instituted, only one law of nature survives. This is the law that imposes on human beings the obligation to obey civil laws.

Thus, if a conflict were possible between civil law and natural law, 'the citizen who obeyed the latter rather than the former would violate the general law of nature which prescribes obedience to civil laws' (Bobbio, 1993, p. 165). Civil law is established on the basis of the law of nature, but once it has been established, the norms of the system derive their validity from the authority of the sovereign and not from the particular laws of nature. Hobbes admits only two exceptions to this duty of obedience: (a) when the sovereign commands subjects to offend God; (b) when he commands subjects to honour himself as if he were God. In this way, Hobbes deploys the most sophisticated ingredients of natural law – the state of nature, individual rights and the social contract – to develop a logically consistent theory of obedience to the state.

I shall attempt to demonstrate in this chapter that classical liberal scholars who seek to justify limited government by reference to Hobbesian arguments logically must fail to do so and, almost inevitably, end up at some point on the anarchy–order spectrum with their original classical liberal principles in disarray.

Oppression versus Freedom: The Political Philosophy of John Locke

In order to understand the political philosophy of John Locke, and to distinguish it from that of Thomas Hobbes, it is essential to return to the concept of the state of nature which is the starting point in Locke's genetic account of the rise of civil societies. For Locke's concept of the state of nature differs fundamentally from that of Hobbes in moral as well as in strictly positive characteristics.

The social characterization of the state of nature in Hobbes is unambiguous. Life is 'solitary, poor, nasty, brutish and short', a condition of war 'of every man against every man', a war in which there is no industry, no culture and no real society (Hobbes, 1946, chapter 13, paras 8–9). The moral condition of individuals in that state is less clear, although it is evident that they have no moral rights or obligations at all in the ordinary sense – 'the notions of right and wrong, justice and injustice, have there no place' (ibid., chapter 13, para. 13).

Locke's social characterization of the state of nature is much less bleak than that of Hobbes: 'Want of a common judge with authority, puts all persons in the state of nature' (Locke, 1960, II, p. 19); 'Men living together according to reason, without a common superior on earth, with authority to judge between them, is properly the state of nature' (ibid., II, p. 19). Locke consistently claims that wherever no one is entitled to settle controversies between two persons, wherever there is no authorized referee to judge between them, those persons are in the state of nature. It is important to note that this is a sufficient and not a necessary condition.

It is also important to note that what is at issue is not the presence or absence of effective government. Individuals according to Locke may be living under effective, highly organized government and still be in the state of nature, if the government is illegitimate with respect to these individuals. At the very least, it is necessary to build into the definition the absence of *legitimate* government. To deal with this concept it is necessary to take account of Locke's moral characterization of the state of nature which also differs sharply from that of Hobbes.

Locke's definition of the state of nature clearly incorporates moral elements, making use of such notions as legitimacy and voluntary agreement. Individuals are endowed with full-blown moral rights and obligations defined by the law of nature, which is eternal and immutable (ibid., II, p. 135). Although the particulars of the law of nature are not defined in any detail, their general form is clear. They are duties to preserve oneself and others, by not harming persons in their lives, liberties and properties. Persons enjoy in the state of nature their full complement of *natural rights*, which correlate with the natural duties of others to respect those rights.

Each individual is born to this set of rights and duties and receives them fully on reaching maturity (ibid., II, pp. 55, 59). Natural rights are a 'grant or gift from God' (ibid., I, p. 116), which individuals possess intact until they consent to enter a legitimate civil society, surrendering some of these rights in the process. However, private contracts between individuals are fully consistent with the state of nature. Such contracts may alter the existing structure of rights and duties among mature individuals, save only for those that in principle are inalienable. In this sense, consent 'carves the boundaries of natural law' (Simmons, 1993, p. 25).

What is the social characterization of the state of nature? Locke sets out two contrasting situations. At one extreme, he describes the state of nature as 'a state of peace, good will, mutual assistance and preservation' (1963, II, p. 19). At the other extreme, he describes it as 'a state of enmity, malice, violence and mutual destruction' (ibid., II, p. 19). Both descriptions are of *possible states* of nature, but neither is of *the* state of nature (Simmons, 1993, p. 28). Where individuals almost always abide by the laws of nature, the state of nature will be one of peace, goodwill and the like; where individuals typically disregard the law, the state of nature will be one of enmity, malice and the like.

Since individuals almost always fall between these two extremes, the social characterization of the state of nature in the *Two Treatises* (1963) is a mixed account, or as Locke puts it, 'one of mediocrity'. It is a state of limited safety and considerable uncertainty, a state of significant but not desperate inconveniences, a state to which only certain limited forms of political society will be preferable. Locke, in distinct contrast with Hobbes, focuses more on the moral than the social characterization of the state of nature. For Locke, the only intelligible choice is between some limited form of government and anarchy. The absolute government favoured by Hobbes is clearly worse than the worst consequences of anarchy.

In one respect, both Hobbes and Locke share the same view. They are fundamentally opposed to political naturalism which holds that the natural condition of humans is a *political* condition; that individuals naturally are subject to political authority; that there can be no understanding of morality or social understanding except within the context of some form of political organization. Contemporary political naturalists take their inspiration from Aristotle or Hegel. Locke was more concerned with defenders of the divine right of kings, like Filmer (1947), whose patriarchal theories of authority defended the autocracy of the House of Stuart.

The Lockeian assertion that each individual is born free in the state of nature correctly recognized that we are not born into political communities, even if we are born into the territories of such communities. We are not naturally citizens. We must do something to become citizens. The claim that our natural moral condition is non-political 'is a refusal to accept mere accidents of birth as the source of substantial moral differences among persons' (Simmons, 1993, p. 38). It is from this compelling foundation that Lockeian political volunteerism begins and develops. It is from this perspective that Nozick's (1989) retreat into communitarianism can be seen to be philosophically flawed.

Locke clearly depicts the state of nature as a state of '*perfect freedom* to order their Actions, and dispose of their Possessions, and Persons as they think fit, within the bounds of the law of Nature, without asking leave, or depending upon the Will of any other Man' (1960, II, p. 4). In this sense, his political philosophy clearly runs on the freedom versus oppression and not on the anarchy versus order spectrum. It is important to note, however, that Locke's state of liberty is not a state of licence. The state of nature has a law of nature to govern it, which obliges every individual. No individual 'ought to harm another in his Life, Health, Liberty, or Possessions' (ibid., II, p. 6).

The law of nature essentially reflects the moral claim of each individual to negative freedom and the duty of each individual to uphold the negative freedom of all others. To this end, each individual has an executive power to punish the transgressors of the law of nature 'to such a Degree as may hinder its Violation' (ibid., II, p. 7). Indeed, those who transgress the law of nature to a sufficient degree may forfeit their own rights to life, liberty and property. The constant danger of the state of nature degenerating into a state of war is the chief reason advanced by Locke for preferring a limited government (civil society) to the state of nature.

Locke was fully aware of the inconveniences of the state of nature 'which must certainly be great' since men may be judges in their own case. Yet, this is a much better situation than that in which men are bound to submit to the unjust will of another. At least, in the state of nature, if any individual judges wrongly in his own or any other case, he is answerable to the rest of mankind. By agreeing to leave the state of nature and to enter into civil society, the individual necessarily sacrifices his right to judge and to punish the breaches of natural law by others. This is no mean sacrifice and it will not be countenanced unless the civil society is strictly limited with respect to the authority that it subsumes.

Civil societies and governments do not possess rights naturally; only individuals have that capacity. For Locke, there is only one possible process by which such political rights can be secured. Only voluntary alienation by the rightholder – consent, contract, trust – can give another person or body political power over the rightholder: 'Men being … by nature, all free, equal, and independent, no one can be put out of his estate, and subjected to the political power of another, without his own consent' (1960, II, p. 95); 'No government can have a right to obedience from a people who have not freely consented to it' (ibid., II, p. 192).

Locke's wording makes it clear that by 'consent' he means the actual personal consent of each individual. Hypothetical contractarianism plays no role in his political philosophy. Once actual consent is abandoned as the ground on which civil society is made to rest, we also abandon much of what is most compelling about classical consent theory – namely the clear, uncontroversial ground of obligation on which it relies, and the high value of self-government with which it remains consistent (Simmons, 1993, p. 78). Societies that refuse to permit or fail to facilitate free choice of political allegiance are simply illegitimate, however many such societies might actually exist.

Locke's emphasis on personal consent does not imply any special commitment to democratic government. Consent, for Locke, is the source of a just government authority and its citizens' obligations. It does not determine the form that the government will take. Democracies may be legitimized by consent; but so may oligarchies and monarchies, hereditary or elected. Consent is given to membership in the society. The majority then determines the form of government to be entrusted with the political power given to that society. However, a separate, special consent (1960, II, pp. 138–40) is always required to resolve the issue of taxation under any form of government.

That all individuals possess certain natural rights that are inalienable is a thesis closely associated with Locke as strictly limiting the competence of government. It is important, however, to look more closely at the concept of inalienability. One view, closely associated with resisting oppression, is that an inalienable right is a right that no man can take away. A different and more extensive view is that it is a right that cannot be lost in any way, whether voluntarily or involuntarily.

According to Simmons (1993, p. 103), neither of these interpretations of inalienability is true to the 17th and 18th centuries employments of the concept. Revolutionary authors typically viewed inalienable rights as rights that no citizen could be understood to have given away. This view confirms with Locke's rule that '[n]obody can give more power [rights] than he has himself' (1960, II, p. 23). We can only alienate rights that are not connected with the preservation of ourselves or others.

From this perspective, governments cannot have the power to take our lives (unless we commit an appropriate crime), to deprive us of property at will, to rule by arbitrary decrees, or to tax us without our consent, because all of these amount to arbitrary powers that might endanger our lives if exercised maliciously. Each such transfer of power would be contrary to the natural law of preservation, 'which stands as an eternal rule to all men, legislators as well as others' (ibid., II, p. 135). In this sense, Locke's limits on government power should be construed to imply that we cannot transfer to government rights that we ourselves lack. Only in this sense does Locke construe the moral limits on government to be limits set by the citizens' inalienable rights.

Precisely because Locke's philosophy is focused on the freedom versus oppression spectrum, the *Two Treatises* may be viewed as a work designed 'to assert a right of resistance to unjust authority, a right, in the last resort, of revolution' (Dunn, 1969, p. 28). It is Locke's attempt to evaluate the moral consequences of governmental transgressions of its limited authority. Locke's employment of strong claim rights allows the revolutionary a moral high ground to stand on in resisting government (Simmons, 1993, p. 152). When Locke's citizen defends his rights, those who oppose him also wrong him by breaching their duties to respect his rights. Crucial to this judgement is Locke's argument that rights can only be alienated by those who possess them; and that certain rights are inalienable in the sense defined above.

Locke employs two distinct lines of argument in justifying a popular right of resistance to oppressive government. In his first line argument, he justifies such resistance on the ground that, under certain conditions, a state of war exists between the people and their government. Here Locke focuses, naturally, on the case of tyrannical executive power

(James II). However, he also notes that the legislative may also intro-
duce a state of war with the people 'using force upon the people
without authority and contrary to the trust put in him' (1960, II, p. 155).
In such cases, the oppressors forfeit all rights under the law of nature
and may themselves be lawfully killed, or used at will by any other
person.

In his second line argument, Locke notes that when governments act
contrary to the terms of trust 'by this breach of trust they forfeit the
power the people had put into their hands' (ibid., II, p. 222). Such a
breach of trust need not involve either a basic breach of natural law or
the forfeiture of all natural rights. Governors who breach their trust
reduce themselves to the status of ordinary persons without authority
(ibid., II, p. 235).

Being thus deprived of their referee, the common judge over them
all, the people might seem to be returned to the state of nature as a
consequence of the misconduct of their government. Locke, perhaps
incorrectly, rejects this inference. 'The usual and almost only way' the
political society itself is dissolved 'is the inroad of foreign force making a conquest upon them' (ibid., II, p. 211). Otherwise, political society remains and the government actually 'dissolve themselves' leaving
the people morally free to seek new avenues for securing their rights
(Simmons, 1993, p. 163).

The Shift to the Anarchy versus Order Spectrum

It is now possible to explain the apparent retreat from classical philosophy evident in the writings of Robert Nozick and John Gray in the very
year (1989) that witnessed the final collapse of classical liberal's arch-
enemy, Marxist–Leninist philosophy. I shall attempt to explain this
inexplicable change of course not as a retreat but as a shift of focus
from the freedom versus oppression to the anarchy versus order dichotomy. It is entirely possible that this shift of focus occurred uncon-
sciously rather than explicitly on the part of Nozick and of Gray. The
consequences, in any event, are profound.

Robert Nozick

In 1974, starting with a strong assumption of value pluralism (p. 309),
Nozick concluded that there was indeed a Utopia, one best society for
everyone to live in, even though there would not be one kind of community existing and one kind of life led in Utopia. Utopia is a frame-

work for utopias, 'a place where people are at liberty to join together voluntarily to attempt to realize their own vision of the good life'. Utopia in this sense is the Lockeian minimal state. This morally favoured state, 'the only morally legitimate state, the only morally tolerable one' (Nozick, 1974, p. 333) is the one that best realizes the Utopian aspirations of untold dreamers and visionaries:

> The minimal state treats us as inviolate individuals, who may not be used in certain ways by others as means or tools or instruments or resources; it treats us as persons having individual rights with the dignity this constitutes ... How *dare* any state or group of individuals do more. Or less. (Nozick, 1974, p. 334).

In 1989, this vision of Utopia was denied by Nozick as 'a book of political philosophy that marked out a distinctive view, one that now seems seriously inadequate to me' (Nozick, 1989, p. 17). A careful reading of *The Examined Life* suggests that Nozick has shifted focus from the freedom versus oppression to the anarchy versus order dichotomy in thus denying his early scholarship.

First, in his discussion of different stances, Nozick suggests that the very question, How can I be free? is rooted in excessive egoism. The relative stance, he suggests, asks how one can be related to external reality and prizes determination of action. What would be regrettable, on this stance, would be a determinism that was only partial, one that was not complete enough (Nozick, 1989, p. 161). Second, in his discussion of authority (Nozick, 1974, p. 175), Nozick notes that authority has legitimacy to the extent that those commanded feel obligated therefore to obey. A leader functions to resolve the competition of goals. Only under very special conditions can society avoid the need for leadership of some sort. Third, in his discussion of Plato's degree of reality theory (Nozick, 1989, p. 199), Nozick emphasizes such criteria as being invariant under certain transformations, being more permanent, specifying a goal toward which things move. In all these observations, a yearning for unity or order is clearly apparent.

This yearning for unity takes full shape in Nozick's retreat from the minimal state with all the disorder that *laissez-faire* seems to imply. Democratic institutions now are viewed as vehicles through which we express the values that bind us together, the solemn marking of our human solidarity (Nozick, 1989, p. 287), the constitution of our relational ties. The *zigzag of politics*, that sorry Nozickean retreat from the inspiring vision of the moral minimal state, is the only alternative to

Leviathan for a scholar who has abandoned freedom for order and unity as the supreme goal of mankind.

John Gray

In a sequence of papers published over the period 1976 to 1988, John Gray pursued the ambitious project of defining classical liberalism and giving it a foundation. Although he always reviewed the writings of the great classical liberal scholars – John Stuart Mill, Isaiah Berlin, Friedrich Hayek, Herbert Spencer and James M. Buchanan – in an appropriately critical manner, Gray culled from their contributions ideas that clearly provided the *moral* foundations for the limited, if not for the minimal, state. There was no real hint in these papers that his project would end in 1989 with a condemnation of classical liberal ideology as an inevitable failure: 'Our circumstance, then, is the paradoxical one of postmoderns, whose self-understanding is shaped by the liberal form of life, but without its legitimizing myths, which philosophic inquiry has dispelled' (Gray, 1989, p. 240).

A careful reading of Gray's scholarship, both in his 1989 volume, *Liberalisms*, and in his 1993 volume, *Post-liberalism*, suggests that Gray also has shifted from the freedom versus oppression to the anarchy versus order dichotomy in thus denying his early scholarship. This shift of focus apparently has been driven by the influence of Thomas Hobbes and Michael Oakeshott and by a misunderstanding of the writings of James M. Buchanan.

In his paper on Hobbes (Gray, 1989b), Gray comments that 'there is an arresting contemporaneity about many of Hobbes's insights that we can well profit from' and '[f]ar from being an anachronistic irrelevance, Hobbes's thought is supremely relevant to us, who live at the end of the modern era whose ills he sought to diagnose' (Gray, 1993, p. 3). In Gray's view, 'the modern state has failed in its task of delivering us from a condition of universal predation or war of all against all into the peace of civil society' (Gray, 1993, p. 3). In its weakness, the modern state has recreated in a political form that very state of nature from which it is the task of the state to deliver us. 'In this political state of nature, modern democratic states are driven by *a legal and political war of all against all* and the institutions of civil society are progressively enfeebled' (Gray, 1993, p. 3).

According to Gray, the paradox of the Hobbesian state is that, whereas its authority is unlimited, its duty is minimal – the maintenance of civil peace. Civil peace encompasses that framework of civil institutions whereby men coexist in peace with one another, notwithstanding the diversity of their beliefs and enterprises and the scarcity of the means whereby these are promoted. In this Hobbesian perspective, the liberties of the subjects of a civil society 'are not absolute or inalienable rights, since they may be circumscribed by the requirements of a civil peace in the absence of which they are altogether extinguished' (Gray, 1993, p. 10). Liberties (such as they are) are intimated by the spirit of civil society itself, which is held together only by recognition of the sovereign. The Hobbesian state is the classical solution of the prisoner's dilemma 'in that the Hobbesian contract, by providing for agreed-upon coercion to obey known rules, releases its covenanters from destructive conflict into the peace of civil life' (Gray, 1993, p. 13).

In his paper on Michael Oakeshott (Gray, 1992), Gray notes approvingly that Oakeshott rejected, as a prime example of rationalism in politics, the attempts by Locke, Kant and Mill to fix the proper scope and limits of the authority of government determinantly, once and for all. The proper tasks and limits of government cannot be determined by reasoning from first principles.

Political discourse is not an argument, but a conversation. Gray is especially enamoured of Oakeshott's 'pluralist affirmation of the diversity of modes of discourse and experience, of moralities as vernacular languages whose nature it is to be many and divergent, and of the miscellaneity of practice, which no theory can hope to capture, that embodies his most distinctive contribution to philosophy' (Gray, 1993, p. 46).

Gray captures the spirit of Oakeshott's thought in a single phrase, *a critique of purposefulness*. The image of human life that Oakeshott conveys to him is not that of a problem to be solved or a situation to be mastered. It is our image of being lost in a world in which our vocation is to play earnestly and to be earnest playfully, living without thought of any final distinction. Now, there is a kind of freedom in that image; but it is not the kind of freedom that requires eternal vigilance, that characterizes classical scholarship. Rather it is the freedom of the boat without the compass.

Gray is not content, however, to end his philosophical journey in some Oakeshottian scepticism of human action, viewing philosophical discourse as so much flotsam and jetsam, tossed here and there on the tides of political events. Gray instead seeks out an anchor, in the wake of classical liberal philosophy, in the form of civil society. He anchors the concept of civil society, at least in part, in the scholarship of James

M. Buchanan who, paradoxically, he recognizes as focusing a 'profound moral concern for the fate of free man and free peoples' in his reconstitution of classical political economy (Gray, 1993, p. 47).

Gray is particularly attracted to Buchanan's indirect, proceduralist contractarianism based on methodological individualism but presupposing the cultural inheritance of Western individualism, with its roots in Christianity and Stoicism. In Gray's view, it is this cultural context that enables Buchanan to make the hazardous passage from Hobbesian despair to Humeian hope, from the *Leviathan* of unconstrained majoritarian democracy to the limited government of constitutional democracy.

In his 1990 paper, Gray places at the crux of his enquiry the question: What is the place of liberty in Buchanan's contractarian approach? He notes that Buchanan does not privilege liberty from the outset, that his approach does not issue in a determinate list of basic liberties that are fixed and unalterable. This is not surprising, given the Hobbesian pedigree of Buchanan's political philosophy (Buchanan, 1975).

Buchanan is also clear (argues Gray) that in any plausible real-world situation, contractarian choice will not yield a Lockeian, Nozickian or Spencerian minimal state; nor will it necessarily issue in unencumbered Lockeian rights. Indeed, limited government, according to Buchanan, would surely have some redistributional functions. According to Gray, in Buchanan's system 'liberty is not given the apodictive priority it has been in Kantian-inspired contractarianism, nor is it the case that the role of the state is defined by the protection of Lockeian rights' (Gray, 1993, p. 60).

Nevertheless, suggests Gray, Buchanan's contractarianism is bound to issue, in most real-world contexts, in the enhancement and protection of individual liberty. It does so by virtue of its exploitation of the classical insight that voluntary exchange is mutually beneficial. It does so again because its defence of the market economy is in terms of its contribution to human autonomy rather than to any abstract conception of general well-being or collective welfare. And it does so finally in virtue of its insight that, provided there is a suitable framework of law, the undesigned coordination of the market is superior to any that can be generated by command or coercion.

Gray concludes that Buchanan's contractarianism cannot give universal protection to the personal or civil liberties that are central to the Western individualist tradition. This limitation Gray finds to be both inevitable and even desirable: 'It is far from self-evident, and sometimes plainly false, that the institutions and civil liberties of even limited democratic government are always and everywhere appropriate and defensible' (1993, p. 61). In Gray's judgement, if liberty has a future, it will have been fortified by Buchanan's work. For the final message of Buchanan's thought, as he interprets it, is that if we wish to preserve the precious heritage of Western individuality, we are bound to engage in the project of theorizing the world as it is, without illusion or groundless hope.

Conclusion

In my view, the retreat from classical liberalism on the part of both Robert Nozick and John Gray is completely explained by their shift, in a troubled world, from a preoccupation with the goal of preserving liberty to that of preserving order, from a commitment to the philosophy of John Locke to that of Thomas Hobbes. In both cases, reliance is now placed on some broad-tent notion of civil society as a basis for preserving the political legacy of classical liberal philosophy from the ravages of totalitarian pressures.

I am far from optimistic about this pragmatic judgement for a number of reasons, some of which Buchanan (1975) himself shares. First, if Gray is truly correct about the Hobbesian nature of man, there really is no prospect of a social contract short of that which creates *Leviathan*. All potential parties to a Hobbesian contract, short of one that hands over all authority to a superior being, must surely anticipate that the parchment of that contract will be shredded by amoral individuals in the post-contractual environment. Civil society, in such circumstances, swiftly must collapse into de Jasay's (1985) plantation state, whatever the status of the constitutional agreement.

In this respect, Gray simply misunderstands Buchanan's insight in *The Limits of Liberty* (1975). Surely Buchanan employs the Hobbesian model, in rationalizing contractual consent for limited government as an alternative to anarchy. Like Locke, however, Buchanan employs Hobbes as the *pessimistic scenario* of the state of nature, the threat that leads free individuals into civil society. This does not imply that Buchanan believes Hobbesian man to be the norm. Far from it. All his scholarship on constitutional political economy is predicated on the notion that man possesses Lockeian characteristics, that man searches for release from the prisoner's dilemma of unlimited democracy, that man wishes to force himself to be free. This grievous misunderstanding leaves Gray with a concept of civil society that has little resemblance to the strictly limited state of Buchanan.

Second, Gray, far more than Buchanan, is willing to countenance redistributionist transfers as a legitimate function of civil society. In so doing, he denies the Lockeian notion of the right to property that prevents the minimal state from being mutilated as a commons in which the rent-seeking dilemma leads to a war of each against all.

Third, once attention is diverted from the priority of preserving liberty to the priority of preserving order, the dyke is opened for those who would invade individual rights to do so under the guise of avoiding anarchy. One has only to review the reactions in all branches of government to the tragedy of Oklahoma City to see how quickly opportunities to trample on liberties are seized upon by those who perceive economic or political gain.

Finally, and almost inevitably, those who embrace Hobbesian philosophy tend to focus either exclusively on analysing what is or what conditionally might be (avoiding entirely all moral discourse), or to ignore Hume's naturalistic fallacy and seek to create an ought from an is. Ultimately, of course, such an endeavour is doomed to failure.

In this vale of tears, if one believes in a moral philosophy, one had better articulate it clearly and pursue it with a heart that pumps more than blood. The fine essays in this volume attempt to articulate just such a moral philosophy of the minimal state that is relevant to the new century that now beckons. In my view, these essays bear witness to the fact that classical liberal philosophy is far from dead, indeed that it is alive and well and worthy of the most serious consideration in the post-communist world order.

References

Berlin, I. (1968), *Four Essays on Liberty*, Oxford: Oxford University Press.

Bobbio, N. (1993), *Thomas Hobbes and the Natural Law Tradition*, Chicago: University of Chicago Press.

Bracton, H. (1968), *On the Laws and Customs of England*, Cambridge: University of Chicago Press.

Buchanan, J.M. (1975), *The Limits of Liberty: Between Anarchy and Leviathan*, Chicago: University of Chicago Press.

Buchanan, J.M. (1991), *Analysis, Ideology and the Events of 1989*, Chicago: University of Chicago Press.

de Jasay, A. (1985), *The State*, Oxford: Basil Blackwell.

Dunn, J. (1969), *The Political Thought of John Locke*, Cambridge: Cambridge University Press.

Filmer, R. (1947), 'Patriarcha', in J. Locke, *Two Treatises of Government*, ed. T. Cook, New York: Hafner. Originally published 1680.

Fukuyama, F.C. (1992), *The End of History and the Last Man*, New York: The Free Press.

Gray, J. (1976), 'John Stuart Mill and the future of liberalism', *The Contemporary Review*, 220, September.

Gray, J. (1980), 'On negative and positive liberty', *Political Studies*, XXVIII.

Gray, J. (1981), 'Hayek on liberty, rights and justice', *Ethics*, 92 (I), October.

Gray, J. (1989a), *Liberalisms: Essays in Political Philosophy*, London: Routledge.

Gray, J. (1989b), 'Hobbes and the modern state', *The World and I*, Washington DC. Reprinted in Gray (1989a), pp. 3–17.

Gray, J. (1990) 'Buchanan on liberty', *Constitutional Political Economy*, I (2), spring/summer.

Gray, J. (1992), 'Oakeshott as a liberal', *The Salisbury Review*, January.

Gray, J. (1993), *Post-liberalism: Studies in Political Thought*, London: Routledge.

Hobbes, T. (1928), *The Elements of Law Natural and Politic*, ed. F. Tonnies, Cambridge: Cambridge University Press. Originally published 1650.

Hobbes, T. (1845), 'De Cive (Philosophical rudiments concerning government and society)', in T. Hobbes, *English Works*, vol. II, ed. W. Molesworth, II vols, London: J. Bohn. Originally published 1651.

Hobbes, T. (1946), *Leviathan*, ed. M. Oakeshott, Oxford: Basil Blackwell. Originally published 1651.

Locke, J. (1963), *Two Treatises of Government*, ed. P. Laslett, Cambridge: Cambridge University Press.

Nozick, R. (1974), *Anarchy, State, and Utopia*, New York: Basic Books.

Nozick, R. (1989), *The Examined Life: Philosophical Meditations*, New York: Simon and Schuster.

Simmons, A.J. (1993), *On the Edge of Anarchy: Locke, Consent and the Limits of Society*, Princeton: Princeton University Press.

Before Resorting to Politics

Before Resorting to Politics

Anthony de Jasay

The Shaftesbury Papers, 5
Series Editor: Charles K. Rowley

Edward Elgar
Cheltenham, UK • Brookfield, US

Published by
Edward Elgar Publishing Limited
8 Lansdown Place
Cheltenham
Glos GL50 2HU
UK

Edward Elgar Publishing Company
Old Post Road
Brookfield
Vermont 05036
US

British Library Cataloguing in Publication Data
De Jasay, Anthony, 1925–
 Before resorting to politics. – (The Shaftesbury papers;
 5)
 1. Economics 2. Political science
 I. Title II. Series
 330

Library of Congress Cataloguing in Publication Data
De Jasay, Anthony
  Before resorting to politics / Anthony de Jasay.
  — (The Shaftesbury papers; 5)
  1. Political science — Economic aspects. 2. State, The. 3. Value.
  4. Values. I Title. II. Series.
 JA77.D45 1996
 320.1'01—dc20   95–40188
                                                     CIP

ISBN 1 85898 226 X

Printed in Great Britain at the University Press, Cambridge

Contents

1. Introduction

The Good of Some and the Bad of Others

Why does anyone want to resort to politics and why does anyone put one kind of political order above another? Those who are both very earthy and very frank approve the one they believe is doing the most good for them. 'The way truly to understand history is the way of Princess Mathilde [Bonaparte]. She would not forgive those who spoke ill of Napoleon because, as she explained, "without that man I should be selling oranges on the wharf in Marseilles". The good or the bad done to us, there is the grand criterion of history' (Bainville, 1941, p. 16; my translation). However, it takes more effrontery than most of us possess to be *this frank* and *this earthy*; and at all events Princess Mathilde's 'grand criterion' of political hedonism, by which I approve of the system that favours mainly me, and disapprove of the one that favours mainly others, has no hope of generating a semblance of basic agreement about the respective merits and consequences of political systems over and above the fairly low common denominator of democracy, namely the shared redistributive advantage of a winning over a losing coalition.

Once, therefore, we try to advance toward a beginning of Kantian generality and universalizability, seeking to justify political arrangements by reference to arguments that are morally more compelling than the advantages for some bought at the cost of setbacks to others, the 'grand criterion' ceases to be of help. What makes matters worse is if a type of political order not only has a clear propensity to cause some to gain and others to lose, but if the gainers and losers are always much the same persons, divided by permanent cleavages. '[It] is difficult to see why a loser in the competitive struggle should support the market system when it encourages the development of character traits whose existence in others works to his disadvantage and which he himself does not possess...' (Buchanan, 1985, p. 51). If this argument holds for the market system, it holds equally for the system of the welfare state, a putative antidote to the 'market system', under which burdens are imposed on one class of person and benefits awarded to another, and which is believed, not without reasonable ground, to help develop character traits in one class which work to the permanent disadvantage of the other.

The Pursuit of Values

What is true, in a crude and obvious way, of the system of political hedonism that expects the state to cater for some interests to the relative neglect, if not the actual harming, of the others, is true, albeit less conspicuously and more subtly, of any other political order that fosters one value, or a few, to the relative neglect of the others. Not all values are compatible; most must compete with one another. Secular historical experience largely bears out that liberty has a cost in terms of security, security in terms of progress, progress in terms of equality, equality in terms of respect of rights, and so forth. There are, to use the economist's jargon, marginal rates of transformation between each, indicating, for a particular society and age, 'how much' of one must in effect be sacrificed to get a little more of another. At the same time, every individual with a fairly developed awareness of his own preferences and with some capacity to act upon them coherently, can be construed and understood as having, to use the same jargon, marginal rates of substitution between values, indicating 'how much' of one he would be only just willing to give up for a little more of another, if the occasion arose.

Values, of course, are very large, poorly defined and abstract categories, and it is perhaps contrived language to suggest choices, substitutions and transformations between them, rather than between the objects to which they are attached. To suggest, in addition, that values lend themselves to meaningful quantitative measurement for their substitutions and transformations into one another to have recognizable 'rates' (so many 'units' of one for one 'unit' of the other) may be thought of as an even worse aberration. Nevertheless, people as well as political societies do visibly trade values off against one another, and sometimes do so consciously, on purpose, overtly reasoning about such marginal choices, and that is all the quantitative character my present argument really needs.

A political order 'reveals' its hierarchy of values by what it promotes and demotes. It selects policies that produce more of one value and less of another *as if* it sought to equate its marginal rate of substitution between them to the marginal rate at which they can be transformed into one another in the real world. The latter is a matter of the social and economic facts of life that are given, at least in the short run. To say that policies are chosen to adjust the marginal rate of substitution of any two values to their marginal rate of transformation is to say, tautologically, that the policies are chosen rationally. It is also to say that if the trade-offs they brought about were not the ones sought, the policies would be rejected and different ones adopted.

It is an empirical question whether these marginal rates of substitution between, say, liberty and other valuable ends coincide with those of many, or indeed any, denizens of the society whose political order we are discussing in these laborious and tediously technical terms. Plainly, if they are like people everywhere, namely different from each other, the coincidence will be less than perfect,[1] and the value-oriented political order will be a less than perfect match for the people who live within it and must live with it.

This is, indeed, exactly what we should expect on a little reflection. The design of teleological political orders, intended to equip them for the pursuit of some end, mimics the 'model' of a single actor pursuing some end. However, a single actor making choices that bind others, no matter how sympathetic and well-attuned he may be to the interests and preferences of those for whom he acts cannot possibly pursue the same ends, practice the same trade-offs and replicate the same choices as a multiplicity of actors would severally like to make, except if the latter are all alike in all relevant respects, a condition that is neither likely nor desirable. One cannot both uphold the teleological design that biases the particular order to favour, say, liberty over equality or vice versa, and avoid overriding the value preferences of some constituents who are invited and expected to accept this order. There is nothing, no discernible mechanism, that would make global social choice coincide with the best available choice of each individual consistent with the best available choice of every other – which is the equilibrium solution of ordered anarchy.

The Pursuit of Happiness

Some communitarians first of all, and probably socialists too, would say that this is as it should be. It is only right that politics should serve to promote certain values at the expense of others, and that this should leave some people adhering to values the community rejects, less than satisfied. Politics must serve the common good. We may disagree about what the common good happens to be, that is about the 'object level' political question. We may even disagree about the meta-level question, that is the proper manner of ascertaining the common good. We do agree, however, that it is not any kind of sum of the good of everyone, nor any kind of game-theoretic equilibrium in which each does as well as he can consistent with everyone else doing so. Value-neutrality, if it were possible, would be wrong.

Opposed to the idea of the common good is a traditional liberal view, little changed since it was handed down by the Philosophical Radicals, though no longer regarded as an essential indefeasible part of liberalism. In this view, the best political order is one that is most apt to give people what they most want – some kind of 'greatest happiness', no matter which values it is derived from and in what proportions – and that formalizes this goal in the value-neutral terms of utility-maximization. Of course, in properly understood 'utility theory no one aims at utility as such or even cares about it. Utility is postulated as the mathematical expression of the rank or strength of the material ends people do pursue. So long as the relation between material ends can take any logical form at all, ... there is no harm in this view, and very little bite' (Fried, 1978, n 13). Except for the word 'material' (for there is surely no restriction whatever about the ends utility theory handles, be they tangible or intangible, material or moral, or, in Bentham's words, 'pushpin or poetry') there is much to be said for this explanation of Charles Fried's. It makes it clear that utility is not a *rival* of other values. It is *all* the values a person has, taken together, and ordered after having undergone the trade-offs his relative preferences tell him to effect among them.

Translating into common utility language the multiplicity of values that motivate any *one* person's choices does nothing, however, to bring about value-neutrality *among* persons. For it is impossible to pursue 'utility' or happiness as such. One can only pursue specific objects functioning as ends that are expected to make greater or lesser contributions to 'utility'. It is possible to seek ends that are likely to contribute to the 'utility' of two persons at the same time, or for that matter to that of a whole society. But it is impossible to do it 'value-neutrally'. For a collective choice that is a practice of trade-offs between values can conform to the value-hierarchy (marginal rates of substitution) of one person and not of another unless, once again, they think exactly alike.

Whichever way we twist and turn the 'social welfare function' or the 'social choice rule', we cannot square the circle. Value-neutrality, where there is not too much of one thing and too little of another, can be achieved by the individual for himself, but not by a political order for many, let alone for everybody.

The 'Debacle and Ruin' of Liberal Theory

These seem to me among the most fundamental, almost tectonic reasons for the growing loss of credibility of modern liberal theory as a whole. They are inherent in its basic design. The upshot is twofold. First, liberalism is easily colonized by a variety of incongruous doctrines, notably about 'rights' for desirable things and favourable treatment people are asserted to have, to the effect that the adjective 'liberal' is becoming useless, signifying very little that is distinctive of one doctrine and not true of almost every other. Second, liberalism, misstated from the outset as a theory of the superiority of liberty over other 'political' goods, cannot any longer sustain its strong original claim to moral ascendancy over other blueprints of the political order. A former liberal, and perhaps the most prolific present-day commentator of liberalism, now diagnoses '[t]he debacle of the project of liberal ideology' in which there is not anywhere a 'compelling demonstration of the priority of liberty over other political values' (Gray, 1989, p. 261); he finds that 'the liberal ideal itself becomes indeterminate in the absence of criteria for identifying freedom and unfreedom' (op. cit., p. 141) and that 'the strong indeterminacy in liberal principles...spell ruin for fundamentalist liberalism' (Gray, 1993, p. 313).

'Debacle' and 'ruin' are strong words. They seem to claim too much too dramatically, for the case of liberalism is not lost, though I believe it will have to be pleaded along new, firmer and safer lines. Yet its loss of identity, loss of moral vigour and vulnerability to dilution are persuasive evidence that something is seriously amiss that cannot be put right merely by a return to the orthodoxy, such as it is, of the classical sources.

For this reason the present essay, though one of its objects is to deal with what seem to me some of the most potent fallacies that have colonized and perverted liberalism in recent years, seeks above all to look for the rock-bottom of liberal logic. It proceeds by laying bare what seems to me implicit in this logic and proposes three, admittedly sketchy, 'principles of politics'. I claim them to be principles that are entailed in the liberal ethic. Any liberal theory must incorporate them in its foundations and whatever else it contains must be consistent with them. Any such theory will, in that case, be simple, rugged, fairly though not absolutely undemanding in its assumptions about the nature of man and society, and undemanding in terms of its meta-ethics and epistemology. Above all it should be resistant to parasitic ideas alien to its ethic.

Armed with the nucleus, if not with the fully elaborated substance, of such a theory or perhaps theories, I shall in what follows seek to review some contemporary theses about the scope of government, democracy and property that, to my mind, contradict the logic of liberalism, while claiming to be developments and extensions of it.

Notes

1. There is a special case that ensures the perfect match, though there is little to recommend it for all that. Under it, liberty, or (in a more cautious formulation) a set of key liberties, is given lexicographic priority over all other values by the just political institutions of society; no trade-offs are sought or accepted. The lexicographic priority results from the unanimous choice of the parties who contract to be bound by these institutions. The parties are, for this purpose, a single person. His marginal rate of substitution of liberties against other values is infinity.

2. In Doubt, Abstain

Consequentialism 'on Balance'

Taken at large, this chapter pleads for an injunction to restrain consequentialism to its legitimate sphere which in politics is very small indeed. Consequentialism, reduced to its simplest expression, assesses the worth of an action by its results; as a guide to action, it tells us always to take from a set of mutually exclusive options the one that will bring about the best consequence unless there is a sufficient reason for doing otherwise. However, mainstream consequentialism is more absolute than this. For if the reason for not aiming at a certain consequence is sufficient, the consequence cannot be the best, and the real reason why we ought not to aim at it is that *on the balance of reasons* it is better not to do so. Consequent consequentialism, in other words, vanquishes all before it, because it reasons on the balance of *all* reasons. There may be under the widest, most general version of consequentialism, though not under its narrow and strict form, reasons for or against an action that are not its consequences. They are arguably not caused by it yet are its corollaries, so that we cannot seek 'the' result if we do not override the reason that speaks against the action in question. Doing good by lying would be one example incorporating two reasons to be balanced against one another in wide consequentialism; the narrow version would ignore the wrong of lying if it did neither harm nor wrong to anyone. It is nonetheless the case that consequentialism, wide or narrow, proceeds by *adding up* widely or narrowly conceived arguments with due regard to their algebraic sign, positive or negative. The distinction between wide and narrow forms of consequentialism is confined to the kind of arguments that are admitted to the exercise of summing. Utilitarianism, the oldest and most prominent version of narrow consequentialism, operates only with arguments about the extent to which actions cause the preferences of individuals to be satisfied.

The Scope of Government as the Scope for Doing Good

Within the logic of consequentialist ethics, it is incoherent to want to limit the scope of government. For as long as the beneficial conse-quence of the best available political option exceeds its opportunity cost (which is of course the benefit expected from the next-best option), it is incoherent to say that the best option ought not to be exercised. It is like saying that the net increment of good ought to be thrown out of the window, cheating society of it.

A constitution may be no more than a set of procedural rules laying down how political decisions are to be reached – perhaps, more pre-cisely, the conditions that must be fulfilled for a political decision to be binding both for the officers of the state and for its ordinary subjects. These are, to use Herbert Hart's term, the 'rules of recognition' writ large. Beyond them, the constitution may also lay down substantive rules about the admissible content of political decisions. Their effect is to render certain procedurally quite irreproachable decisions inadmiss-ible. For instance, the effect may be to forbid and void a majority vote by secret ballot for indefinite detention without trial, for press censor-ship, or for the taking of property without just compensation. Any such substantive limitation is but 'vain breath' in consequentialist ethics, for it amounts to a *vow* not to do certain things even if, one day, there was sufficient 'on balance' benefit from doing them. However, by what Thomas Schelling calls 'a stunning principle of social organisation' (Schelling, 1984, p. 99), but what seems simply an entailment of the meaning of 'promise', a promisee can always release the promisor from his promise, and if they happen to be the same person the prom-isee cannot coherently both demand and refuse the release. If, then, the action that is inadmissible under the constitution appears to hold out better consequences on balance than any alternative, a consequentialist society cannot, without self-contradiction, allow the power for doing good of its politics to be frustrated by self-imposed constitutional limi-tations. Limiting government, as it were on purpose, would only be rational if the scope for doing good were itself limited, which no doubt it is not.

'Balancing' Incommensurables

Why, despite its pleasing logic, is all this wrong? There are two inde-pendent reasons. The first is relatively mundane: it is that we ignore the full consequences of many of our actions. This, for an individual responsible only to himself and his family dependents, imposing his will on no one else, dealing with them only by means of voluntary exchanges or gifts, is not a very grave moral problem. Politics, however, is different. It involves the use of what is, for practical purposes, an irresistible power, 'the monopoly of the legitimate use of force', to impose the will of some on all, including on those who would reject it if they could. For politics, therefore, the Hippocratic precept applies with particular stringency: *first, avoid doing harm*. A state that acts on the consequentialist logic, and ignores out of hubris, bad faith, or sheer lack of perspicacity, its own ignorance of the consequences which may in time turn out to be far from good, will fritter away the legitimacy of its monopoly of force – if indeed it ever had it.

The second reason is more fundamental and, to my mind, if anything more compelling. It is that among the multiple consequences, functioning as multiple reasons for or against, only some are commensurate. Those that are, suffer from our partial ignorance of what they will in fact turn out to be: but this handicap could in principle be attenuated if we learned more about the future. Those, on the other hand, that are not commensurate, defy any consequentialist logic even in principle, and even if all knowable knowledge were known. Between the good and the bad consequence, where neither is either greater or smaller than or equal to the other, no balance can be struck, and consequentialist reasoning is simply out of place.

The central place where consequentialist reasoning is incompetent to penetrate is the interpersonal balancing of 'utility'. This is more than somewhat ironical, since nine political decisions out of ten have such balancing as their unspoken justification; a policy is adopted because, though it imposes costs on some, it brings greater benefits to others.[1] The cost, seen comprehensively and taking everything into consideration that the policy influences unfavourably, is the diminished utility of some. The benefit, reckoned in the same comprehensive way, is the increased utility of others. The reason why we cannot proceed to a straightforward addition, with due regard to sign, is not (as many astonishingly still persist in thinking) that we 'lack sufficiently detailed utility information' and don't know how much to add and how much to deduct, but if only we had the 'information' we could strike a balance. The reason is that there is no information to be had and no balance to be struck. The good of different persons is incommensurable.

Avoid Doing Harm

Let us be very clear about one thing. The value judgement that it is better if a certain subset of a society gains and another loses than if neither gains and neither loses is just that – a value judgement and a perfectly legitimate one at that. So would the contrary judgement be. Neither has more analytical or empirical support than the other. The 'ought' is not derived from any kind of epistemic 'is', for before making the value judgement between two policies, we have not measured nor compared differences between the utility gains and the utility losses of two groups of individuals. Once again, we have not done so, not because we 'lack the data' but because the project of comparison is nonsensical and could not be proceeded with. Policy recommendations that insinuate some kind of 'is' backing up their 'ought' – the classic example is the more or less tacit suggestion that a more even distribution of national income 'must' have a greater utility – lack either honesty or intelligence. Policy recommendations courageously disclaiming support from facts, surmises, or reasoned forecasts, and resting squarely on some overt and partisan value judgement alone, must stand up against rival value judgements. This is a contest that cannot be decided inside consequentialism, if it can be decided at all. Its result must, at all events, be subordinated to the moral precept about the use of the fearful instrument of legal coercion: first, avoid doing harm.

Commission and Omission

Nothing that I can see authorizes the setting of the commission of some harm on the same footing as the omission of doing some good. On the contrary, harming and benefiting the same person, let alone different persons, are sufficiently heterogeneous to be held prima facie incommensurable in any relevant and non-trivial sense. An action whose consequences combine such 'incommensurable' elements cannot, then, be characterized by *one* on-balance consequence, and compared with another action and its consequence, because a combination of non-homogeneous consequences resulting from an action cannot be expressed as a single net balance.

The consequentialist calculus, in other words, is inapplicable wherever a consequence of an action within a set of alternatives contains incommensurable elements. By and large, commissions and omissions, and interpersonal gains and losses, defy such calculus. Choosing one alternative from such a set is a value judgement, and must never pretend to be a judgement of fact.

It is dubious in the extreme that a political authority is entitled to employ its power of coercion for imposing value-choices on society, on its subsets and on individual members. Its sole guiding principle in such cases can only be: *When in doubt, abstain.* That the choice could be justified by a value judgement shared, for example by a voting majority, does not remove doubt, especially if outside the majority rival value judgements are held. It may be observed that the respect of this guiding principle, unless it were complemented by other deontic rules about what governments must do irrespective of the consequences (and unless these rules mandated government actions even if the consequences were not unambiguously welcomed by all concerned), would compress politics to the vanishing point.

Cognitivist Authority

If consequentialism were to be a valid rule of choice in all cases, the value judgement by which the choice is in some cases (in fact in most cases that really matter) made, would itself have to be a valid one. But whether one judgement putting a valuation on a consequence, among rival judgements putting different valuations on it, is valid or not is itself a question to be resolved, under consequentialism, on consequentialist grounds. It can normally only be resolved by a value judgement which has, in turn, to be validated. This leads us into an infinite regress. To avoid it, we can close the loop by postulating a valid value judgement that, on cognitivist authority, finds in favour of on-balance reasoning in evaluating consequences. (One such possible value judgement could, for instance, assert that we ought to impute interpersonal levels or differences of human well-being to levels or differences of some measurable, homogeneous resource endowment, electing the latter as a proxy for the former.[2]) The doctrine then rests on circular logic, for the alleged correspondence between two sets of interpersonal differences, one measurable, the other not, is not a finding of fact, but a judgement about how we should evaluate such differences.

The Presumption against Coercion

If consequentialism is circular, depending in all cases involving harm or interpersonal comparisons on a value judgement about its own validity, the standard argument for letting the state do all the good we can find for it to do, and accordingly allowing politics to have unrestricted scope, falls to the ground. Its collapse releases and activates the basic presumption against coercion, a presumption that can be derived either from an axiom about the practice of choice, or from a social convention of 'live and let live', of letting each do what he will if doing so involves, roughly speaking, no harm to others. Accepting, and acting on, this presumption also presupposes a value judgement, but it is one that demands far less of our moral credulity than any consequentialist alternative I can think of.

The presumption against coercion must always mandate *some* restriction of the domain of politics, removing at least some alternatives from the reach of social choice. Otherwise the presumption would have no effect on the use of coercion, and it is difficult to see precisely what would be meant by it in that case, unless it were that while coercion can legitimately be used to realize any socially chosen alternative whatever, in the face of the presumption social choices should only be made upon strong provocation and strong justification, while in its absence any justification would do. This difference is verbal, slippery and vague, it does not work intersubjectively, and has no place in a political doctrine that is meant to be resistant to Princess Mathilde's and other interested parties' attempts to twist it in their own favour.

Giving real effect to the anti-coercion presumption, then, means at least some non-procedural, strictly substantive limitation of social choice. It takes too much faith in political man's rectitude to believe that such limitations will generally, let alone always, be respected; after all, they are 'only' vows, promises to ourselves, and temptations to break them come dense and fast in public life. It is a very unsafe political order that must rely heavily on a substantive constitution. The major danger, as the history of constitutions and especially of that of the US convincingly shows, is not the open breach of a substantive rule, but its 'evolution', its reinterpretation, small step by small step, its twisting out of all recognition in the span of a few decades.[3] In view of this experience, some kinds of constitutional limitations look more likely than others to stand up against the temptations of the times, simply by virtue of their lesser twistability. An indiarubber rule, for instance, that subjects government actions to the test of fairness, and makes statutory distributions of burdens and benefits unconstitutional if they do not respect the condition of fair shares, must be practically unbreakable, for the understanding of what are fair shares is sufficiently flexible and malleable to accommodate the whole range of politically feasible distributive policies. By comparison, a fixed bar on aggregate public expenditure of all kinds, limiting a certain definition of it to a fixed maximum share of a certain definition of national income, however blunt and arbitrary it may be, is less twistable. It can no doubt be circumvented in relatively minor ways by stretching the definitions, but probably not in massive proportions; if public expenditure as defined exceeds the permissible percentage of national income as defined, the rule is openly broken, ringing the alarm bell, provoking at least some embarrassment, some blame, and some modest impetus for a revision of policies.

Lowering the Stakes

The 'when in doubt, abstain' principle will more effectively guide (and curb) the state in a body politic that is not yet permeated by, or has already shaken itself free from, consequentialist ethics and cognitivist meta-ethics. Such arcane matters in the realm of thought may not seem burningly relevant to practical politics. However, in the long run they probably matter more than they seem. The liberal disposition so attractively demonstrated by the Scottish Enlightenment, by Humboldt, Constant and Bastiat, was inspired by implicit deontological rules of liberty and property. In the edifice of liberal ideology erected by 19th-century philosophers and economists, an edifice whose design was wide open and, as I would contend, positively invited invasion by alien squatter elements, the deontology was largely replaced by essentially utilitarian justifications. Liberty and property became instrumental, means to other, more nearly final ends and values. As other means came to be seen as equally or more efficient in maximizing the same values, or as the hierarchy of values appears to have shifted, liberty and property, and the conventional rules upholding them, progressively lost their morally inviolable character. It would be extravagant to affirm that the hubris of consequentialist and cognitivist thought caused the loss; but it is plain that it gave intellectual coherence and ethical backbone to the process.

At first blush the 'in doubt, abstain' principle looks not a liberal but a conservative one; for cases of reasonable doubt about policy abound, and if instead of resolving them, in doubt we abstain, it is the status quo we may be thought to protect. The theorem that 'utility' is inter-subjectively incommensurate, hence interpersonal comparisons presented as findings of fact are gibberish, appears likewise to justify the status quo at least by default.[4] However, it is an unwarranted diagnosis. For cases of reasonable doubt abound, not only about policy changes but also about policies already in force. Civil society is tightly shackled and heavily steered in its legal, cultural, and perhaps most particularly in its economic dimension by literally countless institutions, statutes, rules, state properties, regulatory interventions and administrative practices, that are imposed on it by fiscal or other coercion. A benign view of government sees them as self-imposed by the citizenry, 'socially chosen', but even so for some reason needing to be enforced by a dominant central coercive power that, by virtue of its monopoly, is different in kind, and not only in degree, from the lesser coercive powers scattered across civil society. With regard to such of these institutions as are, in the light of the foregoing arguments, in reasonable doubt, the principle calls, not for leaving them as they are, but for dismantling them. In that it is not a conservative, but a liberal principle.

Dismantling certain state and state-enforced institutions by repeal, privatization and, at the margin, by reduced scope and reduced budgets for continuing programmes, has an interesting and I believe far-reaching by-product: it lowers the stakes that can be gained or lost by exerting some influence on the redistributive aspects of governing. (I speak advisedly of the 'redistributive aspects' of governing, instead of referring to the government's 'redistributive measures', in order to exclude the inference that there can be government measures that are not redistributive. Every policy measure either produces benefits that have an incidence on individuals or imposes burdens that must be allocated among them, or both at the same time; and it is not logically impossible but hardly imaginable that they could leave the distribution the same as it would be if the measure had not been taken. This is a fact of life, whose truth does not depend on any redistributive intention. Whether redistribution is the primary objective of some government activity or its more or less accidental by-product, is often impossible to determine anyway.) The more the stakes are lowered, the more the nature of such policies as subsist is transformed. This is the converse of the case of a large role of government in the regulation of industry and commerce, in taxation, transfers and the production of public goods, very fully explored by public choice theory under the heading of 'rent-seeking'. When potential 'rents' are getting progressively more miserly, interest groups have less of a stake in preserving the stakes, the industry of seeking rents goes into decline, which ought by a feedback effect to reinforce and accelerate the lowering of the stakes, hence the slimming down of 'rents'. This scenario will probably never be played out on a real political stage, but that need not stop us from pointing out that it represents a plausible conjecture about the practical effect that the progressive espousal in our social ethics of the 'when in doubt' principle would have.

Between 'Must' and 'Must Not'

A recognition that consequentialism as a guide to political action backed by coercion is unsound, flatulent and unable to live up to its pretensions, would leave only deontological rules potentially standing. The most important rule, overshadowing all others, is undoubtedly the negative one imposing on the state the general duty of abstention from using coercive power for purposes whose consequentialist justification is of the on-balance kind and where the sign of the balance is open to reasonable doubt. Is there anything further to say? Are there, in the shadow of the negative rule, positive ones laying on the state the duty to use coercion in order to accomplish certain things?

If there are no things requiring coercion that the state *may* but *need not* do, i.e. if there is no optional middle ground between what must and what must not be done by coercion, it suffices to define what the state must do. If what it must do can be specified and justified, things it must abstain from are defined by the same token: they are all the things whose achievement involves coercion and that the state has *no duty* to do. Positive deontological rules yield, as a residue, the negative one: 'abstain'. In a severe political deontology, treating coercion as a very grave matter not to be taken lightly, and for that reason admitting no discretionary, optional areas of the political domain, there is only 'must' and 'must not', but no middle ground open to doubt, hence no latitude either for deciding whether the doubt is reasonable or not. Putting it differently, if the optional use of state coercion is excluded, so that the only uses of it that are permitted are mandatory ones, the description of the mandatory area adequately describes the prohibited area as well: the latter is whatever is not covered by the former.

Certitude about what must be done would do away with the need to resort to the potentially controversial finding of 'reasonable doubt' about the occasions where abstention by the state is its duty. However, this ideal can hardly be attained. The very reason why reasonable doubt has an irreducible element of subjectivity, militates also against an uncontroversial, agreed position about the cases where it is certain that the state has a duty not to abstain, but to act. Given all the things that the state could do, any degree of indeterminacy in the subset labelled 'must' entails the same indeterminacy in the complementary subset labelled 'must not'.

The indeterminacy is not resolved by the usual liberal device of enunciating a list of 'musts' – the prevention of harm, the protection of rights, the production of public goods – both because each of these purported duties of the state is poorly defined and indeterminate in itself, and because it is by no means proven that these functions are totally and intrinsically political, and could not wholly or partly be fulfilled by non-political, non-coerced, cooperative arrangements. Swallowing them whole and uncritically as the archetypal and irreducible duties of the state is to swallow a hook by which individuals in a civil society find themselves committed to a form of political life that many find overwhelming and unduly intrusive. The three duties of harm-prevention, rights-protection and public-goods production, between them are sufficiently broad and have sufficient capacity for expansion by reinterpretation, to leave no part of life outside politics and no resource whose use is not subject to non-unanimous coercive collective choice.

Inviting Coercion

Recourse to first principles in political ethics suggests a path, albeit a narrow one and poorly signposted, out of this thicket of fuzzy definitions and indeterminacies. The first principle that seems to me the least demanding, hence the easiest to subscribe to though no doubt less easy to put into effect, is that applying coercion is legitimate when it is positively invited by the prospective coercee.

For an isolated individual, the only case when it is not absurd to bring down coercion on his own head is when he thinks he needs help to overcome his own weakness of will. The case is well known and can be taken as read. In every other case he would be silly to ask to be coerced to do what he wanted to do, and sillier still if he asked to be made to do what he did not want to do.

Interactions of two or more persons, however, can create situations ('prisoners' dilemmas') where inviting coercion is the rational thing to do, given certain expectations about the actions of the other persons or, more fundamentally, about their rationality. The object is to transform a non-cooperative 'game' into a cooperative one by improving the credibility of promises. There is, to be sure, an argument to the effect that this is only half the battle. Making agreements fully credible by enforcing compliance presupposes that agreements are reached in the first place; this is the basis of what Jules Coleman calls 'thin contractarianism' (Coleman 1988, chapter 10). 'Thick' contractarianism, by contrast, recognizes that bargaining about the distribution of the prospective surplus to be produced by overcoming a prisoner's dilemma is itself liable to fail, and there may be no agreement to comply with. This type of theory, then, contends that the emergence of market solutions is prevented by 'pre-market market failure' (ibid., pp. 262–76). To resolve this more 'fundamental' (p. 267) failure, an antecedent 'political association' is necessary to lay down a 'property rights scheme', including rules of property, liability and tort.

How the scheme allocates property rights in the pre-market situation, i.e. under what distributive conditions all participants will agree to a political association that will enforce the scheme, is thought to be a bargaining problem of great complexity. The claim that rational behaviour will lead to a universally agreed property rights scheme is not very plausible (p. 267). The upshot is that the state exercising coercion without the prior consent of its subjects may be necessary for Pareto-optimal resource allocation.

The problem, it seems to me, arises from the wholly artificial starting position where distribution is, so to speak, up for discussion, and there are no established, pre-existing property relations. (It is worth stopping here to note that while in the theory that Jules Coleman calls 'thick contractarianism' people bargain *ex nihilo* about distributing unowned wealth among themselves, and likely fail to reach a bargain solution, in the contractarian theory of Buchanan and Tullock, and of David Gauthier, the base line from which bargaining starts is one where wealth is already owned. The solution does not establish a 'property rights scheme' *ex nihilo*, but modifies the one that already exists in the state of nature.) A grand bargain to decree who shall own what is then necessary and may well fail to be reached. But there is, of course, no call for such an overall bargain, for patterns of ownership emerge and evolve over time in virtue of unilateral acts (see pp. 37–41) and bilateral contracts, and can be sufficiently determined by them. The 'thick theory' with its 'pre-market market failure' creates its own difficulty.

'Market failure', or more precisely the possibility that people may not succeed to base schemes of corporation on contracts, but may need coercion, or ties of affection and solidarity, is a vast field of study that occupies the better part of game theory. The most we can do here is to allude to some of its more robust conclusions. The situations where it can be rational for me to invite coercion have at least one common feature. It is that the best outcome of the interaction for each of us is obtained if neither of us seeks the best outcome for himself. Contract is the most important of such situations.[5] The best outcome for me is if the other party performs and I default. Second best both for me and the other party is if we both perform. Mutual commitment to seeking the second best by each will ensure the best possible for all. If each is coerced to respect his commitment, each can have full confidence that none of the others can take advantage of his trust. Let us note, for consideration presently, that coercion, let alone coercion by a single central political authority, is not a necessary condition for commitments to be credible, and that instead of 'full' confidence, partial, probabilistic confidence in the other participants may be sufficient for the best outcome for each to be obtained (or at least approximated in a mixed strategy equilibrium).

From the condition that for coercion to be legitimate it must be invited by the prospective coercee, it is only one step to hypothetical invitation, the crucial first step in social contract theory. Its argument refers to a contract situation where, assuming the parties were rational, they *would* invite coercion if it were absent (i.e. if the invitation were not redundant to the citizens of an existing coercive state) and if they were not too numerous to communicate and agree among themselves on a jointly binding invitation, i.e. if 'transactions costs' were not too high.

'Transactions costs', default and free rider temptations, and 'hold-out' temptations that can obstruct the solution of bargaining problems, are the three sub-optimal unfruitful situations where it is conceivable that rational persons caught in this type of predicament might rather escape from it under coercion than remain in it and escape coercion.

However, it is not good enough that they conceivably might, or that under certain types of mutual expectations, whose presence inside their heads we cannot verify, it would be rational for them to wish to do so. Hypothetical invitations have no better standing than hypothetical contracts. What is needed for the application of coercion to be above moral suspicion is that the prospective coercees *do* actually invite it. The way to provoke this, hence to test the legitimacy of the state, is for it to stand back and not to proffer political solutions, by legislation, regulation and taxation, to such tasks as the enforcement of basic social conventions (notably concerning torts, externalities and the amenities of civilized conduct), of contracts and the provision of public goods. It is only when politically imposed and publicly financed solutions are not readily available that those concerned can tell whether voluntary 'grassroots' solutions would or would not work, and the necessary conventions to stabilize them would or would not emerge soon enough; and only if they really do not is there an ethically defensible case for calling in the state to help. Finally, and here we have come full circle, it is only by first withstanding these tests that certain tasks become duties the state must assume, duties about which there could hardly be reasonable doubt.

Notes

1. There are two unsophisticated variants of this formula. One states that the policy benefits more people or more voters than it imposes costs upon. This is the democratic variant. The other states that the benefits, in terms of money or 'wealth', exceed the costs. This is the cost–benefit approach of the workaday economist, as well as of the judge walled in by the 'Law and Economics' perspective.

   I am not suggesting that because they are unsophisticated, these variants should never be used. They seem to me to have some grounding in common sense in some, essentially non-political, morally not acute contexts. But they cannot bear the weight of the heavy guns of sovereign prerogative and lawful coercion – at least morally they cannot.

2. Utilitarians think that the basis for interpersonal comparisons can be found in 'how desirable certain things are', in knowing 'what makes life enjoyable and how [a person] with his individual differences is placed to exploit his possibilities' (Griffin, 1986, p. 188); 'comparisons involve a general profile of prudential values' (op. cit., p. 120), i.e. objective entities.

   One of the premier utility theorists, John Harsanyi (1977, pp. 58–9) proceeds by linking each person's preferences to objectively ascertainable general causes or variables and using them as a proxy for everyone's preferences, which then become homogeneous and comparable.

   The avowed non-utilitarian goes much the same way: 'workable criteria for ... the relevant interpersonal comparisons must, I believe, be founded on primary goods or some similar notion' (Rawls, 1982, p. 170).

   The common strategy is to save interpersonal comparability, i.e. aggregation, by replacing heterogeneous, *personal* predicates by homogeneous and *impersonal* ones. But the substitution is exactly that: it replaces something with something different without furnishing any conclusive proof that they are not really, relevantly different. Instead, it slips in an arbitrary value judgement that rules them relevantly the same.

3. There need be no scheming, nor stealth, nor any conscious partisan ideological effort involved in these processes. Constitutions are expressed in language and their meaning shifts with the ebb and flow of public opinion and public understanding of the language (cf. Epstein, 1985, p. 20).

4. There is, in fact, a clear distinction between the effects of the 'when-in-doubt' principle and the status-quo-protecting Pareto principle. (On the conservatism of the latter, cf. Peacock and Rowley, 1979, pp. 24–5.) The former relates to doubt about the algebraic sign of the difference that the state-enforced institution or policy measure makes to the goodness of an overall state of affairs. There is doubt whether it is positive or negative. The presumption is against the maintenance, and not only

against the novel introduction, of some state-enforced feature of the state of affairs, and the burden of proof is on those who advocate its preservation if it already exists or its introduction if it does not. The Pareto principle, by contrast, creates a presumption against any change in the state of affairs and puts the burden of proof on the advocates of change to show that it would not make anyone feel worse off or that no one would object to it.

5. Every executory contract is of course a single-play game of prisoner's dilemma with 'default' as the dominant strategy. The received wisdom is that contracts would be 'vain breath without the sword' – at any rate so spoke Hobbes and we can, I think, safely go along with him this far – *and* that the sword must be that of a monopolist of the use of force – which does not follow at all. 'Swords' of the contracting parties, and of their neighbours, peers, colleagues, associates, competitors, customers and suppliers are deterrents to default that are not demonstrably more inefficient than monopolist enforcement by the state. Many historical episodes show that the private enforcement of customary contract law thrived whenever the state for one reason or another was unable forcibly or amicably to displace conventional co-operation.

What default is to contract, tortious acts are to social conventions about respect for life, limb and property. Their incentive structure is a prisoner's dilemma and trespass, larceny, 'conversion' represent the dominant strategy. The received wisdom is that without the strong arm of the protective state, we would make each other's lives unliveable and society would founder in 'anarchy'. This of course does not follow from anything, except perhaps from the vague feeling that the state must be serving some purpose, and if we could have order without it, it would prove to be a useless creature and would wither away. The reason why the institution of contract does not need the state either for its emergence or for its survival, and why in reasonably healthy communities life and property are broadly respected, and social conventions sanctioning breaches of such respect with ostracism, mutual assistance, 'civic policing', etc. are maintained, is basically simple. Default and tort are dominant strategies in single-play prisoners' dilemmas only. But in real life there are very few genuinely single-play games. Most of life's social relations are in reality probabilistic repeated games. Every player who expects to live another day runs some risk of meeting some player again in some game or another.

3. The Feasible is Presumed Free

The Freedom to Choose and the Things one is Free is Choose

The question whether freedom is valuable or a free society is good, ought not to enter at all into a properly thought-out political doctrine, liberal or other. It should be resolutely ignored. Whichever way the question were answered would, it seems to me inevitably, steer us in a teleological direction, and undermine the foundations on which the society that we could consider free might stand and survive. What Richard Epstein says of civic virtue and happiness goes almost certainly for freedom too: 'to make it the direct end of human conduct is to guarantee that it will not be obtained' (Epstein, 1985, p. 344).

An answer that freedom is *not* valuable is eccentric, nobody (or as good as) is prepared openly to voice it, and though it has intrinsic interest, we will not let it detain our argument. Answers affirming that it *is* valuable are of two sorts.

In one view, freedom is a final value. Arguments to show that it is valuable are neither possible nor necessary. There is nothing else more fundamental than itself, that could commend it and impart value to it.

This, of course, is a view that effectively stops argument, which is perhaps to be welcomed, but at the same time exposes freedom to the most devastating kind of relativism. It may seem valuable, perhaps very valuable to me, but nothing obliges you to agree with me, especially if you grew up in a different culture. On such intellectual foundations, freedom will be safe, if at all, only in a political community where it is already deeply ingrained; but it will not have the force freshly to colonize other, less free, polities.

The other kind of possible answer is that freedom is valuable for what it does for us: it is not a final, but an instrumental value. Having it enables us to choose what we prefer[1] and protects us from being made to choose what we do not prefer. Some call this the absence of coercion (Hayek, 1960), the ability to lead one's life according to one's own lights, non-subjection to the arbitrary will of another (Hayek, *passim*), an enabling condition to carry out one's life plan (Rawls, 1971), pursuing one's own projects (Lomasky, 1987) or autonomy (Raz, 1986). Probably little attention should be paid to such expressions and little is gained by an exegesis of their more or less significant differences. They all give freedom an instrumental role. However, defending freedom instrumentally by discovering some other, more nearly final, value to which it contributes, merely postpones the relativist devastation. For any instrumental value gets its worth, at one or several removes, from a final one. If no value is non-instrumental, no instrumental one could be valuable either, for an instrument that is merely a means to another instrument is worthless unless the latter is valuable; but the latter is worthless unless it is more than merely a means to yet another instrument, and so on. Value could only be recognized and found at the end of an infinite regress, that is to say nowhere. Consequently, any disability that final values suffer due to their finality and that freedom as a final value would suffer with them, is transmitted back to the corresponding instrumental values, including freedom if it *were* an instrumental value.

Furthermore – and this is the major disability – as and when attempts are made to give an account of what freedom is *for*, the concept bursts at its seams, starts to expand and risks absorbing other values that, on the evidence of our ordinary language, are distinct. There is presumably a reason why different words are used in ordinary language to denote them. This reason should be respected and they should be kept distinct.

Since freedom, whatever else it is, is *also* the absence of deliberate man-made obstacles to action, 'being free to do something and being able to do it' (Plant, 1992, p. 124) cannot be properly dissociated. Before we know where we are, the freedom of ordinary speech and freedom as the set of the alternatives among which we are free to choose are confounded. We find ourselves saying that richer, more attractive alternatives, as well as greater knowledge and the ability to discern them, mean more freedom. Money, brains, looks, talents, opportunities are all part of freedom, they all pass under the spreading umbrella concept that swallows up much that ordinary language knows by separate words. One depressing end result is that we now call, without the least semantic embarrassment, both the freedom to choose and the set of things available to be chosen by the same name of freedom, distinguishing between them only by the misplaced adjectives 'negative' and 'positive'.

It is not inevitable that discourse about freedom should degenerate into discourse about all good things *and* that the latter should also be called 'freedom'. But the confusion is difficult to avoid, and current practice, for instance the frequent claim that 'welfare rights' are a derivative of freedom, and valuing freedom implies recognizing them, does all it can to make it worse confounded.

A Deontological Frame

Neither the confusion nor the effort it would take to dissipate the worst of it, are really necessary. The awkward, shapeless and unruly concept of freedom that seems deeply infected by consequentialist thought, can be sidestepped altogether. In its place, it is a simple task to fit a frame of familiar deontological rules. Those who wish can call the space framed by the rules 'freedom', but nothing is lost if this is not done.

The basic rule is that a person is presumed free to do what is feasible for him to do. This presumption is subject to two compatibility conditions. One relates a person's proposed actions to his own obligations, the other to harm to others. Where these conditions are satisfied, the presumption that feasible actions are admissible has the effect of relieving the defendant of the burden of proof that his action is in fact admissible, and must neither be hindered nor sanctioned. The burden of proof is clearly placed on the plaintiff instead, who challenges the admissibility of the action. This is in harmony with fundamental rules of action in both Roman and common law. A well-known rule is that the accused is presumed innocent until proven guilty; another is that possession gives rise to presumption of title. Remarkably, this harmony ceases in the realm of public law. Citizens are apparently not *as a rule* presumed to need no permission to do what is feasible for them to do. Instead, actions seem to be presumed forbidden unless specifically permitted, and citizens are given civil 'rights' under constitutional provisions, and entire 'bills of rights', to that effect. Indeed, these 'rights' are incoherent unless seen as suspensive conditions of a tacit presumption that everything not covered by them is forbidden by legislative discretion if not by legislative *fiat*. The affirmation of these 'rights' grossly ignores the norm at the root of liberal thought, that whoever proposes to stop another from doing what is feasible must show a right to prohibit or obstruct the particular feasible action.

The rule and its two conditions have intuitive appeal but like the value of freedom that is self-evident to lovers of freedom but not to non-lovers, this appeal too lacks universality. However, two other, less relative arguments support it. One is epistemological. There are two rival presumptions: 'everything is admitted that is not specifically excluded', and 'everything is excluded that is not specifically admitted'. Whichever hypothesis is adopted, either the list of excluded, or the list of admitted actions is sufficient for identifying any action as either admitted or not. Both are not needed for guidances in choosing actions. However, the list of feasible actions is indefinitely long. Compiling the full list of interdictions is, under ordinary circumstances, a less onerous task than compiling a full list of permissions; enumerating what we must not do, and monitoring that we do not do it, are less exacting than listing what we have a right to do, and monitoring that we do not do what we have no right to do. However, if no lists of either kind are readily available, distinguishing between what is admitted and what is excluded becomes a matter of probabilistic inference, and in the extreme case where neither a priori grounds nor indirect, circumstantial evidence favour certain actions over others, putting one's proposed action in one category rather than another becomes a random choice. Discovery of admissible actions, then, is more likely, and the risk of mistaking an excluded action for admissible is less likely if the first presumption prevails than if the second prevails. The worst of both worlds is if there is a list of excluded actions, a list of 'rights', and an unspecified zone about which no clear presumption exists, allowing free play to political discretion. Such a configuration is typical of para-totalitarian government.

The other argument is that the presumptions of admissibility and of inadmissibility are not morally equivalent. In a borderline case, the first presumption permits a proposed action to take its course unless a good cause is shown why it should not. Harm and contrary obligation constitute such causes under the suspensive conditions of the 'feasible is free' principle. If the action is harmless and breaches no obligation, it is free. Harm or obligation has to be proven to stop it. The second presumption stops the proposed action unless good cause is shown why it should be allowed to take its course. Let us suppose for argument's sake that there is symmetry between the suspensive conditions of the two presumptions. Both presumptions are suspended only with respect to harms and breaches of obligation, and nothing else. For the second presumption, this means that *unless* it can be shown that the proposed action *is* harmless and breaches no obligation, it must *not* take its course. If the universe of harms that the particular action must not cause is not clearly and unambiguously bounded, it is impossible to prove (i.e. verify) that the action would be harmless. The universe of imaginable harms is too vast and ill-defined for every possible harm to be enumerated, examined, and its chance eliminated. Likewise, if the universe of obligations is not strictly circumscribed, it is impossible to prove that there is no obligation that the action would be in breach of, i.e. no right that it would violate. If both universes are properly and narrowly bounded, proof is possible in principle but hard to produce in practice.

There is, in addition, a built-in invitation to object to proposed courses of action simply because the objection costs little and has some chance of succeeding or being bought off. This rewards motives that can be cynically selfish, busybody, or merely frivolous. Extravagant claims of harms and rights by third parties get leverage and bargaining power under this principle that is probably out of proportion to their moral worth. Even if an action is not challenged for ulterior motives or out of sheer busybodiness, the formal requirement to show that it would cause no harm and breach no obligation (i.e. that no one's right could be opposed to it) is sufficient to stop any and all action and freeze everyone in impotent immobility – or would do if it were taken quite seriously. As it is, it merely suffices to render ordinary processes of social cooperation excessively legalistic, litigious, costly and precariously dependent on judicial, administrative and regulatory review.

The Meaning of Coercion

When we say that a person should be presumed free to do what is feasible for him to do, subject to the 'harm' and 'obligations' conditions, we risk creating a false impression, for 'free' could well be understood to mean 'costless'. Plainly, an action that is both harmless to others and is not in breach of an obligation, can be socially costless in the sense that it need use no resources that others could have used instead, and create no negative externalities for third parties. But individually being free to do something is never costless, for doing it loses the doer the opportunity of doing any of the other mutually exclusive alternatives. His cost of doing one thing is the forgone value to him of not doing the next-best thing. This is of course a recognition of an analytic truth[2] that economics owes to the Vienna School (Wieser), that has done to cost what the recognition that 'utility' cannot be added or subtracted across persons has subsequently done to welfare (Leube, 1994, p. 370). Its significance for the present purpose is in clarifying the concept of coercion, often left nebulous in ethical theorizing about state power; it seems more promising to clarify the meaning of coercion than that of freedom, and it achieves no less.

Coercion is an intentional act by A, whether actual or threatened, whose effect is so to change B's set of feasible alternatives as to make his chosen alternative different from what A presumed B's preferred alternative to be. Successful coercion must make B act otherwise than A thought that he had intended to act. It achieves this by intrusion into B's feasible set. Successful coercion alters the cost of alternatives so as to make B choose as A wishes, and not as A thought that B wished.

The object of coercion can be of two kinds: either to induce B to take a particular alternative ('I will hit you if you do not listen to me'), or to dissuade him from taking one ('I will hit you if you listen to her'). Coercion operates by intentionally deforming an existing option, e.g. 'not listening to him' into 'not listening to him *and* getting hit'. It is of course possible that B did not really prefer 'listening to her', was not going to, and the threat of being hit if he did was quite unnecessary. But A did not know this, and from his point of view coercion was effective. Enforcement of a norm of behaviour even after conforming to the norm has become second nature, would correspond to this pattern; it would confirm the enforcer's belief in the importance of his coercive function.

It is important to appreciate that the concept of coercion is not simply qualitative, binary, absent or present. It matters whether the threat is to be hit on the head with a heavy hammer, on the knuckles with a ruler, or on the cheek with a lady's fan. It would be absurd to call the last threat coercion. Doing so would trivialize a matter that is intrinsically grave, that conventional linguistic usage should encourage us to regard as grave, and that must continue to have, as it has had in the past, overtones of the politically incorrect. How about having one's knuckles rapped to encourage one kind of behaviour? Should this be regarded as coercive – and does it depend on rapping them hard enough? Obviously, since we want the idea of coercion to be confined to serious matters which requires us to ignore trifles, we must assess intrusions into the feasible choice set in quantitative terms. What is and is not coercion must be treated as a matter of the degree of intrusion. Hence we cannot escape the usual 'where to draw the line' problem. Where does trivial interference end and coercion, with all the weight the word should carry, begin?

The law would draw the line where the threatened coercive act, if carried out by a private actor, would be an actionable tort. Much the same line should serve to separate trifles from serious harms to others.

This line, though rough and ready, seems good enough for most purposes, but not all. It fails to capture cases of moral bullying and blackmail, it is not clear where it would put various cases of the threatened use of economic power, and it is altogether silent on the exercise of the state's power over its citizens.

...And How not to Stretch it

Economic power, acting on the options of others by the (albeit implicit) threat of its use, is often cited as coercive. No amount of conceptual clarification will persuade the average wage earner facing his supervisor, or the small business man anxious to keep the custom of a much bigger one, that he is not being coerced in certain bargaining situations. It is nonetheless worth pointing out that with such a usage, coercive acts spill over, ethically speaking, from the domain of right and wrong to the domain of the putatively equitable and reasonable. Legally speaking, it would classify as coercion acts or the threat of acts that 'deprived' a person, the employee or the small businessman, of an option he did not have in the first place. He may have expected to strike a certain bargain, or renew it on the old terms. He may have considered that this was a reasonable expectation, and third parties may have thought his expected terms equitable.[3] For all that, however, the bargain on the hoped-for terms was never an available alternative in the feasible set of the 'economically weak' party, and not having it in the first place, he was not deprived of it when the stronger party presented his unexpectedly tough terms. A bargain over terms is a contract, and a contract, depending on at least two parties, is never in the feasible set of only one of them;[4] only an unexpired offer of one party is in the feasible set of the other.

Stretching the concept of coercion beyond *existing* options, so as to make it cover *reasonable expectations* as well, is of course not a matter of the improper use of logic and language. Between stretching and not stretching a concept, we choose as we see fit. One usage is not true and the other is not false. Adopting one or the other is a matter of political and legal judgement. It is quite conceivable that some way down the road we are travelling, political thought will have evolved to the point, and legislation will have been put on the books to the effect, that the terms of *all* contracts between parties of disparate wealth or 'economic strength' are to be subject to court approval, and the threat of nonrenewal of an expiring contract on the same or better terms will become tortious coercion. This is not yet standard practice. It would be stupendously inefficient if it became the standard, though that is perhaps no reason for expecting it not to happen. Nor is it the principal argument against putting the thwarting of expectations on the same footing as the spoiling of actual options. The main argument, it seems to me, remains the rock-bottom distinction between what the first party *is* free to do with his endowments without violating the 'harm' and 'obligation' conditions, and what he, no matter how reasonably, *hopes* to be able to do, subject to a second party's agreement. If withholding the reasonably hoped-for agreement is deemed coercive in cases where the first party is 'economically weaker' than the second, and if coercion has legal consequences, the first party's 'freedom' becomes incompatible with that of the second party. Any principle that entails this incompatibility renders the system of justice self-contradictory. It is an unjust principle, both if justice means concordance with 'natural right' and if it means the respect of rights resulting from agreements.[5]

If coercion is held to be a grave enough injury to call for redress, extending the scope of its meaning is a grave matter, too. Freedom of contract can no doubt produce harsh terms on occasion, as Hayek's oft-cited parable of the thirsty man in the oasis and the extortionate price of water shows, and as many other situations of monopoly and monopsony tend to produce on a less cruel scale. If such results are to be prevented, the prophylactic remedy is to be sought in the causes of monopoly and monopsony. They are less intractable in our type of economic environment than in the desert oasis. Doing away with the freedom of contract in cases of transactions between 'strong' and 'weak' parties, on the grounds that a person's reasonable expectations, especially if he is weak, should enjoy the same protection as his effective options, looks like a remedy that is worse, morally more objectionable, than the alleged wrong it would be designed to right. For it is hard to conceive that loading the system of justice with mutually contradictory elements can possibly contribute to more perfect justice.

'Having no Alternative'

In ordinary speech, a person is said to 'have had no alternative, he was coerced'. What is usually meant is that though there was at least one alternative, i.e. to resist the coercion, it was too painful, too unpalatable, too costly for him to accept. It is worth making this point in the face of the barrage of rhetoric about capitalism, industrial society, materialism, racism, sexism, city life, suburban life, alienation or, more grandly still, 'the system', leaving people with 'no alternatives'.

There is, however, a special form of coercion that literally leaves no meaningful, non-casuistic alternative. If someone puts an armlock on you and calls 'say Uncle or I will break your arm', and if you are heroic enough, you can clearly choose not to say Uncle and have your arm broken. But what of the command, by someone much stronger than you who is holding you by the scruff of the neck by the waterside, 'jump in or I will throw you in'? Whether you jump or are thrown, you end up in the water; you had no real alternative, though you did have a casuistic one.

This special case is significant, for it is a simulation of the kind of coercion a state, possessing sovereign power, can and does exert in a vast number of everyday cases. The fiscal laws decree that a person in given circumstances must surrender a given part of his income or wealth for public purposes. Short of removing himself, this income and his assets from the legal reach of the state – an option that is not available to most ordinary people – the solvent individual, however ready to envisage costly alternatives, simply has none once he has exhausted all possible legal recourse. It is no use his accepting to be fined or to go to prison, he will be made to pay regardless, if need be by a lien on his income or seizure of his assets, just as the person who would not jump was thrown in regardless. Interestingly, every other coercive threat of the state, designed to ensure obedience to the law, is of the more general kind, which leaves the subject a genuine choice between two unpleasant options, in this case between obeying the law or breaking it and risking punishment. Whether anything ulterior and sinister about the state's differential intent can be read into such differential treatment – whether paying tax is the one duty the state *really* wants its subjects absolutely to fulfil – is something about which more extended speculation would be otiose.

In Lieu of Freedom-Talk

At this point, I will try to wind up what I think needs to be said about the deontological rules of politics in lieu of speaking about the politics of freedom.

Each individual is endowed by circumstances with a set of actions it is materially feasible for him to carry out. Some are inadmissible because they would cause harm to others that would be of a degree and a kind to constitute, by the long-standing conventional norms of society, *torts* and call for remedy. Others are inadmissible because the individual, by contracts he concluded with others, has undertaken not to choose them; they would constitute defaults, *breaches of obligation*. Every other feasible act of his is admissible. Among them, there are some he has undertaken to carry out, *at the option of others*, as his side of a promised exchange. He does not choose them, others choose them for him. These contracts or para-contractual undertakings to perform as promised if called upon to do so, define his contingent obligations.

The counterpart of his obligations are rights of others, while his *rights* are nothing else but obligations to him accepted by others. The exercise of the right and the fulfilment of the corollary obligation describe *the same event* in different words, just as 'A collected his loan from B' and 'B repaid the loan to A' describe the same event. The evidence of an obligation is the contract, and as between obligor who bears a burden and obligee who expects to benefit from it, the burden of proof is on the obligee, the claimant of the right, for it is in his interest, and not in the interest of the burden-bearer, to prove the claim. Every genuine right of one person has the agreement of another as its source, cause and evidence. The deontology of rights is their epistemology.[6] We know what they are by the way their existence is revealed, namely by the contract. Without it the consent of the bearer of the burden would be alleged and hypothetical at best, and the deontology of rights would rest on nothing more substantial than unilateral claims to benefits at the expense of others who never declared their willingness to assume them.

A brief digression seems to be called for here. What do we mean by 'every genuine right' having agreement as its source? How about the right of the unemployed to unemployment benefit, or of the child to instruction in a state school? In what sense do these rights spring from agreement, and are they 'genuine' or not? The common-sense answer is that the monarch or the legislator has agreed that the state should provide these things and place the corresponding burden on the tax-payer. An instance, the state as tax collector and welfare dispenser, has been interposed between obligee and obligor; there is no direct evidence that the obligation of the latter is voluntarily borne. On the contrary, there is a presumption that it is not. Does this deprive the putative right in question of the attributes of a 'genuine' right? Although the unemployed can until further notice successfully claim their benefit and the children their instruction, their right is specious for all that, not because the obligation is involuntary, but because it is *ex gratia*, non-contractual, subject to repudiation, hence precarious. The benefit is undoubtedly an entitlement for the time being, but unlike a right, it can be modified or reduced or withdrawn altogether without the rightholder's agreement, and without other cause than a decision of the lawgiver based on a judgement of expediency. Genuine rights, of course, cannot be curtailed or withdrawn without the rightholder furnishing cause or giving his consent.

With torts and obligations taken care of, the set of admissible actions becomes a residual: an admissible action is the exercise either of a right (entailing the fulfilment of someone else's obligation) or of a *liberty*. A liberty is any feasible action that is neither a tort, nor the breach of an obligation, nor the exercise of a right. In order to be feasible, a person must be able to perform it without another person being required to perform *onerously*. Some liberties are exercised all by themselves: I can go for a walk on the common without requiring anybody's active coop-eration. Others depend on someone else exercising a matching liberty: I can only contract to buy a house if the owner is willing to sell at my price, and if he is, his action, though required for the accomplishment of mine, is not onerous. On the other hand, my going for a walk *and* singing loudly as I walk must surely be onerous for the other strollers on the common, but it requires their onerous *forbearance*, not their onerous *action*, hence on my proposed definition it passes for a liberty of mine (if local convention does not decree it to be a nuisance).

Contrast this with one of the senses in which Nozick uses 'right' in his *Anarchy, State and Utopia* (1974, p. 92): 'rights, that is permissions to do something and obligations on others not to interfere'. Rights, of course, are not permissions but claims for performance by another. Yet liberties are not permissions either; if they were they would be most confusingly misnamed. Who would be competent to grant permissions and on what authority? And assuming an authority to grant or withhold them, why is its or anyone's permission required to do anything what-soever? The only reason is if there are grounds for objecting to the thing being done, for surely no permission is needed to do it when no objection can stand against doing it. If there are objections, a positive permission might have the function of overriding them as insufficiently strong or unfounded. However, strong and well-founded objections are gathered under the 'harm' and 'obligation' headings. I propose to take it that the two together exhaust the set of valid objections. Suppose, however, that they do not, and that there are other contingencies where a feasible action that is neither a harm nor the breach of an obligation, might yet be objectionable and require permission. Under the presumption that the *feasible is free*, it is for the objector to prove the validity and strength of his objection. If he fails, the proposed action needs no permission, and if he succeeds, it ought not to get it. It is only under the opposite presumption, namely that everything is forbidden unless it is permitted, that this logic is reversed and the permissions that Nozick (and others including, however deplorably, constitutional texts as well) call 'rights' make sense and become necessary.

Coercion fits into this scheme in a way that is by now fairly evident from the foregoing. Coercion may be applied either to the inadmissible or the admissible subset of the set of feasible actions. Applied to the inadmissible subset, it will characteristically function to deter tortious harms and breaches of contract. It may be administered by agreement among some or all of the parties interested in maintaining the security of life and property and the respect of contracts. Social conventions that are not self-enforcing yet survive, operate in this way by self-administered coercion, and the sort of political doctrine sketched in this essay, inspired by properly agnostic, hippocratic and minimalist principles, will consider this legitimate, though space does not permit a fuller explanation of the reasons why. If it is the case that certain social interactions, *as well as* the cooperation needed to enforce Pareto-optimal solutions for them, are single-play prisoners' dilemmas (a contingency which is possible though it looks farfetched), social conventions to overcome them would probably fail to take root and state coercion would be necessary. If it were invited by the parties, it would be legitimate; the conditions and the problem of testing the credibility of such invitation when the status quo is not the state of nature, but some social order that already incorporates coercion by the state, has been touched upon earlier (pp. 16–19).

Coercion applied to the admissible subset of actions is prima facie illegitimate. It deforms the values and hence the opportunity costs of rights and liberties, and does so by threatening or committing torts. Coercion, then, must be deterred in the same way as torts. It is possible that certain public-goods problems cannot be overcome by contract, perhaps because transactions costs in large-number situations would render such contracts unprofitable.[7] Under such circumstances coercive interference by the state with admissible actions covered by rights and liberties, might be just as legitimate as coercion to deter torts and to ensure the execution of contracts. However, these circumstances are unlikely to be as prevalent as is assumed in the received theory of why society needs the state, and the deontology of politics must on no account be based, as it so often is, on the facile supposition that the circumstances in question do in fact generally prevail.

Notes

1. Amartya Sen (1993, p. 39) has pointed out the difference between the availability of alternatives and the availability of the best alternative. He rightly distances himself from the view that removing everything from a feasible set except its best element is not a real loss for the chooser, since he wishes to choose the best element anyway. If freedom is purely instrumental, it does not seem to matter that less preferred alternatives are removed as long as the preferred one subsists. If their removal matters, freedom must have some kind of intrinsic, non-instrumental attraction.

2. That the cost of having (or acquiring) something is the value of the best of the forgone alternatives, is a proposition entailed in the concept of cost, and can be analytically derived from it. In ordinary language, this concept is called 'opportunity cost' to distinguish it from historical cost, i.e. the money or goods against which the acquired thing was originally obtained. Only the latter can be 'objectively' ascertained, but it is not a significant or very useful concept – except for tax accountants.

3. This is a version of Hayek's case (1960, p. 136) of the oasis in the desert where the owner of the only well charges an unheard-of price for water. Hayek considers that a traveller arriving in the oasis is being coerced by the well-owner. He must think that the traveller had reason to expect that water will be sold at an affordable price. It is this reasonable expectation that the well-owner has destroyed. However, he has not destroyed or worsened any actually existing option of the traveller. The latter's expectation about the price of water in the oasis was simply mistaken.

4. This point has been made to me in a private communication by Dr Hardy Bouillon. It is made, in somewhat different language, in his *Freiheit, Liberalismus und Wohlfahrtsstaat*, (1995).

5. The principle is unjust in terms of justice as the respect of rights resulting from agreements, even if the agreement were of the dubious hypothetical kind imputed to individuals behind a 'veil of ignorance'. I do not think the imputation can stand up to critical scrutiny. However, if it were accepted, it would supposedly mean that the parties have agreed to recognize rights to 'equal maximum freedom' compatible with the same freedom for others (Rawls, 1971, pp. 60, 250) and to give this principle absolute priority over distributive considerations. How, then, can the freedom of contract be accorded to the poor but denied to the rich? The only way out is to exclude the freedom of contract from the scope of the freedom or freedoms of which each party must have a maximum compatible with the same for every other. Many contemporary liberals, notably Dworkin, do exclude the freedom of contract from the list of freedoms to be maximized or even safeguarded.

6. Charles Taylor, while deploring moral scepticism, correctly observes that one defence against it is 'a pervasive feature of modern intellectual culture, which one could call the primacy or the epistemological: the tendency to think out the question of what something *is* in terms of the question of how it is *known*' (Taylor, 1993, p. 208).

7. This statement is certainly not intended to mean, and I trust it does not mean, that

high transactions cost is a sufficient condition for public-goods problems to defy voluntary cooperative solutions, nor that low transaction cost is sufficient for public-goods problems to have such solutions.

4. Let Exclusion Stand

Exclusion or Fair Shares

It is a widely accepted tenet of modern politics that justice demands the benefits of social cooperation to be shared in some fashion agreed to be fair. It is one of the tasks of politics to procure agreement on what is fair. Another is to see to it that benefits are in fact shared in the agreed fair manner.

As it stands and before it is interpreted, this tenet is perfectly general and consistent with any imaginable manner of distributing benefits. For one, it is consistent with the prevailing pattern of ownership of the factors of production and with every owned factor receiving benefits equal to its marginal product. Under this alternative, it is at least implicitly deemed fair that lawful possessions and voluntary exchanges should determine who gets what. The result is what might be called a primary or 'natural' distribution, (except that 'natural' distribution, just like 'natural' right, is a persuasive label full of subliminal suggestion, and is best avoided). The role of politics, if there is one, is then confined to upholding the customs and laws of property and contract; and it is not certain that even this limited role is indispensible; for nothing, neither deductive reasoning nor experimental evidence, proves that property and contract cannot be adequately and economically protected by extra-political means.

Under any other of the countless possible conceptions of what is fair, politics is called upon to play a deliberately redistributive role, and fairness is invariably interpreted as a norm requiring politically decided and enforced adjustments in distribution. The propertyless, the weak of will, the short of talent and short of luck are deemed to be excluded from the benefits produced by social cooperation, or at any rate to share insufficiently in it. Collective choice backed by the power of the state, must therefore be employed to *break down exclusion*, and make the better-endowed give up a part of their property or income in favour of the less well-endowed. Let us remind ourselves in passing that giving up part of the income from property is tantamount to giving up part of the property, for it is the capitalized value of the income it yields that provides its exchange value, hence the opportunity cost of replacing the lost income.

'Breaking down exclusion' is a pleasing goal, especially if it is done to bring about fairness, the more so as we are likely to benefit from our particular idea of it. Its pursuit is one of the principal temptations that make people have recourse to politics. Since it creates gainers and losers, it willy-nilly implies a 'balancing' between the good of some and the bad of others. As such, it cannot serve as a warrant for the use of coercion. Any attempt to justify it must be undertaken on consequent-ialist grounds. However, such grounds, as argued in Chapter 1, p. 9, are insufficiently firm and should not be admitted in any ethically well-founded political doctrine.

The Problem of Original Ownership

There is another, more direct and less general, moral argument in defence of exclusion, or of the categorical nature of property, whose ownership entails no obligation to share it with others and to include non-owners in the benefits it produces.

Once property is owned, its voluntary transfer from one owner to another takes place either in exchange for value received or as a unilateral gift. A new pattern of ownership results from the agreement of the parties (for accepting a gift or a bequest is also a matter of agreement), and as such it is uncontroversial: the transferee's title is no worse than that of the transferor. Each owner owes his title to the agreement of the previous owner, along a chain of valid transfers stretching back into the past. However, the legitimacy of the chain can be called in doubt if a link is defective. The very first link, in fact, has not ceased to excite controversy at least since Pufendorf and Locke – for what is the standing of subsequent transfers if the purported first owner was in fact a usurper and his title was invalid? If original ownership is moot, it is highly contestable that someone can ever become the rightful owner of anything that was previously unowned. If what is unowned cannot be legitimately appropriated, legitimate ownership is forever impossible, since no one can become the rightful owner of something that was previously unowned.

Since every present-day title would be precarious if a fault in any preceding title, no matter how far back along the chain of transfers, could serve as ground for invalidating it, custom, and more lately the law, forestall the chaos that would result by imposing a statute of limitations. But this is strictly a matter of expediency, and the passage of property from unowned to owned status, no matter how far back it is supposed to have been accomplished, can still be open to challenge in moral justice if not in law, for there is no agreed statute of limitations on moral claims. The legitimacy of what is indifferently called 'first taking', 'first appropriation', 'original occupation' or 'first possession' does for this reason have a significance for present-day exclusion and for what passes for the theory of private property, that is quite out of proportion to the quantitative share, in today's stock of wealth, of the things that can be supposed to have been *first appropriated* rather than subsequently *produced* from owned inputs in accordance with mutually agreed contracts, and remaining *unconsumed*.

The problem of accepting that something unowned and at least contingently accessible to all should, by virtue of some private act, become owned and access to it excluded except by the permission of the owner, has been stated in these terms: 'the idea that individuals can, by their own unilateral actions, impose moral duties on others to refrain from using certain resources and that the moral force of these duties can be transmitted by processes like exchange and inheritance, is a very difficult idea to defend in an unqualified form' (Waldron, 1988, p. 253).

Depending on the precise nature of the unilateral action of the prospective owner, and on the access non-owners have previously enjoyed to the resources in question, separate arguments are available according to cases to answer this charge. The basic defence, however, is quite general and straightforward. It is that if a prospective owner *can* in fact perform it, taking first possession of a thing is a feasible act of his that is *admissible* if it is *not a tort* (in this case not trespass) and violates no right; but this is the case by definition, i.e. by the thing being identified as 'unowned'. Taking exclusive possession of it is, in terms of our classification of possible acts, a liberty, and as such only a contrary right can obstruct or oppose it.[1] The opponent of this simple thesis is trying to have it both ways: he is *both* asserting that the thing has no legitimate first owner from whom a second or *n*th owner could have legitimately obtained it by agreed transfer, *and* that there is nevertheless somebody, who has been and still is entitled to use the thing and therefore can validly object to being excluded from it. But an entitlement to use the thing is an at least partial antecedent ownership claim needing an owner, or the permission of an owner, before it can be made; ownership cannot both exist yet not exist. If, on the other hand, the objectors have been using the thing without being entitled to it, because no third party had excluded them by taking first possession, and because they were unable, unwilling or uninterested to perform the act of taking first possession themselves (whatever that act may consist of), their enjoyment of the thing was precarious, not vested. Its appropriation by a third party may have deprived them of an *uncovenanted advantage*, but it did not violate their *rights*.[2]

What, then, is the act whose performance constitutes appropriation and vests ownership in the performer? There is in fact not one act but two alternative ones, depending on the type of access non-owners have, prior to the act, enjoyed to the thing. One could be labelled 'finding and keeping'; the other, despite its possible misleading historical connotations, 'enclosure'.

'Finders Keepers' and the Moral Arbitrariness of Luck

A thing of value lying unnoticed in a ditch by the wayside could be found by anyone who passes. If it is found by a person who then hides it or takes it home for his own exclusive use, it is appropriated by him and has become his putative property. Maintenance of his ownership is conditional on his successful exclusion of all others who would seek to make use of the newly discovered property in question without the owner's permission. Exclusion involves costs, some once-for-all, some continuing, which can be considered as part of the price of ownership. The thing appropriated by the finder can obviously no longer be found and freely used by anyone else. Anyone who was at all likely to pass that way in the indefinite future has, by the act of the finder, lost some, no matter how small, probability of finding the thing, i.e. some probability of enjoying an advantage. Admittedly, if all accept the rule that the finder is keeper, i.e. that first possession confers ownership, the mathematical expectation that the non-finder may one day also find a valuable thing becomes worth more to him, for he could then keep the thing, and no one would challenge his control of it. This would reduce the exclusion cost of protecting his ownership. But the bird that has just slipped out of his hand might have been too painful a loss to be offset by the chance of secure possession of the bird in the bush, once he catches it. Nothing ensures that the expected utility of a finders-keepers rule will tell him to leave well alone, in the hope that tomorrow it will be his turn to catch a bird, or to find something else.

Is this a ground for challenging the *fait accompli*, disputing the title of the finder in the thing, or for making recognition of his title subject to some bargain? Trading the respect of private property against some redistributive compensation, so that the new owner must in effect purchase the acquiescence of the propertyless in his ownership, is an idea that underlies a large body of modern political thought. It is sometimes alleged, not only that such a bargain is ethically required to justify property, but that it is an empirical fact, and the necessary condition of the social acceptance of capitalism. No evidence has to my knowledge ever been offered for the belief in some implicit bargain of this kind, and in the nature of the case none could be offered. Our present interest, however, is not in the truth of the empirical proposition that respect for property is obtained, or can only be obtained, by compensating the propertyless, but in the ethical proposition that such compensation is due.

If finding useful things were mostly a matter of luck – which in certain basic but not very important cases it clearly is – the ethical proposition could be reduced to requiring that the lucky compensate the unlucky. There is no particular reason to confine the application of this norm to cases of 'finding' property; every bit of luck in every case where luck matters in shaping a relevant outcome, would carry a moral liability to compensation.

The force of the claim that the lucky ought to compensate the unlucky reposes on the belief that whatever is 'morally arbitrary' ought not to come to pass and calls for redress. However, we may readily concede that the effect of luck on the distribution of good things is morally arbitrary, without being led to draw any conclusion about redress; the step from the one to the other is a moral *non sequitur*. Moral questions are strictly about right and wrong. The random hand that destiny impartially deals to each of us is arbitrary, and it is manifestly lucky for some, unlucky for others, but it is not a matter of right and wrong. It is a matter of the way the world is made. Redress cannot be called for on moral grounds. At best, remedy could be called for on grounds of compassion or love-thy-neighbour.

It is a category mistake to believe that every distribution is either right or wrong; some, perhaps most, may simply be arbitrary, and this characterization need not imply anything about their moral quality. Only certain distributions, arising out of relations of trust and responsibility, are matters of distributive justice.[3] The relations between finders and non-finders, owners and non-owners are not, a priori, such relations. Hence finders-keepers poses no question of justice, and creates no liability to compensation or redress.

Finding by sheer luck is a limiting case. Finding as the pure result of incurring finding costs, where the scale or intensity of the 'search' by would-be finders is pushed to the point of equality at the margin between the value of the mathematical expectation of the find and the finding cost, is the opposite limiting case.[4] All cases of finding are presumably situated between these limits, with only a minority sitting on either borderline. The nearer an actual case lies to the search-optimizing ideal where marginal finding cost is equal to the probability-weighted marginal value of the find, the less reason popular opinion would be likely to have to question the legitimacy of the resulting ownership or to ask that, in return for respecting the finder's find, non-finders be compensated. However, if this is how popular opinion sees the justice of the matter, it is in a muddle, and not for the first time either. Questions of the justice of finding, of chance, exclusion cost, desert and profit do not really lend themselves very well to resolution by popular opinion. They are, for that very reason, best handled in a well-ordered society as matters of rigid custom or strict law (though not necessarily statute law) rather than of equity. This seems to me necessary, even if barring considerations of equity loses us the capacity flexibly to adapt rules to particular cases.

'Enclosure' and Exclusion Cost

A useful thing may be there for all to see, with neither chance nor finding cost being necessary to realize its existence; yet it may not have been appropriated, its use may not be reserved to any defined set of persons, and any chance comer may have free access to it. The squatter who takes the thing, or carves out a portion of it, can establish first possession by excluding everyone else's access to it. He puts up a fence, patrols the boundary, has fearsome dogs, manhandles trespassers and utters more or less credible threats against all who would try to dislodge him. He 'encloses' the thing and incurs exclusion costs. By analogy with finding costs in the preceding section, 'enclosure' is advantageous up to the point where the marginal exclusion cost is just equal to the use value of the enclosed thing to the encloser;[5] but there may well be opportunities for profitable enclosure where the thing can be appropriated at a marginal exclusion cost falling well short of its marginal use value, leaving an 'unearned' surplus; these cases are analogous to the windfalls that accrue when finding a thing is at least partly a matter of good luck, rather than of spending resources by way of finding costs.

The analogy with finding, however, is incomplete. Those who, however casually and sporadically, used to enjoy access to the unenclosed thing, now lose an actual benefit, and not merely the probability of an opportunity. In the preceding section, it was argued that no compensation was due for the latter, since the non-finders were not *entitled* to a find. It is arguable that the excluded are not entitled either to be included, since they have done nothing to secure their liberty of continuing access to the unenclosed thing against another's liberty of taking exclusive possession of it. The enclosure worsens their situation, but does not violate their rights. But this argument may possibly be faulty, for it ignores the force of such contingent circumstances as precedent and the possible 'common pool ownership' character of free access.

Both points are somewhat involved, and full justice cannot be done to them here. However, the following brief considerations should suffice for the present. Prior to its enclosure, some people used the thing merely in passing, on an *ad hoc* basis. Others, however, used it regularly enough for their access to amount to established precedent. They have no title, but they have some kind of reliance-based claim against the enclosure, and some compensation for their loss of usual access seems to be due in return for their acceptance of the exclusion. It may even be that access was not really free to all comers, but was informally shared by a closed set of people, and all those outside the set were virtually excluded in the sense that had they attempted access to the good, the attempt would have been opposed, or endured only under protest. This situation is perhaps not commonalty or 'common pool ownership' properly speaking, and if it had been, the problem of first possession and the passage from unowned to owned status would not have arisen, since the thing would not have been unowned. But an unowned good regularly used by an identifiable closed set of persons is sufficiently close in character to the village common to render compensation in case of enclosure mandatory. It is fairly clear that enclosure of a common, and even of a quasi-common, could only secure voluntary acceptance if compensation came close to offsetting the reliance-based damages suffered by the quasi-owners. Yet their acceptance of the exclusion is necessary for what is, effectively, a transfer of title rather than the appropriation of an unowned thing. Acceptance on their part, in turn, may reduce the necessary exclusion cost. It is an empirical question whether it would reduce it by an amount greater or less than the compensation; in a world where compensation was settled by mutual agreement rather than statutory means, its amount would tend to approximate the exclusion cost the agreement has saved.

First Possession as Liberty that has Prevailed

The reader must step carefully around here to avoid possible confusion. It was said that to the extent that the taking of first possession by 'finding' and 'enclosure' was a feasible act, it was also admissible, hence a liberty, since the thing possessed was by definition previously unowned and no one had a prior right to it. Those deprived of its use by exclusion lost an opportunity, or an actually enjoyed advantage, but in so far as the advantage was not vested either by agreement or by customary regular usage (encouraging and justifying reliance on continuing non-exclusion), this was not sufficient ground in justice for denying the passage of the thing from unowned to owned status. The liberty of the finder and encloser not being opposed by a contradictory right, it must be suffered to prevail.

This nutshell argument, however, provokes an obvious counter-argument meant to shatter the nutshell. Let us admit, it might run, that taking first possession is a liberty, since it is both feasible and unopposed by a right. Prior to their exclusion, however, the access of all comers to the unowned good was a liberty, too: it was feasible and unopposed by a right. Rights prevail over liberties, but in this set of relations between persons and acts, no rights figure at all. They are *ex hypothesi* altogether absent. This is precisely the problem; we want to defend a particular theory of how and why rights can arise and fill this void. The theory of ownership by first possession expounded in this chapter affirms that the liberty to find and to enclose should prevail. But why should it prevail over a contradictory liberty, that of all comers to have free access to the as yet unowned thing? The clash of the two liberties is at best a draw. At worst it is the liberty of freely using the unowned thing that should prevail, for it represents the status quo, and that should not be changed without a good argument in favour of the change. Consequently, only two possible conclusions subsist. Either unowned things must forever remain unowned, or the loss of those who lose the advantages of free access to them – and they may on a strict reading include society as a whole or even all humanity – must be compensated. But this attack involves a muddle about the nature of liberties as distinct from rights. Rights must all be mutually consistent; it is fraud to assume two obligations whose fulfilments are mutually contradictory, like selling my house with vacant possession to Jack and granting a lease on it to Jill. Indeed, a theory of rights that holds clashes between rights possible is seriously wrong.[6]

Rights cannot, but liberties can and do clash. There is nothing in their logic to prevent that. We are both free to voice our opinion at a public meeting, we both start to shout, and either none of us is heard, or you shout louder than I and prevail.

But not all clashes are tolerated by a given, conventional system of liberties. Some clashes would have results that mature social conventions or law have long declared unacceptable. My shooting at anything that I dimly see moving in the wood would clash unacceptably with your liberty to pick mushrooms in the wood. The liberty to pick mushrooms is, for obvious reasons, accorded priority; hence I am not at liberty to shoot and must not shoot. Shooting you carelessly is a tort, not a liberty. It is feasible but not admissible. However, the clash between free access to an unowned good and exclusion from access to it, is a clash between two liberties, and not between a liberty and a tort. More accurately, the latter is not a tort under the type of social conventions, customs or laws that are respected in our type of civilization, though of course there is no telling that it will not become one if our civilization goes on changing and our sense of right and wrong changes with it. Pending such changes, however, excluding others from a previously unowned good is no more tortious than was its previous unexcluded, promiscuous use. Whichever of these two liberties prevails *de facto*, prevails. If exclusion is successful and just claims for compensation on grounds of reliance are satisfied, the thing passes legitimately into the ownership of the finder-encloser. The fundamental reason is that there is in this case no principle of right or wrong at work to compel the *de facto* result to be overridden, which perhaps also explains why the dictum 'possession is three parts of the law', though emphatically not the whole law, does not generally strike us as an immoral guide used by cynical courts.

The Contingent Incidence of Exclusion Costs

In both of the above scenarios, the act of first possession is completed by the exclusion of non-owners, and it is the owner who bears the exclusion cost. But this need not be the case. Anyone else can bear it, or be made to bear it, or some of it on the owner's behalf. It is strange that in all mainstream theories of property, as in theories of the state as producer of the public good of law and order, it is invariably 'society', the sovereign or the 'government' which assumes the exclusion cost or, as the matter is usually but less pertinently put, 'protects and enforces property rights'. One of two assumptions seems to be made: that only society or its proxy can do it, or that only it can do it efficiently. The first assumption is hardly tenable and I propose to dismiss it. The second is, empirically, an open question; it may or may not generally be the case, and experimental proof seems unobtainable. However, even if it were true and could be *known* to be true, it would still not follow that a randomly chosen owner, or local association of owners, or all owners as a class, could do no better than to entrust the exclusion function wholly to the state.

From an owner's point of view, inasmuch as this property is not protected by the unrequited service of others, the rational choice is to have as much and as good protection of it, and of his associated rights, as to equate the marginal return from better protection to its marginal cost. He does this by buying it, hiring it or producing it himself in the form of self-help. The appropriate inputs are different for different types of exclusion; the lock, the fence, the safe, the electronic tag on merchandise in the shop provide one kind of barrier to unauthorized access to private property, the anti-racketeering squad, the Serious Fraud Office another, the recourse to peer group help, to arbitration, or to action at law yet another. Every kind of barrier has more or less close substitutes that perform a comparable though seldom identical service. In the real world at least some of them are nearly always performed 'in house', by self-help. No matter how efficient the police, the super-market still makes its own costly arrangements to prevent people from carrying off its wares without paying for them. Other functions are 'contracted out' to specialized providers, guard services, credit infor-mation bureaux, quality assessors, rating agencies. Yet others may be dispensed with by dint of avoiding the kind of transaction that would call for them: thus, contract enforcement costs can be saved by not dealing with fly-by-night parties, nor with notoriously litigious ones.

Some services, particularly those that involve adjudication of dis-putes about who owns and who owes what, and with enforcement of the findings, are usually performed by institutions of the state. But this need not be so, and it is difficult to make a plausible case that alterna-tive arrangements would be less efficient and less impartial. The state has, over the centuries, increased its 'market share' of these services, but this is not in itself proof that it is the superior provider. The relative efficiency of the state and its potential competitors is obviously 'path dependent'.[7] The assertion of centralized sovereign power at the end of the Middle Ages enabled states to establish and protect their monopoly of certain lucrative aspects of exclusion, for other potential providers of such services were put at a disadvantage by virtue of their disarmed and subject status. The state, moreover, can become and remain a monopolist without possessing any of the supposed merits of the 'monopoly of the legitimate use of force'. History, both past and contemporary, is rich in examples where it abuses its sovereign power and gets away with providing a law-enforcing and property-protecting service that is neither efficient nor impartial.

What one needs to retain from this is that the assumption of exclusion cost by society, by owners, or by both in some proportion, is a contingent fact, not a necessary truth arising from the immanent features of social life. This is worth stressing again and again, for the contrary belief, namely that property owes such security as it ever has to the collective effort of society to protect it, is deeply embedded in the post-Enlightenment consciousness. Indeed, it is thought by most of those who think about the matter, and *a fortiori* by those who teach it, that society is prior to property and the state is prior to the 'market'. This belief, and its equally unsupported twin that ownership and voluntary exchange could not exist without a pre-existing 'institutional infrastructure' that can be characterized as a Hobbesian social contract, are mutually entailed (see p. 17). They have profound consequences for the evolving shape of liberal doctrine and for political practice; for they rationalize the basic disposition of political man to consider the system of private property as an unspoken contract whereby 'society' affords security of tenure to property owners, and in return justifiably gains a decisive say in the distribution of property and of its fruits, warranting some 'socially chosen' breach of the principle of exclusion.

Contract and the 'Right to Contract'

Property, according to the simple taxonomy of rights and liberties put forward in Chapter 3, is properly speaking not a 'right' (nor a 'bundle of rights') but a liberty to act upon owned objects. The liberty to act upon them includes the classic triad of use, usufruct (if indeed these two are really distinct, which I am inclined to question) and disposition.

The most important liberty of disposition is of course the freedom of contract, whereby an owner transforms some of his liberties to use the benefit from his property into obligations for himself and rights for others; for example, a lease obliges the owner to renounce the liberty to use his property in certain ways, and vests a right to use it in the lessee, the owner being obliged to cede possession.

Note that while the owner had *liberty* to use, the non-owner needs a *right* to use, which the lease confers upon him. Using 'liberty' for the one and 'right' for the other, though perhaps pedantic, underlines the fundamentally different nature of these two relations, the second of which depends upon agreement while the first does not. Likewise, an employee who enters into a labour contract exchanges his *liberty* to do as he likes during working hours against an obligation, and his employer gains the *right*, within the limits fixed by contract or custom, to direct him to do as *he* likes during working hours.

This sounds, and is, trite. The sole point of stating it is to drive home the understanding that a liberty is first of all a matter of feasibility, a *fact of life*, while a right is a matter of another party's obligation that he has *agreed* to assume. A reminder to this effect is not altogether redundant, for like property itself, the freedom of contract is also coming to be regarded, in modern social theory, as a privilege the parties enjoy by the grace of society, which gives them 'rights' to engage in the practice of contracting, forbears to interfere with it if the terms are 'socially acceptable', and enforces compliance. The last of these supposed contributions, as I have argued in connection with the enforcement of exclusion, is merely a contingent fact. It may or may not be the case or it may partly be the case. There are many alternative ways, some more powerful and some more costly than others, ranging from self-help and group convention to bought help, for enforcing compliance. The first two alleged collective contributions to the institution of contract, namely granting the right to contract and refraining from interference with contracts, however, beg a conceptual question. Can one be granted a right to a liberty – and is non-interference with a liberty, e.g. with the freedom of contract, a matter of social forbearance, that could be withheld or extended at society's pleasure? Even the usually crystal-clear Richard Epstein, surely not a legal philosopher one would expect further to confuse an already confused issue, seems to lean towards an interpretation of the concept of contract that requires the parties to be *entitled* to do what they are free to do: 'if one asks why C and D are entitled to enter into a contract with each other, the answer presupposes that the rest of the world has a duty not to interfere with the formation of their agreement...C's right to enter into a contract with D cannot be acquired by a contract between themselves...again collective recognition of the entitlement lies at the root of the common law' (Epstein, 1985, viii). Much as one must hesitate to disagree with Epstein on the common law, or indeed on all matters of common sense, on the face of it he gives comfort to a curious and curiously illiberal understanding: for it is surely inconsistent with both common sense and liberal doctrine that C must first acquire a right to contract, or the collectivity must first recognize his entitlement to do so, before he *can* contract with D.

It is not clear why the parties need a *right* to enter into an agreement they consider both agreeable and mutually binding and are capable and competent to conclude. The agreed exchange of binding promises, to which the parties need no 'right', entitlement or authorization from anyone, is logically prior, and distinct from the enforcement of performance should one of the parties attempt to default on his promise. Suppose 'society' through its agent, the state, offers the parties to enforce the contract in case of need. They have the choice of accepting this offer or resorting to some alternative arrangement, depending on whether the enforcement cost demanded by 'society' is higher or lower than the cost of private, peer group, or any other possible provider of enforcement, and also on which is more effective and rapid than the other. Is it the acceptance of society's offer by the parties, or the mere making of it, the assurance of its availability, that renders the making of the contract subject to an entitlement which must be 'acquired'? And is it this offer that entails a 'collective recognition' without which the rest of the world could interfere with it at will? If it is not the offer, then what is? And what if the offer is declined – or if it is not made at all, as was the case in the Praetorian 'formulary' law of republican and early Imperial Rome?

If the contract is an institution under customary or formal law, it is surely anomalous that its very existence should somehow be made dependent on what is no more than one of its contingent features, i.e. a particular mode of enforcement. Do men and women have to 'acquire a right' to marry, a 'right' society has a right to grant (hence also to withhold) by virtue of the legal protection it provides for the institution of marriage, and the legal facilities it offers for dissolving it? Surely, these protections and facilities, such as they are, do not *make* the institution, however much they may *shape* it and enhance its convenience. Legal support does not create the institution. If, on the other hand, the contract is a voluntary agreement before it is an institution, it is difficult to see why the parties should have to acquire a prior 'right' or entitlement to conclude it, and what would happen if their 'entitlement' were not granted collective recognition. Would reciprocal promises cease to be binding? Isn't this confusing an obligation with one of the several means to which recourse can be had if it is not respected? It is incomprehensible on what grounds the parties' 'right' to contract, i.e. to carry out a feasible joint action that is not a tort nor the breach of an obligation, does not go without saying but needs to be questioned, and why such a question requires an answer.

If anything is questionable and requires an answer, it is the collectivity's right to subject the freedom of contract to an 'entitlement', to be granted by itself, and to be withheld in certain circumstances. I am far from claiming that there are no such circumstances. In cases of force, fraud and unconscionability, it is perfectly arguable that some formal or informal body or institution which may be, though it need not be, the collectivity, society or the state, should have authority to release a party from a contractual obligation and protect him from the other party's attempt at enforcing performance. For this, however, force, fraud, unconscionability or some other weighty ground must first be *shown*. The onus of proof is not on the parties to show that their contract provides *no* such grounds. The recognition that there may exist a class of contract-dissolving grounds in no way permits the conclusion that the freedom to contract when some such ground is *not shown* is a social privilege, a 'right' granted by society to the contractors, and that society's 'duty not to interfere' is a corollary of the right it has granted them.

The Mirage of the Common Pool

'Contract is a social privilege granted to individuals' takes its place alongside 'the state is prior to the market' and 'property rights are defined and enforced by the political authority', to form the threesome of half-truths and misunderstandings which helps legitimate the politics of redistribution. For redistribution may be the chosen aim of a teleologically inspired political ideal, and consequentialist ethics may provide it with a case for holding that one distribution is recognizably better, more just or more uplifting than another. But if contract is free, if the source of property is first possession and contract, and if the distribution of benefits and burdens in society at any time is the result of the preceding pattern of ownership and a continuous process of voluntary exchanges that modify it, interference with contracts, imposed exchanges, and forced and unrequited transfers of property, would be prima facie illegitimate intrusions into liberties, and violations of recognized rights. Coercive redistribution could perhaps still be legitimized after a fashion – perhaps after the frank and forthright fashion of Princess Mathilde Bonaparte (cf. Introduction, p. 1), perhaps by claiming that contracts between unequals are to be classed as made under duress, or perhaps by resorting to more windy, obscure and pompous formulations, some of which will be looked at in Chapter 5 – but the ideology concocted from such disparate elements is hardly a heady brew. The troops will not march far on it. How much more liberating is an ideology that leans on a non-exclusive conception of property; for if owners do not *really* own it, but *share* ownership with society, if the terms of contracts are subject to social approval, and if a certain pattern of distribution must obtain before the processes of voluntary exchange become legitimate,[8] no (individual) liberties prevail in the matter of property, no (individual) rights arising from voluntary agreements are violated by involuntary transfers, and redistributive politics, restrained, if at all, only by expediency, can be underpinned by what promises to be a coherent ideology. On a closer look, however, the promise remains sorrowfully unfulfilled.

The foundation stone of this ideology is the inchoate intuition that the accumulated stock of wealth is owed to the entire history of social cooperation since the day our ancestors climbed down from the tree. It is a common pool, and it is absurd that some individuals should be allowed to exclude others from particular parts of it that they claim as their 'absolute' private property. They may, to be sure, practice a measure of exclusion, but not on their own terms, and no more than society, the co-owner, will countenance. Why, then, allow owners *any* degree of exclusion – why not go all the way and declare that all property, or all property that matters (productive wealth) is 'social', and its use and disposition entirely a matter of 'social choice'?

The ideology, it seems to me, reveals an odd fault line here. The whole stock of accumulated wealth is owed to the whole sum of social cooperation over time. It is this debt, owing to prior contributions, that creates social ownership, and supports its primacy over individual claims today; social ownership is a matter of justice, of *suum cuique*, and its ground is apparently deontological. However, like any common pool ownership, 'social' ownership loosens the link between the bearing of burdens and the enjoyment of benefits: it permits those who have sown only a little to reap much, leaving little to reap for those who have sown much. It punishes good and rewards bad husbandry. In less biblical language, it is a hotbed of inefficient factor allocation, free riding and the worst kind of principal–agent problems. The remedy, of course, is not merely exclusion, for a common pool also excludes those left outside it. Social ownership, too, excludes other societies than ours. To be free from the vices of the common pool, it must be exclusion under single or several private ownership. It does not matter whether it has one owner or many, the equity in a property must be clearly divided and each share must separately belong to one natural or legal person. The efficiency gain of private over common pool ownership generates a surplus. The difference between the redistributionist and the socialist ideology is that the former believes in the efficiency gain, does not feel like throwing it out of the window, and therefore accepts, on consequentialist 'on balance' grounds, the exclusion implied in private property. In the final reckoning, it ends up with property that is both excluded and shared, both private and public. This is a schizophrenic understanding of property, which is deontological for its 'socially owned' and consequentialist for its private *persona*. Such, I submit, is the contemporary liberal conception of property, which underlies the modern liberal redistributionist ideology. Whatever else it is, it is not coherent.

Moreover, the deontologically derived social *persona* is but a figment of a feverish imagination. The stock of wealth at large is said to be owed to society at large, because it is impossible to trace or undesirable to break down society's global contribution into the myriad of bits and pieces, past and present, contributed by each cooperating individual. How to tell who made what, who invented, innovated, improved what – and to what extent it were his efforts that produced a given increment of wealth, to what extent those of everybody else, his teachers who taught him, his doctor who cured him when he was ill, the policeman who kept him safe, and the literally countless others whose contributions were all necessary for him to make his contribution? How to trace each contribution to the contributor?

But the answer is relatively simple. The 'tracing' has already been done at the time the contribution was made, and has duly left its permanent mark on the ownership structure of the 'stock of wealth'. It does not have to be done a second time. The producer, the inventor, the teacher and the policeman all contributed what they did in exchange for value received. This value may or may not have been equal to the

marginal product of each, but though the question is intrinsically interesting, and I do not know how to answer it, I do not think I have to. It
suffices that each gave and received what he did in the course of
voluntary exchanges, which constituted valid transfers of title to the
goods and services in question. Some of what each received he con-
sumed. The remaining bit, if any, he added to the 'stock of wealth'
simply by virtue of the fact that he did not consume it, and it was
clearly labelled as *his* contribution of the exchange value thereof, because he held title to it. If he neither sold it nor gave it away, nor
bequeathed it to his heirs, it is still clearly labelled as his. Every other
bit is likewise labelled with the name of its contributor or his legal
successors. No unowned bit is unaccounted for.

Arguably, every bit is interdependent with every other, and none
could have been contributed without all others also being contributed at
the same time, or earlier. But this no more means that every bit is 'owed
to society' than that every bit is owed to every other. *Nothing is owed*:
everything has been paid for, one way or another, in a manner and to an
extent sufficient to call forth the contribution. There is no further common pool-type claim overhanging the lot, for no payment must be
claimed twice. He who sees an overhanging claim in favour of 'society'
is seeing a mirage, or the wishful image of one.

Notes

1. Rousseau is worth quoting here '...the positive act which establishes a man's claim
   to any particular item of property limits him to that and excludes him from all
   others...in so far as he benefits from this right, he *withholds his claim*, not so much
   from what is another's, as *from what is not specifically his*' (Rousseau, 1762,
   pp. 186–7, emphasis added).
2. It will be noted that this position is opposed to the one taken under Lockean
   inspiration by Robert Nozick. For the latter, '[t]he crucial point is whether appropriation of an unowned object worsens the situation of others. Locke's proviso that
   there be enough and as good left in common for others is meant to ensure that the
   situation of others is not worsened' (Nozick, 1974, p. 175). He distinguishes between two kinds of worsening: the loss of opportunity and the loss of actually
   enjoyed advantage. If the proviso means that neither kind of worsening must take
   place, it cannot be satisfied in a finite world. If only the second kind of worsening is
   barred by the proviso, Nozick believes that the institution of private property and
   the market economy whose proper functioning it permits, are sufficiently beneficial
   to enable the proviso to be satisfied.
   This, of course, will remain a matter of judgement. It is possible that first
   appropriation improves the situation of most people in the long run, but worsens
   that of some or perhaps of most in the short run, calling for a balancing judgement. I believe that setting conditions which then require such balancing to be
   performed, is undesirable. The position developed in the text does not require that

nobody loses as a result of first possession, as long as the losses were not vested interests.

3. The reader may note this departure from the well-known position of Hayek, for whom the notion of distributive justice is itself a category mistake. Plainly, however, there are questions of distributive justice in the treatment of children by their parents, in the marking of examination papers, in the allocation of scarce under-priced public housing, in sharing out the burdens of a joint undertaking, and so forth. Here the relations of trust and responsibility largely determine the appropriate distribution, and deviations from it are prima facie unjust. 'The concept of distributive justice is applicable within the context of limited associations, with limited and definite aims held in common. Such aims give guidance how the fruits of common activities should be distributed' (Lucas, 1980, p. 220).

4. It is not immediately obvious where, between these two limiting cases, Israel Kirzner's (1978) particular conception of the finders-keepers principle fits in. It seems to me that it can best be fitted in by equating the input of the finder's entrepreneurial acumen, his scarce talent for discovering arbitrage opportunities unseen by others, to the incurring of a resource cost. But I am in no way claiming that Professor Kirzner would agree with this interpretation, for it could call into doubt the existence of his 'pure' profit.

5. Judge Posner makes a related but somewhat different point: 'the pattern by which property rights emerge and grow in a society is related to increases in the ratio of the benefits of property rights to their costs' (Posner, 1992, p. 35).

6. John Gray (1989, p. 148) believes that we lack a theory of acquisition that can help in adjudicating 'apparently conflicting property rights', and illustrates the conflict by the following example. The catch from a certain fishing ground falls because of industrial pollution by a coastal plant. The 'right' of the fishermen to fish in their traditional fishing grounds conflicts with the 'right' of the industrialist to employ a polluting process.

    In fact, no rights are involved, hence none can conflict. The fishermen's liberty to fish is intact, but there are fewer fish. Whether compensation is due to them for the negative externality they suffer is a question of prevailing liability rules. They may favour the fisherman or the industrialist. We may consider a particular liability rule just or unjust. But if the fishermen have had property rights in the grounds, the industrialist would have violated them by killing their fish. There would still be no conflict of rights, apparent or real. The fishermen would win an action for remedy and the industrialist would desist or compensate.

    Consider an amended example. The fishing grounds have an owner; he leases them to the fishermen, and unbeknown to them also sells an easement to the industrialist to pollute it with his effluent. There is a conflict of two putative rights, but only because the conflicting obligations have been fraudulently assumed.

7. Cf. Ellickson (1991, p. 253): 'Once an informal control system has been established among neighbours, for example, their marginal cost of referring additional disputes to it may be lower than before. Conversely, *once the state has assumed the major role*, even more state control may be utilitarian' (i.e. efficient) (emphasis added).

8. Onora O'Neill (1982, p. 321) thinks it plausible that in order to guarantee that the process, for instance the process of voluntary exchange, is followed, the outcome of the process must fall within an 'acceptable' range. We must ask what happens if the outcome falls outside the range – for instance if voluntary exchanges give rise to a very unequal distribution of wealth. We can only speculate about how O'Neill would answer the question. She might say that under such conditions the poor might consider the share of the rich unfair, and would violently or 'democratically' upset the applecart of voluntary exchanges that produced the unfair outcome. Of course they may or may not try to do so, and may or may not succeed. But this has nothing

to do with the *legitimacy* or otherwise of exclusive private property and freedom of contract. It concerns its *capacity of survival* under conditions of extreme inequality, which is an interesting empirical question, but not germane here.

If she does not mean survivability, what does she mean? Could she mean that unless the process of voluntary exchanges produces acceptable outcomes, it is not a voluntary process? Whether the outcomes are acceptable to an outside observer, a philosopher of social justice, is of course quite irrelevant. It is the parties to the exchanges who count. Yet if 'acceptable' signifies 'acceptable to the parties', the statement is analytic: if I enter into a contract whose terms are unacceptable to me, I entered into it involuntarily (but then why did I?). Acceptability of the outcome to all parties 'guarantees' that the process is followed, but guarantees it tautologically, since we have just defined the voluntary process as one that produces acceptable results. Unacceptable results *mean* that the voluntary process was not followed: some other process was.

None of this is helpful. Nor does it bear out O'Neill's suggestion that *both* process *and* outcome may have simultaneously to satisfy certain conditions in a satisfactory theory of just distribution. It is hard to see why we should bother with the process if we know what outcome would be 'acceptable'. This would be like insisting on having an election, although only the election of the right candidate would be acceptable. Why not bring about the right outcome directly, by giving to each what he ought to have?

5. Confronting Community and Equality

Why the Resort to Politics?

If the argument of the four preceding chapters is by and large coherent, we have drawn up and defended the ground-plan of an ethical theory of considerable robustness as a guide for regulating social coexistence. Its raw material is agreement, and convention, which is agreement at one remove. It is based on simple propositions. Costs and harms to some cannot generally be offset by benefits to others to yield an alleged balance for justifying the imposition of the will of some (however many) on all. Liberty is a matter of feasibility subject to the avoidance of torts and respect for obligations. Torts are defined by convention. Rights are not found in nature, nor ascribed by social choice. They are agreed by those who must bear the matching obligations. Property originates in a liberty, it remains a liberty, and its growth and distribution are the results of agreements. Coercion is prima facie a tort. Coercion by the state is not a tort by convention but it is a morally grave matter, especially where the state has an effective monopoly of the use of force. There is a presumption against it; it is clearly legitimate only if invited by those subjected to it. Doubt about an issue creates a presumption to abstain, and against resolving it by coercion.

There is, as a corollary of these propositions, a manifest presumption against politics. The politics of unanimity is fatuous and unnecessary. Non-unanimous politics is prima facie wrong, because it involves resort to coercion. Choice mechanisms that purport to rank all social alternatives, or at least to select the best one among all, by reference to the non-unanimous preferences of the members of society, are attempting to square the circle and must generally fail on their own terms. The choices they do produce are defective as composite expressions of the preferences they are supposed to reflect.

Before resorting to politics, a great deal can be decided by agreement and convention; there is, moreover, another great deal that need not even be decided, because it proceeds as a matter of course as people exercise their liberties without requiring the active cooperation of others. Regarding politics as a last resort, a desperate remedy to be used when all else fails, is far from being the sickly symptom of the negation of man as a social being, and of an unnatural 'atomistic' and 'abstract' individualism, whatever that is intended to mean. On the contrary, it is man as a social being who has the least need to resort to politics, precisely because he commands the difficult civic skills and virtues of voluntary cooperation, of finding bargained solutions, of maintaining valuable conventions and keeping free riding within tolerable bounds.

It is these skills that atrophy and vanish when politics takes over. They start to atrophy before it does, because its real or even potential availability is liable to lead to the abandonment and breakdown of voluntary solutions. This is likely to be the result of the combination of two factors.

There is, first, the recognition in modern democratically governed societies that whatever the constitution may say on the subject, the scope of politics is effectively restricted only by a falling expected marginal net benefit, a winning coalition and its constituent interest groups, which take turns to be 'decisive' within the coalition in matters affecting their particular interests, associate with its marginal expansion.[1] As long as its marginal benefit is still positive, it pays a winning coalition to bring state influence to bear in favour of a coalition member and to the detriment of a non-member.

Second, in any bargained solution of a cooperation problem, be it a labour contract, a scheme for maintaining a public park, or an agreement for sharing water between irrigation and municipal use, the ability of the parties to enlist political allies is usually different. The party with better access to political processes, and greater assets (such as voting strength, public sympathy, etc.) to bring to a potential new coalition, may often have an incentive to let a potential private bargain fail, or to have an actual bargain overriden by public regulation, as well as to arrange to shift privately-borne burdens on to the general taxpayer. It is a matter of taste whether we ascribe such goings on to the natural tendency of social beings to seek social solutions to social problems, or to the ruthless utility-maximization to be expected from the model of individualist 'economic man'. Whoever of the two is really at work (assuming for the moment that they are really two different persons) the effect is that resort to politics intrudes into the area that civil society could order non-coercively by agreement and convention, or that orders

itself as a matter of course.[2] The intrusion is often deplored on instrumental grounds. The balance of informed opinion tends to hold that it is
bad for efficiency, although there is, and no doubt will always be, a die-
hard view that only 'too much' intervention is inefficient. This controversy is no concern of this chapter. The reason is not that the question
of expediency is unimportant or irrelevant to the course of liberal
thought. Both the Scottish Enlightenment and the Philosophical Radicals paid great attention to it, in some cases so great that less might
have been more. Regardless of its importance, however, I think it is
worthwhile to leave efficiency strictly on one side for once, and to
pursue a little longer an argument concerned mainly with liberties,
rights and coercion, that judges politics above all in terms of right and
wrong, just or unjust.

It may be that the main driving force of expanding politics is base
self-interest. The hypothesis is at least consistent with the evidence.
Most of politics, at any rate, can be explained and predicted in those
terms. Significantly, however, there is in modern western political thought
an intense and perhaps growing interest in theories of public morality
that would justify and legitimize the expansion of politics by appeal to
normative categories. Two of these categories, community and equality,
seem to me particularly worth subjecting to the acid of deontological
political ethics outlined in the first four chapters. The present chapter
aims at a confrontation of this kind with two texts, a chapter in Robert
Nozick's *The Examined Life* (1989) standing for the communitarian,
and Bruce Ackerman's *Social Justice in the Liberal State* (1980) for the
egalitarian position.

The Indivisible Common Good

As this is not a work of exegesis I will not try to render a critical
account of the many strands of communitarian thought, but only con-
front what seem to me the two essential versions, one of which I find
fully intelligible, the other almost wholly unintelligible.

The intelligible version, as far as I can judge, owes its existence to,
and derives its logical basis from, the indivisibility of certain goods.
For 'goods' we must sometimes read 'ends' or the 'values' that characterize these ends, but the communitarian thesis is clearer if stated in
terms of goods only: there are no doubt many goods that are unambiguously indivisible and large, while it is a moot point whether there are
many values that cannot be pursued by individuals acting separately,

and whose presence, as it were, on the social scene cannot be augmented in small increments by individual action.

Be that as it may, indivisibility on a large scale of worthwhile goods seems clearly to necessitate joint community undertakings on a correspondingly large scale before we can have them at all; increments short of some massive minimum are irrelevant and unfeasible. We must mobilize a massive common effort to rebuild the cathedral. It is no use rebuilding a row of bricks here, half a column there. The effort has a definite scale. It may be too large for the joint forces of those who, keen cathedral lovers, would actually volunteer to work at it. Besides, individual motivation could never get it rebuilt, for the usual social dilemma would stand in the way; all would like to have the cathedral, but each would prefer someone else to go and work at rebuilding it. The orthodox pointer to the way out, in the language of methodological individualism, is to reduce the attraction of the free-rider option by some coercive measure, or close it altogether (as is the case with taxation that is strictly non-optional). In communitarian language, the same way out is described as the organization of a common effort in pursuit of the common good. There is much that is thoroughly attractive in this language. It appeals to a sense of identification with a community whose members are aware of its past, feel concern for its future, and that has a stable character of its own that inspires affection and pride. A residue of such a sense is still present in many, and may survive for some time the passing of genuine communities capable of inspiring affection and pride.

The common good functions in this setting as a good of the community that is *not* a more or less plausibly contrived aggregate of the preferences of its individual members. It is not derived from any assumption of the individual maximization. As such, it is not seen to be a public good under another name, and its achievement is not completely analogous to the solving of the public-goods problem. The latter, whether it is resolved by invited coercion or by voluntary cooperation that leaves room for some free riding,[3] is a problem in individual maximization in a collective setting. The common good, by contrast, is the holistic maximand of the collective entity itself. No attempt is made to impute it to a set of individual motivations, perhaps because it could not be done (if it could, what would communitarianism be *for*?), perhaps because it need not be done.

Liberal doctrine does not easily make room for the common good. Affirming its existence and nature seems to be a metaphysical proposition; intellectually it belongs to a world where methodological individualism is very much at a loss to find its way. Above all, since the common good is not, and does not even purport to be, some vector or sum of individual preferences, individuals have to be coerced to do what the community requires them to do, and this offends against the liberal presumption that resort to politics is prima facie wrong *because* coercion is wrong. Yet the argument from indivisibility to the common good is at least coherent, and does not depend, as do some other communitarian arguments, on gratuitous assumptions and morally implausible, excessively demanding value judgements. Moreover, the gate it opens to the intrusion of politics, though it seems to me too broad for the safety of society, is not so broad as to let politics invade it beyond all measure; for the ground opened up to politics is, after all, confined to genuine indivisibilities, and among them only to those that have some worth in the eyes of a morality that has resisted the wear and tear of a community's history.

The 'Solemn Symbolism' of Enforced Uniformity

Such redeeming features are altogether lacking in another kind of communitarian justification of expanding the domain of politics. In a single chapter of a book that is otherwise little concerned with the legitimate use of coercion, Robert Nozick (1989) advances bewildering reasons why it is generally right to force dissenters to behave as if they consented, in order to stop them spoiling some 'solemn symbolism'.

This surprising conclusion is prepared by first claiming that one of the *raisons d'être* of democratic institutions is to express, in a solemn and official way, our autonomy, to allow a 'symbolic affirmation of our status as autonomous and self-governing beings' (Nozick, 1989, p. 286). Individual autonomy and liberty are valuable, not simply because of what they let the individual choose to do or have, but because they 'enable him to engage in pointed and elaborate self-expressive and self-symbolising activities' (sic) (op. cit., p. 287). This is somewhat obscure, but must be taken on credit, together with the statement about democratic government being, not a rule-bound means for imposing the will of a majority on a minority, but 'a solemn marking of our human solidarity' (ibid., p. 287) a vehicle of 'the symbolic importance of an official political concern with issues and problems, as a way of marking their importance' (ibid., p. 287). These solemn symbolic and self-expressive characteristics of political action seem to lend it an intrinsic value independently of what it does for and to people in the less mysterious, non-symbolic sphere where it functions to distribute benefits and impose burdens.

Here, Nozick remembers that in his libertarian days, he used to consider merely the purpose of government, which, though important, was too narrow a criterion. He does not wish to imply now that 'the public realm is only a matter of joint self-expression; we wish also by this actually to accomplish something' (op. cit., p. 288) but even the purpose of politics is too narrowly conceived if we do not bear in mind the politics of *meaning* (ibid., p. 288).

What, then, is a broad enough view of politics as enriched by its meaning? It must be seen as our means 'to express and instantiate ties of concern to our fellows' (ibid., p. 288) in particular by helping the needy. Why, however, must we achieve this by means of politics? And is it for *expressing* our wish to help that we need political action, or for actually helping? If it is the latter, what is to stop each of us who wish to help going and doing it? If it is the former, why must we insist on doing it 'jointly and officially – that is politically' (op. cit., p. 287)? What is wrong with expressing our wish to help individually, for instance by actually helping? The answer that seems to be forthcoming puts a baffling, and quaintly communitarian, case.

Left to themselves, some individuals would help the needy, others would not. Those who would not, clearly 'have a right' not to, but it would be shameful if they did not. However '[t]heir fellow citizens...may choose to speak for them to cover up that lack of concern and solidarity' (op. cit., p. 288). They may do this by deciding that the needy shall be helped, not by willing individuals each doing as much as he sees fit in ways he thinks best, but by collective action, the unwilling being taxed with the willing to contribute. Nozick takes it for granted, no doubt rightly, that there is a majority for this solution. It lends 'a fig leaf' to cover the shame of the unwilling, since now both they and the willing contribute as if they were both equally willing. 'The point is not simply to accomplish the particular purpose' of helping the needy, but 'to speak solemnly in everyone's name' (op. cit., p. 289). That to provide public welfare with the means exacted by taxation imposed by a majority on a minority is 'to speak solemnly in everyone's name' is a stunning finding, that many would find hard to credit, if not downright ironic. Nozick nonetheless assures us that state welfare is, and voluntary contributions are not, a 'solemn marking and symbolic validation' (ibid., p. 289) of our ties of concern and solidarity.

Even if all this is meant seriously, which we must however reluctantly assume, it does not amount to much of a ground for putting welfare on an involuntary basis, especially as Nozick is prepared to concede that just as much and as good may be accomplished voluntarily. None of his argument is based on the adequacy or quality of help to the needy. The real reason why unwilling contributors must not be allowed to get away with it is not that 'shame must be covered up', the feelings of the needy must be spared, or welfare must be more securely and reliably funded. It is, instead, that allowing minority dissent on this matter to manifest itself would inflict a moral loss on the majority. It would, of all things, leave it 'bereft of a society validating human relatedness' (sic) (ibid., p. 289). Having gone this far, I will, albeit grudgingly, go a step further and try to read some kind of meaning into this phrase. It might mean that while one strain of communitarianism feeds on the indivisibility of certain goods, this strain feeds on the indivisibility of the community itself: if it does not speak with a single voice, and does not adopt a single uniform line of conduct with regard to key issues, it ceases to be a community, or rather does not begin to be one. We lose the 'solemn' experience of having it. The single voice rarely sounds and the uniform conduct rarely comes about all by itself. It must be brought about, and one possible definition of politics, democratic or not, is that it is the one known non-violent means of bringing it about in a society. Nozick is characteristically radical about its use, though while in his libertarian incarnation he was radically minimal-statist, in his communitarian one he is radically maximal-statist. He would wish the whole possible range of 'ties of concern and solidarity' to 'get expressed' in the political realm, no matter how intense and how extensive they might be: '[n]o principle draws the line' (op. cit., p. 292) and that, one is moved to observe, is mainly what is wrong with this peculiar and peculiarly argued plea for drawing politics into areas where is does not strictly belong.

When a Distribution is 'Up for Discussion'

Since the natural world is rich in apparently random asymmetric features, it is not a normal expectation that the distribution of these features among men of a particular class should be non-random, symmetrical, let alone equal. Valued relationships, sources of intangible satisfactions, as well as the power of disposition over material goods, are in the nature of things unequally distributed. We usually say that this is due to two reasons: to accidents of physical, social or personal history, i.e. essentially to luck, and to the unequal distribution of opportunities and talents for gaining control over these sources of satisfactions. Inequality of outcome, then, is partly a matter of luck, partly a matter of inequality of opportunities and talents. The latter inequalities, in turn, can again be attributed to the same two types of reasons, namely to the luck of having opportunities and talents, and to the unequal abilities and efforts people deploy to make the best of them. The abilities and efforts deployed, however, are again partly a matter of the luck of having them in the first place, and only partly a matter of our conscious will and application. Having a stronger will and more application, in turn, is partly a matter of luck, etc. etc.

At each successive turn, in other words, inequalities can be ascribed to luck and to a non-luck residual, which at the next turn can again be broken down into luck and another, more remote and indirect, non-luck residual. The operation can be repeated indefinitely: the further we push the inquiry into the ultimate causal determinants of a distribution, the larger looms luck and the further the volitional element recedes into the uncertain distance. Precisely the same pro-forma analysis can be carried out upon the inequalities of burdens, dissatisfactions and frustrations, with ill-luck progressively crowding out negligence and imprudent conduct, as we climb higher from one link to the next along the chain of causation.

The analysis, however, is essentially introspective. It does not discover, nor explain, any empirical fact. Each time the analyst imputes some result partly to luck and partly to non-luck, he merely describes his own thought-processes and the limits of his knowledge. He can more or less confidently attach such names as 'opportunity' or 'talent' to causal factors he can identify in a first approximation, and call 'luck' everything else he cannot put a particular name to. In earlier days the blessings and trials of Providence used to serve where good and bad luck serve today. The choice of vocabulary ought not to affect the underlying issue, but of course it does: while it sounds merely silly and fatuous to declare that 'God's blessings are undeserved' or 'the effects of unknown causes are morally arbitrary', declaring that (unequal) natural endowments are morally arbitrary and hence both undeserved and unjust is, strangely enough, widely considered a promising first step in John Rawls's popular theory of distributive justice.

My object in recalling how we blame luck for the success of others is not to enter into a debate on the moral merits of the case, especially as I am unable to see how the effects of unspecified causes can be classed as deserved or undeserved, but to suggest a way of understanding the basic disposition behind much or most modern normative liberal theory. If the *de facto* distribution of good and bad things in society is chiefly a matter of luck, and we have, by virtue of the very meaning of luck, no satisfactory account of why some people are luckier than others, it is natural to attach little or no moral significance to the status quo. Existing distributions gain no initial presumption of legitimacy from existing. They do not serve as starting points, not even as starting points for criticism and reform. Instead, distributive justice and the principles regulating it are derived as if there were no distribution to start with, only an undistributed mass to be disposed of justly among possible claimants, each standing there empty-handed. There are only *pari passu* claimants, there are no prior owners; there is a pie to be shared out, but no one has provided it to begin with. The entire question of distribution is wide open and up for discussion. This initial condition, once granted, tells us where the burden of proof lies: 'It places the burden of articulation squarely upon those who *seek* an inegalitarian distribution of worldly advantage' (Ackerman, 1980, p. 16, emphasis added).

Equality as the Product of Talk

The discussion, whose issue will determine how a hitherto undistributed mass of 'manna' is to be divided among all who ask for it, must be 'neutral dialogue'. Ackerman, in claiming that he is constructing normative liberal theory, stipulates the 'dialogic' technique for reaching conclusions others seek to derive from hypothetical agreement among the participants, or from an overall synoptic view of the good of each and the good of all. 'Neutral dialogue' has a rule, and if no party to it can produce an argument why he should get more manna than another without violating the rule, all ought to get equal shares. This is, in Ackerman's graceful term, 'constrained dialogic liberalism'.

It is incomprehensible why 'neutral dialogue' should be accorded this particular role, or any role for that matter. Why should a distribution be the product of talk? Nor is it at all clear why, if it is really talk that must be decisive, 'neutral' talk has a better claim to decide the matter than, say, adversarial debate. Neither, to be sure, has a very strong claim, but one looks less weak than the other. Ackerman argues that any distribution or, as he sometimes calls it, any 'power structure' must be tested to see whether questions about its legitimacy are suppressed, or answered in an illiberal way, i.e. whether 'it would support a thoroughgoing Neutral dialogue...the only way to do this of course is to write imaginary dialogues...' (Ackerman, 1980, p. 20). The 'of course' is apparently to justify a relentlessly repetitive series of such dialogues through the long book that leaves the reader perplexed about what each adds to what has been said before.

It is the rule that makes neutral dialogue neutral that is at the heart of the perplexity. 'Neutral dialogue', Ackerman lays down with what can only be described as confident unconcern, 'begins with the affirmation of a right to equal shares' (op. cit., p. 13). This of course is to incorporate the 'presumption of equality', the foundation stone of all egalitarian theory, into the definition of what type of 'dialogue' conforms to the rule. The right to equal shares can only be overruled by a reason that is itself neutral: 'I should get at least as much of the stuff we both desire [as you] – at least until you give me some Neutral reason for getting more' (op. cit., p. 58). However, all reasons the parties manage to advance are immediately unmasked and shot down as non-neutral. This is not hard to do, for it turns out that the rule of neutrality simply prohibits claims to unequal shares. Only if someone is 'better' than another should he have more power over resources (op. cit., p. 15); but 'Neutrality forbids me from saying that I'm any better than you are' (op. cit., p. 15).

This is circular reasoning, and in quite a small circle at that. The question of shares is settled in advance by requiring neutrality and defining it as *implying* equal shares. Neutrality is the hat, equality is the rabbit that has been put in it. Pulling it out at the end of each imaginary dialogue is unsurprising and has little or no entertainment value. It would have been more economical to dispense with the hat, leaving the rabbit freely gamboling on the scene. For all that is being done is the repeated and quite elementary manipulation of a tautology: since neutrality entails equality, neutrality requires equality or, for choice, inequality violates neutrality.

In less stringent variations on the same theme, Ackerman finds that while equality has at least something rational to say for it, nothing speaks for inequality (op. cit., p. 58) except the claims of genetic handicaps (op. cit., p. 130) and cultural disadvantages,[4] i.e. that liberal social justice permits equality to be qualified by some measure of positive discrimination in favour of the 'genetically dominated' and culturally deprived. Recognizing these claims provides added scope for employing the 'technology of justice', namely redistributive politics.

Ackerman notes that 'traditional' liberals are eager to constrain political power but forget that the 'private' entitlements (his quotation marks) they seek to defend from the encroachments of politics, are 'defined and enforced' by the very same political power. He asserts the ubiquitous thesis of 'modern' liberalism that it is the state or 'society' that confers property rights, and what it gives it can also take back. Without 'the powers of government...there is no reason to think that those presently advantaged by the distribution of "private" rights would remain so' (op. cit., p. 19); therefore they have little to complain of if the powers of government are, from the day neutral dialogue is introduced, used to deprive them of their advantages. This line of reasoning can be seen as a defence against objections to the initial presumption of equality, under which there are no pre-existing claims to 'manna' by its providers and producers, for all of it is an as yet undistributed common pool. Even if this strange starting point is rejected, 'liberal justice' can as good as reconstruct it from the status quo by recourse to the fail-safe device meant to deflect all deontological criticism of redistribution. It is the standard thesis, that whatever prior claims exist, they exist by the grace of society that recognizes and protects them, and hence society is entitled to de-recognize and unprotect them in the name of 'dialogic neutrality' or, one would guess, in the name of anything else it was disposed to put in its place. The fallacy that confuses an institution like property, marriage or contract, with its contingent legal protection, and the second fallacy that mistakes a *de facto* monopoly of enforcement for an intrinsic necessity, are busily at work here under the surface.

Since each person has a 'conception of the good', he has a right to 'dialogic recognition'. By neutrality, he is at least as good as every other, which is 'reason enough' for him to have an equal share of 'material reality' (sic) (op. cit., p. 171). But it does not follow that his 'control of material reality' must take the form of 'individualistic property', an institution that has 'an uncertain place in liberal theory' (ibid., p. 171).

One would have thought that how 'material reality is controlled' is a matter to be left to the freedom of contract. Justice in the liberal state, however, will have none of that: it requires that 'the claims of free contract be appraised against the background of power relationships established by the transactional framework and the distribution of wealth, education and ability' (op. cit., p. 199). For all the windiness and opacity of this statement, the meaning manages to transpire that the contract is free to the extent that the just society approves of its terms. It is wholly on a par with Ackerman's more general contention that a process is acceptable if and only if it produces an acceptable outcome – a surprising position to take for a proponent of justice by the process of 'dialogic neutrality' and of political decisions by majority rule (pp. 178–9), the procedural method *par excellence*.

Thus, for Ackerman, the liberties of individuals are subordinated to somebody's consequential calculus (where 'somebody' stands for whomever accepts his rule of neutral dialogue): 'if...a just structure evolved without conscious direction, it would be possible to defend a laissez-faire position' (op. cit., p. 163). If not, not. 'But...the end of exploitation will come only through self-conscious political action' (op. cit., p. 263). Moreover, among several just structures, we 'should choose the one preferred by the majority over the one thrown up by the invisible hand' (ibid., p. 263, note), despite the obvious fact that the former is imposed upon a minority.

In any event it is hard to see the point of these observations. Why should one pretend to entrust the production of social outcomes to procedures – whether the procedure is 'neutral dialogue' or freedom of contract, *laissez-faire* or voting – since we, the liberal majority, altogether determined to employ the power of politics to enforce the equality of manna, have decided from the outset to accept only some[5] and reject the other outcomes these procedures are liable to generate? Why not forget about these procedures, and directly agree to have the acceptable outcome? The question is rhetorical in the real world, where agreement on outcomes is no doubt harder to achieve than agreement to procedures. But it is not rhetorical in the comic, yet somewhat frightening, cloud-cuckoo-land that Ackerman chooses to call the liberal state and that politics on the rampage appears to be trying to bring about.

Notes

1. Both the expansion of the scope of the state, and the marginal benefit the group expects to derive from it, should be understood generally with due regard to sign, i.e. negative expansion and negative benefit should be considered together with the positive.
2. A part of the area that 'orders itself' without bargaining, agreement and convention is, of course, a market where both sellers and buyers are 'price-takers'. However, it is only part of the area, and perhaps not a very large part. The 'market' is invested with such near-mythical force and significance in one strain of vulgarized anti-collectivist discourse that it is surely salutary to remember that civil society can function in many other spheres, as well as in and through the 'market'.
3. The basic mechanism at work here, if the conditions for its successful operation were fulfilled, would resolve the problem in the following way: a public good is

characteristically indivisible ('lumpy'). Hence there is a marginal contribution to its cost which is decisive: if that contribution is not forthcoming, the good is not provided. Voluntary cooperators are induced to contribute by their probability-weighted expectation that their particular contribution might be decisive. Free riders do not contribute, taking the risk that their missing contribution might cause the good not to be provided.

Contributors and free riders are both self-selected, moved by their own preferences for the public good and their subjective expectations about how the whole group will split between cooperators and free riders. Contributions in the first instance are pledged; if too few are pledged, the good will not be provided and the contributions are not made. The more a given individual expects others to take the risk of free riding and not pledge, the more reason he has to pledge.

Contributing is to insure against the failure to provide the good; free riding is to earn a return for bearing the risk the contributors insure against.

4. Ackerman puts high demands on liberal education. He condemns Milton Friedman's school voucher proposal, because, by giving powers of choice to parents, it would enable them to have their children 'force-fed' on the values they happen to have (Ackerman, 1980, p. 160). In fact, however, the problem is not confined to parent power over children; any adult power generates the same tyranny. He observes that '*any* system in which the elder generation uses its superior power to "educate" the young is coercive' (op. cit., p. 162). Is the solution, then, to have only the powerless young educate the powerless young? Ackerman does not say; instead, somewhat lamely, he concludes that the problem subsists 'if not handled with sensitivity' (op. cit., p. 166). Recommending 'sensitivity' has at least one merit, namely that it is impossible to disagree with it.

5. Ackerman is perfectly explicit (1980, pp. 293-7) that the 'outcome indifference' implied in majority rule does not apply to 'illegitimate options', e.g. to a majority decision in favour of unequal inheritance (ibid., p. 294). In other words, he would restrict majority rule by substantive rather than procedural constitutional rules: voting for the wrong alternative would be void, and voting down *this* constitutional rule would also be void.

Nobody would be more cheered about the future of mankind than I if such rules were generally feasible. There are excellent reasons why generally they are not. By the very definition of an endogenous constraint, society cannot bind itself never to unbind any self-imposed constitutional bind.

There is, at best, only a limited range of distributive outcomes that can be placed out of bounds if society's lasting commitment to respecting these bounds is to have a modicum of credibility. A permanent majority in favour of equalizing inheritance is perhaps credible. A permanent super-majority against equalizing it is hardly credible.

References

Ackerman, B.A. (1980), *Social Justice in the Liberal State*, New Haven and London: Yale University Press.

Bainville, J. (1941), *Reflexions sur la politique*, Paris: Plon.

Barker, E. (1947), *Social Contract*, London: Oxford University Press.

Bouillon, H. (1995), *Freiheit, Liberalismus und Wohlfahrtsstaat*, Tübingen: J.C.B. Mohr (Paul Siebeck).

Buchanan, A. (1985), *Ethics, Efficiency, and the Market*, Oxford: Clarendon Press.

Coleman, J.L. (1988), *Markets, Morals and the Law*, Cambridge: Cambridge University Press.

Ellickson, R.C. (1991), *Order without Law: How Neighbours Settle Disputes*, Cambridge, Mass: Harvard University Press.

Epstein, R.A. (1985), *Takings: Private Property and the Power of Eminent Domain*, Cambridge, Mass: Harvard University Press.

Fried, C. (1978), *Right and Wrong*, Cambridge, Mass: Harvard University Press.

Gray, J. (1989), *Liberalisms: Essays in Political Philosophy*, London: Routledge.

Gray, J. (1992), *The Moral Foundations of Market Institutions*, London: Institute of Economic Affairs, Health and Welfare Unit.

Gray, J. (1993), *Post-Liberalism: Studies in Political Thought*, London: Routledge.

Griffin, J. (1986), *Well-Being, Its Meaning, Measurement and Moral Importance*, Oxford: Clarendon Press.

Harsanyi, J. (1977), *Rational Behaviour and Bargaining Equilibrium in Games and Social Situations*, Cambridge: Cambridge University Press.

Hayek, F.A. (1960), *The Constitution of Liberty*, Chicago: University of Chicago Press.

Kirzner, I. (1978), 'Entrepreneurship, Entitlement and Economic Justice', *Eastern Economic Journal*, **4**, 1, 9–25.

Leube, K.R. (1994), 'Begreifen und Verstehen', in K.W. Noerr, B.

Schefold and F. Tenbruck, *Geistewissenschaften Zwischen Kaiserreich und Republik*, Stuttgart: F. Steiner Verlag.

Lomasky, Loren (1987), *Persons, Rights and the Moral Community*, New York: Oxford University Press.

Lucas, J.R. (1980), *On Justice*, Oxford: Clarendon Press.

Nozick, R. (1974), *Anarchy, State and Utopia*, New York: Basic Books.

Nozick, R. (1989), *The Examined Life: Philosophical Meditations*, New York: Simon & Schuster.

Nussbaum, M. and Sen, A. (eds) (1993), *The Quality of Life*, Oxford: Clarendon Press.

O'Neill, O. (1982), 'Nozick's Entitlements', in J. Paul (ed.), *Reading Nozick*, Oxford: Blackwell, 1982.

Peacock, A. (1979), *The Economic Analysis of Government and Related Themes*, Oxford: Martin Robertson.

Peacock, A. and Rowley, C.K. (1979), 'Pareto Optimality and the Political Economy of Liberalism', in A. Peacock (1979).

Plant, R. (1992), 'Autonomy, Social Rights and Distributive Justice', in J. Gray, *The Moral Foundations of Market Institutions*, London: IEA Health and Welfare Unit.

Posner, R.A. (1992), *Economic Analysis of Law*, 4th ed., Boston: Little, Brown & Co.

Rawls, J. (1971), *A Theory of Justice*, Cambridge, Mass: Harvard University Press.

Rawls, J. (1982), 'Social Unity and Primary Goods', in A. Sen and B. Williams (eds), *Utilitarianism and Beyond*, Cambridge: Cambridge University Press.

Raz, J. (1986), *The Morality of Freedom*, Oxford: Clarendon Press.

Rousseau, J.-J. (1762, 1947), *The Social Contract or Principles of Political Right*, in E. Barker, *Social Contract*, London: Oxford University Press.

Schelling, T.C. (1984), *Choice and Consequence*, Cambridge, Mass: Harvard University Press.

Sen, A. (1993), 'Capability and Well-Being', in M. Nussbaum and A. Sen (eds), *The Quality of Life*, Oxford: Clarendon Press.

Sen, A. and Williams, B. (eds), (1982), *Utilitarianism and Beyond*, Cambridge: Cambridge University Press.

Taylor, C. (1993), 'Explanation and Practical Reason', in M. Nussbaum and A. Sen (eds), *The Quality of Life*, Oxford: Clarendon Press.

Waldron, J. (1988), *The Right to Private Property*, New York: Oxford University Press.

Index

Classical Liberalism in the Age of
Post-Communism

Classical Liberalism in the Age of Post-Communism

Norman Barry

Professor of Politics
University of Buckingham

The Shaftesbury Papers, 6
Series Editor: Charles K. Rowley

Edward Elgar
Cheltenham, UK • Brookfield, US

Published by
Edward Elgar Publishing Limited
8 Lansdown Place
Cheltenham
Glos GL50 2HU
UK

Edward Elgar Publishing Company
Old Post Road
Brookfield
Vermont 05036
US

British Library Cataloguing in Publication Data
Barry, Norman, 1944–
    Classical liberalism in the age of post-communism. – (The
    Shaftesbury Papers; 6)
    1. Liberalism   2. Post-communism   3. Classical school of
    economics
    I.Title   II. Series
    320.5'1

Library of Congress Cataloguing in Publication Data
Barry, Norman P.
    Classical liberalism in the age of post-communism / Norman Barry,
    — (The Shaftesbury papers; 6)
    1. Liberalism.   2. Liberalism—History.   3. Civil society.
    4. Post-communism.   I. Title.   II. Series.
    JC574.B37   1996
    320.5'12—dc20   95–40188
                                                                          CIP

ISBN 1 85898 256 1

Printed in Great Britain at the University Press, Cambridge

Contents

Preface

I am indebted to Charles Rowley, General Director of the Locke Institute, for first suggesting that I write this book. His help and encouragement have been invaluable. I learnt much from a Locke Institute colloquium on classical liberalism which was sponsored by the Liberty Fund and held at Boston in June 1993. I am grateful to all the participants at this event for providing a lively discussion of some of the ideas that are analysed in this book.

I am especially grateful to the directors of the Social Philosophy and Policy Center, Bowling Green State University, Ohio, for allowing me to use their offices over the Christmas of 1993. Fred Miller, Jeffrey Paul and Ellen Frankel Paul provided their usual congenial and intellectually stimulating environment.

At Buckingham, I have improved my knowledge of economics and the social sciences from long conversations with Martin Ricketts, Professor of Economic Organisation at the University. He is particularly adept at working through the connections between political economy and social philosophy.

Finally, I must express great thanks to my secretary, Mrs Anne Miller, for her excellent work in preparing the manuscript for publication.

1. Introduction

It is a curious irony that in the aftermath of the collapse of communism, and the intellectual disintegration of the edifice of Marxism, the doctrine of classical liberalism should be in the same precarious state as it has been throughout much of this century. Its appeal to the intellectual class is no greater now than it was in the heyday of collectivism and much of its theoretical armoury, most notably its exposition of the necessity of market relationships if any sort of efficiency is to be achieved, has been subtly appropriated by exponents of doctrines whose aims are very different. Apparently, the market can be harnessed to serve social agendas and political purposes some way removed from those of the founders of the doctrines of individualism, private property and limited government.

What has occurred in the West is the rise of what Anthony de Jasay (1991) has correctly called 'loose' liberalism. This has consisted of a series of depredations of original classical liberal doctrine, not only in terms of successive policies which are alien to the tradition, but also by the corruption of the *language* in which these departures from individualistic orthodoxy are expressed and justified. Thus, the demand for individual freedom, which was once thought to be indissolubly linked to economic liberty, the exercise of which is almost certain to produce some inequality, has now become a licence for the state to maximize a notion of *equal* liberties; constitutionalism, which hitherto had provided a theoretical barrier to state intervention, has become a threadbare protection, in America especially, against a state powered by the democratic will; individual rights, which historically functioned as indefeasible side-constraints on political action, boundaries that determined the space within which individuals could pursue their self-determined goals, have lately become welfare entitlements, the granting of which requires positive action by the state; and justice is no longer a concept that describes the procedural rules under which individuals may contract with some predictability but has now become annexed to various 'end-states' (particular distributions of income and wealth) which the state may legitimately impose on a nominally free order.

The *desiderata* of the new flexible liberalism all concern freedom itself and the role of the state has been recommended to extend beyond even the promotion of equal liberties to the maximization of freedom as 'autonomy' (Raz, 1986; Gray, 1992). This means not merely the absence of restraint, and the possibility of uncoerced action within a protected sphere, but the creation of economic conditions in which individual choice is apparently a *true* reflection of options (Raz, 1986, pp. 409–10). In other words, social circumstances may coerce just as much as identifiable individual agents and restrictive laws do and it is the duty of the state to remove these allegedly freedom-reducing conditions.

In this context, the current fashion in political theory for 'communitarianism' (MacIntyre, 1981; Sandel, 1982; Walzer, 1983) has a little more intellectual respectability, or at least honesty.[1] For the communitarians attack the doctrine of individualism head on, they do not distort the concepts and language in which it was originally formulated but explicitly reject them. Their strictures apply just as much to the liberal egalitarians, who have appropriated the word liberalism while discarding its defining features, as they do to classical liberals. Communitarianism is specifically addressed to that universalism which is a feature of much liberal philosophy.

The most significant feature of communitarianism's rejection of liberal individualism is its frontal assault on the doctrine of the 'self' that underlies it. To the extent that classical liberalism has traditionally been founded upon certain more or less permanent features of the human condition (e.g. scarcity, limited altruism and an all-pervading ignorance with which human action has to cope) its quasi-scientific implications are never limited by time and place but offer prescriptions of a more or less universal application. Again, the purely ethical claims that it makes derive from a moral ontology which relates to abstract persons rather than to members of identifiable groups, sociologically-understood communities or ethnic associations. The communitarian claim, however, is that 'the kind of society in which people live...affects their understandings both of themselves and how they should lead their lives' (Mulhall and Swift, 1992, pp. 13–14). This inevitably introduces a strain of relativism into normative argument which is alien to almost all forms of liberalism.

The various claims embodied in the above statement can be reduced to the proposition that the *abstract* individual (of either classical liberalism or liberal egalitarianism) is an inadequate focal point for the construction of a coherent social philosophy; our institutional arrangements and social policies cannot conceivably be understood as products of individual choice and that the individualistic programme cannot be simply exported to communities whose cultural traditions may be quite unreceptive to its apparent *asocial* foundations. Political and economic arrangements are received not chosen and it is our interpretation of them that must inform whatever judgements we might make about distributive criteria, the limits of the market or the permissible bounds of personal liberty. From this perspective the constitutional constructivism (and, ultimately, libertarian economics) of James Buchanan (Buchanan and Tullock, 1962; Buchanan, 1975) or the 'thought experiment' of Rawls (1971), which is designed to generate a rationally acceptable and socially just redistribution of resources, are equally condemnable.

The current difficulties of establishing liberal market orders in post-communist society may lend a superficial credence to this point of view; the impression is that the classical liberal order itself is rooted in particular historical circumstances which, by definition, do not always prevail and cannot be easily transported. However, if the communitarian claim is that liberal economics has historically neglected the institutional (legal and political) framework in which market transactions take place, it is simply false: the literature, from Adam Smith to Hayek and beyond, is replete with explanations of such necessary social structures, and accounts of their emergence. Only in the driest of technical, neo-classical economic theory is 'abstract' man completely abstract. The fact that this institutional framework can and does vary from society to society is not a surrender to relativism (which is a clear implication of communitarian theory) but merely a recognition of that diversity which is a feature of all social arrangements. Indeed, classical liberalism, which merely puts boundaries to coercive state action, encourages such diversity and is compatible with a variety of institutional arrangements as long as certain liberties are protected.

However, the fragility of classical liberal theory has not only been highlighted by liberal egalitarians and communitarians, it has also been a feature of the work of some of its leading exponents. I refer here specifically to the later ideas of F.A. Hayek (1979, 1988). Here that *critical* rationalism which gives classical liberalism its vitality, cutting edge and claim to a qualified universalism, has been almost completely jettisoned in favour of a curious, neo-Darwinistic form of social evolutionism. Although this idea was nascent in Hayek's earlier writings outside economics, the anti-rationalist tenor of those works (Hayek, 1960) was primarily directed at constructivistic and socialistic theories that dispensed with spontaneous market processes in favour of the directions of an *all-powerful* reason. However, in *The Fatal Conceit* (1988) especially, we are asked to submit to the blind forces of tradition in the somewhat optimistic assumption that the private property and free market system would emerge, and be self-sustaining, almost by necessity. The familiar rights-structured, or even utilitarian-based, explanation for a free order seems to have been replaced by a Panglossian belief in the (possibly serendipitous) processes of social evolution. Rational justification for laws and institutions has given way to belief in the apparently benign forces of cultural evolution.

It would appear from this brief and necessarily selective account of contemporary social philosophy that the case for a genuine free market liberalism has not proved to be at all persuasive. It remains very much an 'unknown' doctrine, despite the collapse of communism and the spread of capitalism. The fact that nobody believes in communism any more does not mean that classical liberalism is understood, let alone attractive (it is certainly not 'inevitable', as the later Hayek seemed to imply). It is necessary therefore to reconstruct the doctrine in the light of contemporary social and economic thought: to indicate not merely its serviceability in the realm of public policy but, more importantly, to indicate its relevance to broader philosophical themes and, most crucially, to evaluate its answers to the abiding questions of the relationship between the individual and society.

Note

1. Some communitarian doctrines have conservative and traditionalist elements.

2. Ideology

Classical liberalism, as a normative doctrine, is an amalgam of a number of claims and its rationale rests upon a variety of competing intellectual foundations – 'scientific' economics, utilitarianism, natural rights, Kantian deontology, contractarianism and evolutionism, to name just a few. All of these differing intellectual structures may (though not always) generate a kind of convergence around a commitment to private property, free markets, limited government, constitutionalism and the rule of law. But do these beliefs constitute an *ideology*? Indeed, experience of politics in the 20th century can be used to justify the opprobrium that is so often attached to that word. However, to the extent that the doctrine does espouse a kind of world-view and, in the light of the fact that its explanatory tools have a more or less universal application, it is perhaps not inappropriate to call classical liberalism an ideology.

However, three important qualifications should be made here. First, unusually for an ideology, classical liberalism contains a heavy scientific component. Much of it derives from orthodox resource allocation theory of conventional economics and to that extent has some predictive value: the literature is replete with confirmations of the forecasts it makes about the likely consequences of, e.g., rent control, monetary laxity, and centralized planning. These predictions can be easily formulated in terms of standard Popperian methodology, i.e. as deductions from purported universally-true axioms (Popper, 1957). To the extent that these predictions derive from universally-true axioms they provide a necessary corrective to communitarian theories (and, indeed, liberal egalitarian theories) since the normative conclusions drawn from these doctrines have to be qualified by the conclusions of social science. The most obvious example is the erroneous distinction, derived from John Stuart Mill (1848), between the laws of production and the laws of distribution. Ignorance of the necessary connection between these laws has led liberal egalitarians to ignore the effect on efficiency that policies of social justice always has. As Robbins graphically put it, 'economics deals with the necessities to which human action is subject'

(1935, p. 26). The fact that a variety of social and economic systems are more or less compatible with these necessities should not be used to underestimate their force. Indeed, unlike physical laws, their effect can be resisted – but only for so long. Compared with the credibility of classical liberalism the scientific claims of Marxism are no more than pretensions which have been refuted by events.

The second qualification to the assertion that classical liberalism is a mere ideology is the argument that the doctrine's scope is necessarily limited. It does not provide an overarching theory of the good life; in fact it deliberately leaves the determination of ultimate values to individuals themselves. Indeed, in some versions its subjectivism about economic value is extended even to ethics; moral rules are mere devices to provide security and predictability to actors rather than expressions of higher value. These rules do, however, provide a framework for individuals to pursue a plurality of values. Also, ethical subjectivism is normally qualified by the argument that the rules of justice are not a matter of taste but have a certain objective necessity. They provide that security which is necessary if individuals are to pursue their differing conceptions of the good.

However, just how classical liberals can demonstrate the apparent objectivity of the rules of justice with a generally subjectivist approach to ethics will be considered below, but it is sufficient to point out that the doctrine's commitment to personal liberty precludes that 'completeness' which characterizes the ideologies with which we are familiar. Classical liberalism requires that questions about religion, art and certain types of private moral behaviour should be left to individual judgement. Nevertheless, classical liberalism does suggest decisive answers to certain *institutional* questions, even if it does eschew questions about ultimate value.

The third thing that differentiates classical liberalism from more familiar political ideologies is the most obvious, yet perhaps the most important. This is that it is not attached to a class, party or to any other collective group that might wish to use the state as a mechanism to implement its programme. For one thing, the individualism (both methodological and moral) that underlies it precludes the doctrine from any association with collective ends (except for those public goods which can be derived from individual choice, or at least individually-approved collective decision-making procedures). It is the individual, abstracted from social affiliations of the coercive type (though not those that accrue from voluntary agreements), that is to be liberated, not the group. And, furthermore, that liberation requires, if anything, a transcending of politics and a release from those restrictions that stultify the growth of individuality. Indeed, the variety of classical liberal positions, both in the foundational and the policy sense, indicates that the doctrine consists largely of philosophical and theoretical enquiries rather than of overt political dogma.

3. The Realism of Classical Liberalism

An additional contrast worth making with most other ideologies is that classical liberalism begins with a 'realistic' view of man and his condition. Certain features of the human predicament, although contingent rather than logical, are assumed to be more or less universal, e.g. the predominant (though not all-inclusive) motivation of self-interest, the permanence of scarcity, the infinite range of human wants and the lack of information that confronts all actors. While not denying that the particular form these features take will be influenced by a myriad of differing circumstances, classical liberalism does reject the claim that a change in circumstances will produce a change in man which will render the restraints (law, property rights, and so on) that are required to cope with these contingencies unnecessary. Following David Hume, and the other Scottish Enlightenment thinkers, classical liberalism deals with man as he is, not as he might be: as Hume (1953, p. 146) observed, plans of government which suppose 'a great reformation of the manners of mankind are plainly imaginary'.

Hence the reform proposals that the doctrine recommends are normally designed to correct the predictable effects of the working out of these contingencies. Most notable here is the Janus-like features of the postulate of self-interest: at one level, when it is subject to rules, it points to the possibilities of unforced co-ordination and the unintended production of the public interest, while on another its *unrestrained* operation leads to the classic social dilemma of the automatic production of effects that are destructive of that very same self-interest. Under certain circumstances, rational self-interest dictates that individuals will pursue courses of action that are harmful to themselves. Thus public goods which are desired by (almost) everybody can only be produced by artifice or contract, and not spontaneous processes. Yet as Buchanan (1975) has recognized, how do we stop the Humeian state, limited to the production of public goods and restrained by general rules, degenerating into the Hobbesian state, the unrestrained Leviathan that operates by *command* but whose very existence is the product of rational individual choice?

From its very beginnings, classical liberalism has focused attention on certain *descriptive* features of the human condition, and its normative recommendations have emerged from this analysis. There were, after all, markets already existing for Adam Smith to describe and there were legal orders before there was a jurisprudence to analyse them: all are phenomena that exist independently of man's will. In sharp contrast, one could hardly even imagine communist systems existing in the absence of Marx and the Marxists. Equally, though less dramatically, liberal egalitarianism depends on the same type of constructivism. Ironically, though, classical liberalism does also to some extent; not merely for the production of public goods (which are ultimately rooted in, or derive from, private desires) but also for those constraints on government which make the enjoyment of liberty possible. Markets can exist in orders which deny those non-economic aspects of liberty which individualists value. There is then, despite Hume and Smith's utilitarianism, a deontological strand in classical liberalism (Nozick, 1974) which emphasizes the necessity for these constraints, on individuals as well as governments, irrespective of their immediate consequentialist value (which cannot normally be calculated). Most classical liberals do value liberty for its own sake.

This specifically moral strand in classical liberalism is difficult to identify and occupies a somewhat shadowy position in its philosophy. This is not to say that Hume and Smith were not genuine ethical thinkers but it is true that their moral philosophy was, on the whole, *descriptive*, a sophisticated account of the ethical rules that had spontaneously developed to service a nascent property-based market order. Its claims to universality were always questioned. As MacIntyre (1981, p. 215) put it, 'its appeal to a universal verdict turns out to be the mask worn ... by those who psychologically and socially share Hume's attitudes and *Weltanschauung*'. Furthermore, throughout its history, classical liberalism has had to face the charge that the success of the market system that it described was bought at the cost of morality. Bernard Mandeville graphically, and almost enthusiastically, conceded the point with his claim that 'the grand principle that makes us social creatures, the solid basis, the life and support of all trade and employment without exception is evil' (1924, vol. I, p. 369). Virtue and commerce are forever in conflict and the moral rules that govern trade are no more than conventions that are necessary to make life predictable and secure for transactors. Still, as Adam Smith observed (1976a), why should that normal prudence exhibited in the market be thought immoral? And why should the rules of justice be thought antithetical to commerce?

I shall suggest that a morality understood as a form of convention is not necessarily condemnable, and that there are even universalistic themes within this approach. But the *apparent* moral lacuna in classical liberalism has encouraged its critics and has perhaps contributed to the mutation of the doctrine into liberal egalitarianism. It is a common theme in the post-communist world of ideas that the market has to be moralized by principles extraneous to it. It has encouraged sanitized versions of market economics, as in some theories of the social market economy, to emerge as correctives to the original doctrine; albeit at some considerable cost, not only in terms of adverse effects on productive possibilities which their implementation in public policy entails, but also in respect of intellectual rigour. One should not ignore the corrosive effect on free orders that the influence of such modifications has produced.

4. Spontaneous Order Theory and the Market

The scientific and ethical elements in classical liberalism are closely intertwined, even though its theorists have constantly affirmed the conventional philosophical position concerning the impossibility of deriving an 'ought' from an 'is', of demonstrating the compelling nature of moral judgements from any purported regularities in the social world. Indeed, this now accepted proposition was first formulated by David Hume (1972, p. 220), who nevertheless was both a firm believer in the claim that human behaviour was explicable in terms of regularities ('laws') and an early celebrant of the market system, and its associated order of property rights and the rule of law. His account of the connection between morality and causal explanation is relevant to contemporary classical liberal thought.

In his view, our moral judgements are derived from the passions, not reason; it is the former that drive us to action not the latter (which is confined to a calculative role, either in the realm of logic, or in empirical science). However, he was able to show that certain moral rules would develop spontaneously to service a liberal order and these are compelling not because they can be derived from some religious, or other metaphysical, foundation but because they tended to meet with men's *approval*. They are genuinely moral because they are normative guides to conduct which we are at liberty to ignore; but at a cost. Hence his rules of justice, which comprise basically the inviolability of justly acquired property and the obligatoriness of contract, although they are artificial, and irreducible to a metaphysical concept of natural law, are not *merely* conventional if that means alterable at will. He argues that 'though justice be artificial the sense of its morality is natural' (Hume, 1972, p. 221). It is their appropriateness for civilization and progress, and their consistency with certain unalterable features of the human condition, that justify a qualified claim for their universality.

This is the origin of the anti-rationalist foundations of classical liberalism, an approach continued, perhaps to excess, by F.A. Hayek in the

20th century. It is addressed primarily to that hubris in man which drives him to attempt improvements on quasi-natural processes; most commonly by the use (or misuse) of scientific method. The illusion that the elements of an economic, legal and moral order can be rearranged at will in order to generate some pre-determined outcome has been responsible for most of the catastrophes that are recurring features of the 20th century. The attempt to imitate the staggering success of the physical sciences in exact prediction, and more or less complete control over certain aspects of the environment, by social scientists has been one of the major reasons for these disasters. While one cannot ignore the malign effects of ethnic tensions and the resurgence of communal affiliations on the structure of social order (a fact which ought to dampen the enthusiasm of the communitarians to locate morality uncritically in 'given' communities), the urge of the rationalist to plan and direct events in advance of spontaneity is undeniably a main factor in the decay of civility and the decline of the modest predictability of rules. As Adam Smith observed, in 1759, of the rationalist,

> He seems to imagine that he can arrange the different members of a great society with as much ease as the hand that arranges the different pieces upon a chess board. He does not consider that the pieces upon the chess board have no other principle of motion besides that which the hand impresses upon them; but that, in the great chess board of human society, every single piece has a principle of motion of its own, altogether different from that which the legislature might choose to impress upon it. (Smith, 1976a, p. 263)

What is important here is the fact that because human beings have principles of motion of their own it does not mean that order has to be imposed, that no spontaneous order is possible, or that free actions produce randomness, disorder and inefficiency.

It is true that the history of Western political and social thought may be viewed as a kind of debate between the heirs of Hobbes, who believe that order is a product of design, that individual rational self-interest will produce chaos unless controlled by the terms of some contractual arrangement, and the proponents of spontaneity; but the presentation of this argument in either/or terms has confused the issue. There are, as most classical liberals concede, limits to spontaneous order. Indeed, it was Hume himself who pioneered the theory of public goods with his observation that, because people showed a natural tendency to prefer *immediate* satisfactions, a preference which can be destructive of their long-term interests, they construct social arrangements to correct this defect. In his view, government itself is the paradigm case of a public good (1953, pp. 39–42). There is little indication in Hume, as there is in Hayek (1988), that the blind forces of social evolution will somehow eventuate in a benign social order. However, the admission that circumstances may sometimes generate the necessity for a form of order that appears to owe more to rational design than spontaneity should not be used as a licence to dispense with those co-ordinating processes, both in law and economics, which have historically developed in the absence of a direct controlling will.

5. Market Orders

The painful experience in the struggle to establish market systems in former communist regimes is a tragic reminder of the long-term effect that wildly rationalistic interventions in gradually developing economic systems can have. Property rights, the rules of justice and the rule of law are difficult to re-establish in countries, e.g., Russia, where their nascent and inchoate emergence had been all but eliminated by collectivist planning. In such circumstances, a Hobbesian solution to the problem of order may be unavoidable. But even here it could be argued that certain sorts of rules and values would have developed spontaneously were it not for the imposition of rationally-designed orders. The theory of spontaneous order does rest ultimately on a moral claim to liberty.

There is, however, evidence, of a kind of moral vacuum, concerning the roles of liberty, justice and rights even in societies lucky enough to have inherited (at least partially) the kinds of economic and legal systems described by Hume and Smith. They seem to have instrumental value only and can hence be discarded if occasionally they fail to fulfil that role effectively. The reason why classical liberalism has been vulnerable to contemporary critics, who often call themselves 'liberals', is partly due to this problem and also because the theory of spontaneous order has been misunderstood even in that area in which it has been most effective, i.e., the explanation and justification of market phenomena. It is because of a misrepresentation of the market that critics of classical liberalism can claim the virtues of the exchange mechanism while rejecting most other features of the doctrine. They can be substituted with principles that do not derive from the universal elements in the market system. These principles are normally specifically anti-individualistic.

Thus, John Gray (1992, 1993) can rail against classical liberalism for its unsubstantiated claim to universalism, and unsustainable individualistic ethic, yet at the same time argue for the necessity of markets: 'The epistemic and the incentive arguments for the market are overwhelming' (Gray, 1992, p. 16). In his view the market is a cultural artefact and the form that it takes will depend on the social practices in which it is embedded. It is an error, he conjectures, to suppose that it is analytically linked to a concept of individual liberty (with its primarily anti-statist overtones of classical liberalism) detached and abstracted from particular forms of civil association.

Of course, there is a long tradition in economic thought, most noticeably in the various forms of market socialism, and in the recent appraisals of apparently alternative forms of capitalism in the Far East and in Germany, which does attempt to detach the market from its individualistic foundations. Most versions of this tradition depend on some attenuation of individualistic notions of property ownership, either by reference to straight collective ownership (somehow annexed to choice in the market) or to a version of communitarianism which places certain social responsibilities above individual gratification. In particular, all these non-capitalist doctrines, or severely modified versions of capitalism, are especially critical of the allegedly free wheeling, *laissez-faire* world of Anglo-American economies, inhabited by essentially *anonymous* transactors engaged in 'arm's-length' relationships and governed by formal, and minimal, laws only. This phenomenon is perhaps best exemplified in the market for corporate control where the takeover mechanism (Manne, 1965) determines, to some extent, economic change. It has been specifically attacked for the indifference to moral and communal values that it apparently generates. Almost all the rival market theories have this model in mind for their criticism. It is a model that would appear to have few ethical constraints on the pursuit of individual gratification.

The only specifically moral problem at this level (I leave aside questions of welfare and social justice until later) is the question of the legitimacy of certain actions that are involved in this method of coordination. The whole process may well have an overall utilitarian justification but does it not involve 'evil', in Mandeville's sense, since it seems to depend not merely on the elimination of communal, co-operative or altruistic motivations but, more importantly, on the exploitation of people's *ignorance*? Is one person not being used as a means to the ends of another and is there not therefore a breach of those deontological constraints on human action (which figure strongly in much classical liberal moral theorizing)?

Does not the inequality of information which characterizes all market processes breach rules of fairness? In a familiar example, does a

potential purchaser of an apparently low-valued picture have to reveal
to the owner that he happens to *know* that it is a Rembrandt? Again,
does not the emergence of a monopoly by perfectly natural processes
(and which could be justified as a reward for the superior foresight of a
particular individual) damage unconscionably the freedom of those
thereby excluded, in effect, from the market? It is considerations such
as these that have powered the pro-market opponents of classical liberalism.

Still, despite these possible objections, emphasis still must be placed
on the *creativity* involved in market process, a feature which is likely to
be suppressed by an over-rigorous enforcement of deontological constraints. Creativity is necessarily involved since tastes are never given
but constantly altering in unpredictable ways, and technological possibilities are not costlessly available but have to be sought out by *entre-
preneurs* (Hayek, 1948; Kirzner, 1973, 1979) ever anxious to exploit
the difference between resource costs and product price. Entrepreneurship does not have a supply price and therefore its features cannot be
replicated by some central agency without its creativity being irrepara-
bly compromised. The contemporary attempts to detach the theory of
the market from the elements of human action and freedom described
in classical liberalism are redolent of Christian theories of the 'just'
price, i.e. the long-run price of a product as determined by objective
costs. But what creativity could there possibly be if a market system
were subject to this constraint?

The assumptions about knowledge of costs that lie behind claims of
market socialism (which hopes to dispense with genuine entrepreneurship) are remarkable but not dissimilar ones are made in the contemporary world by those who would impede the operation of market processes on behalf of communal values and expanded concepts of justice.
Whatever moral values they may have are certain to inhibit those co-
ordinating processes of market described by classical liberalism. The
much vaunted communal versions of markets in south-east Asia do not
eliminate entrepreneurship, although it no doubt takes a slightly different form there, least of all do they compromise the competitive instinct.
As I shall show below, the German market economy is not quite like
the Anglo-American one, but its apparent success does not invalidate
the claims of classical liberalism. Evidence of creativity can be found
in some superficially, unpromising examples of market processes.

Hence the claim that the market is a cultural artefact that lacks any
universal application is misleading: it is the different *types* of market

that reflect varying cultures. It is presumably the anonymity of Anglo-American economies, in comparison to the more intimate systems found elsewhere, that encourages their formalistic, indeed perhaps excessively legalistic, nature. The variety of market systems that we witness is not evidence of a lack of universality in the fundamental claims of the original celebrants of those orders.

None of this, then, dilutes the claim of Hume that rules of just conduct develop spontaneously and have a more or less universal application, or Smith's contention that the division of labour is the consequence 'of a certain propensity in *human nature* ... the propensity to truck, barter, and exchange one thing for another' (1976b, p. 25, emphasis added). Those who dismiss the universalistic claims of classical liberalism (e.g., Gray, 1989, pp. 239–64) have to explain how it is that regular patterns of behaviour reproduce themselves if individuals are accorded some freedom of choice, some space in which they can exercise individuality. Of course, this does not conclusively validate the doctrine (especially its moral component) but it does cast doubt on the argument that markets can *only* be understood in terms of particular traditions; as if there were no wider lessons to be drawn from the experience of property ownership and the practice of contracting. As long as rationality is interpreted in a minimalist sense, i.e., as a feature of human action which is concerned with the calculation of the means necessary for the achievement of self-determined human goals, it is a defining feature of individual endeavour. It is only when reason is understood in a maximalist sense, as a purely intellectual device divorced from experience, that it poses a threat to the utilization of knowledge and gradual adjustment to changing circumstances, which are both necessary for progress.

Especially important is the fact that the rules, e.g. of property, contract, and tort, that are necessary for the efficient operation of markets and capitalism have a claim to validity which is independent of specific enactment. Only in a trivial sense are these rules artefacts of society. They are, it is true, not 'given', as facts of nature like the weather, but are the products of human endeavour in a purely social context. However, this obvious truth should not mislead us into thinking that the forms of these rules depend solely on external social or political arrangements, that there would have been no commercial or property law in the absence of the state. The claim that all law necessarily depends on the state no doubt encourages the predominant view that commerce and the market exist somehow by permission of centralized authority.

This leads to the not dissimilar argument that the variety of particular markets and legal phenomena that we see in the world is a confirmation of the claim that their main elements have no claim to universality.

In fact, the literature is replete with studies of the spontaneous emergence of commercial law in the absence of the state (Trakman, 1983; Benson, 1990). Indeed, historically the state is a comparative latecomer: it came after both the law and the market. The myth of the priority of state is no doubt a consequence of the fact that obviously we know so much more about political events. Since the market emerged to serve the needs of unknown people, its development was a response to their very ignorance and its achievements were not the results of the will of a single person or body of persons, it is not surprising that it should have been underestimated as a source of human progress.

The claim that society or the state should regulate contract and property closely has, of course, some foundation in social theory and that foundation does not depend entirely on the argument that these institutions should somehow serve some higher collective (and contestable) purpose. It has often rested on the superficially plausible assertion that contracts are not self-enforcing, that the temptations of the moment may lead individuals 'rationally' to breach them, to the ultimate cost of their own well-being as well as that of society at large. In other words, without coercion, people may free-ride on the institution of contract, thus bringing about its ultimate demise. Even Hobbes could envisage the stability of instantaneous contracting, where the advantages of fidelity to agreements are immediate and tangible. However, he argued that any arrangement which required an element of trust would, under his assumptions, be self-defeating in the absence of an absolute sovereign.

However, modern social theory shows that this is not necessarily so; indeed if the Hobbesian claim were true one wonders how the common law (which preceded the state) could ever have developed. But as Robert Sugden (1986) has demonstrated, rules of cooperation can develop spontaneously. In exchange relationships individuals merely have to co-ordinate their behaviour in order to reap the benefits of cooperation. Communication between the participants and iteration of the 'game of callaxy' (Hayek, 1976, chapter 4) makes it possible for them to overcome the problems conventionally associated with collective behaviour. Furthermore, the exploitation of asymmetries, i.e., the gains that can be made from cooperation between individuals doing different things (as occurs in drivers following the rules of the road) increases the incentives for regularized behaviour. The fidelity to such rules and practices is reinforced by the development of the decentralized forms of punishment in which non-cooperators are excluded from beneficial participation – the tit-for-tat strategy (Axelrod, 1984). Co-ordination games are different, then, from conventional public-good phenomena.

It is true that cooperative practices are more likely to develop in small groups in which the advantages of cooperation are usually visible, and the possibilities of the detection of non-cooperators more easily available than in social situations with large numbers where genuine public-good problems occur. In these circumstances, a public good will be supplied whatever the actions of the participants so that the incentives to cooperate are dramatically reduced. Here there is obviously a role for a more formalized construction of constitutional authority.

Still, we should not discount the likelihood of cooperative attitudes spreading, in an evolutionary manner, throughout a society in the absence of political authority. In modern liberalism, the recognition of the necessity for political authority in one obvious aspect of social life has been used as a licence for it to dominate over areas in which voluntary behaviour has proved to be perfectly adequate. Furthermore, this extension has been primarily not to improve the mechanisms of co-ordination but to impose on free peoples particular end-states, or collective outcomes, which would not have occurred spontaneously. These endeavours have distracted attention away from co-ordinating phenomena that can occur spontaneously and are found wherever people are allowed some liberty of action.

6. The German Market Economy, *Ordo* Liberalism and Classical Liberalism

The failure to appreciate the underlying uniformity of market relationships, and the logical similarity of the rules that govern them, has led to the gradual detachment of the theory of market phenomena from classical liberalism and to the invention of a variety of adjectives that are now used to qualify the noun in the post-communist world. The *Soziale-Marktwirtschaft* (social market economy) is important in this context for two reasons. First, of all the alternatives to classical liberalism it is the only one that has a body of respectable theory and practice (in postwar West Germany) behind it, and second, not only was it specifically offered to the former East Germany, on reunification, as a superior form of economic organization to Anglo-American capitalism, but its influence is spreading elsewhere. There is, however, some confusion about the nature of the doctrine and its connection with classical liberalism. For although the phrase social market economy is used to describe an apparently distinct and specific form of economics, it is actually a somewhat protean expression that obscures more than it reveals.

The first thing to do, by way of clarification, is to distinguish between the social welfare (in the sense of state welfare) implications of German liberal philosophy from its genuinely theoretical components. Western Europe has had a long history of welfare interventions and German market theorists in the 20th century accepted their own Bismarckian inheritance with varying degrees of enthusiasm. Whatever originality German liberal theory had, it was not in its theory of welfare. The key theoretical question is how far the German theories of the market departed from classical liberalism, and whether the differences can offer any general insights into the nature of a free social order.

A distinction should also be made at the outset between the theory of the social market economy and *Ordo* liberalism (although there was some doctrinal overlap): the former was a sophisticated doctrine of a liberal welfare state, as theorized by Alfred Müller-Armack (1965, 1979), and, although it was far superior to the Swedish model, it was ultimately flawed (Hamm, 1989; Lenel, 1989) and eventually slipped into more or less orthodox social democracy. However, the *Ordo* liberals made some theoretically interesting critical observations of classical liberalism, almost all of which relate to the coherence of spontaneous order theory (Barry, 1993a).

The major theorists in *Ordo* liberalism were Eucken (1950, 1951), Röpke (1950, 1960) and Böhm (1960). As the title of their movement implies, their main concern was to demonstrate the conditions for social order (*Ordnungspolitik*), in its economic, social and legal manifestations. It is to be stressed here that what the *Ordo* theorists were trying to explicate was an order of freedom not welfare, although undeniably the latter was an incidental outcome of market processes and to be valued for that reason. The order of freedom was Kantian in origin, i.e. it was a proper legal order which made individual freedom possible, and which had contract and property at its foundation.

The interesting point is that these writers did not believe that the classical liberalism that I have been describing spontaneously produced the order of freedom. Röpke (1950, p. 119) wrote that: 'Like pure democracy, undiluted capitalism is intolerable', and Eucken (1951, p. 93) argued that 'experience of *laissez-faire* goes to prove that the economic system cannot be left to organize itself' and that it had to be 'consciously shaped'. It wasn't that Eucken rejected the underlying features of classical liberalism, indeed contract, tort, property and market relationships featured strongly in what he called the 'constitutive principles' of a liberal order (1950, pp. 80–121). His claim was that if it were left entirely to itself it would spontaneously degenerate. Intervention was not required to create a new and higher social morality, as the liberal egalitarians believe (as also did Müller-Armack), but, in effect, was needed to preserve the original individualist system.

Thus unlimited freedom of contract could ultimately lead to the decline of a contract-based society (Eucken in fact betrayed none of the distrust that modern liberals have for contracts and would no doubt have objected to the statutory-based, and sometimes judicially-derived, qualifications to that ideal) and to the development of *voluntary* market-closing arrangements that shut people out of the exchange process. He also feared that unrestrained *laissez-faire* would generate market power; people would be formally free but their actions would be causally-determined by others. Competition was a public good which had to be protected by the state, or more properly, in Böhm's view, by an effectively organized legal system which allowed individuals to sue for anti-competitive practices. Still, either way there was a general scepticism about the self-sustaining properties of unaided orders.

No doubt the Germans were influenced by the experience of their own country from the late 19th century until the end of the Second World War. Under the *Rechtsstaat* (rule of law state) Germany was more or less *laissez-faire* in economics (leaving aside Bismarck's social welfare state) but had experienced heavy cartelization and voluntarily negotiated market-closing arrangements between producers. Indeed, all this had been given legal validation by a notorious *Reichtsgericht* (Supreme Court) decision in 1897 which had upheld a market-closing contract; that led to a proliferation of similar ones (also German industry was governed by quasi-legal rules which could be said to have developed in a Sugden-like manner[1]). The *Ordo* liberals thought that these were phenomena to which all classical liberal orders were vulnerable.

Traditional classical liberals, for example Mises (1949, p. 346), were dismissive of these claims. Hayek was a little more elusive in his opinions. He was hostile to the social market economy; he described the use of the word social as an 'adjectival frill', or else it masked a substantive aim for a socially-determined redistribution of income (Hayek, 1967, pp. 237–44). However, he was by no means unsympathetic to some aspects of the philosophy of *Ordo* liberalism. In general, though, 'Austrian' economists were of the opinion that spontaneous market processes (especially the pressure of international competition) would gradually eliminate the imperfections that had themselves evolved naturally. Indeed, there is evidence that the problem of cartelization was exaggerated (Wallich, 1955) and that attempts to correct *apparently* market-closing arrangements by reference to imaginary perfectly co-ordinating models of perfect competition actually have adverse effects on those corrective methods that are automatically ('invisibly') operating anyway. It is probably true that the *Ordo* theorists were unduly influenced by American anti-trust law, which has a similar equilibrium theory at its foundation. It is also the case that they were equally concerned by the political effects that cartelization had, i.e. it was probably one of the factors that led to the rise of totalitarianism (at least it made it possible economically) in Germany.

In any event, it is difficult to see how *Ordo* liberalism (and the success of *Ordo*-inspired economic policies in the early years of the

West German republic) significantly dilutes the central claims of classical liberalism; especially the theory that social and economic co-ordination via rules has a universal application. The argument that the market is a cultural and social achievement is no doubt true in a trivial sense but the claim that it is a mere *artefact*, which can be altered or redesigned at will, without there being any serious effect on either co-ordination or the structure of individual freedom, is clearly false. The economic history of West Germany since the late 1960s, when the ideological implications of the social market economy began to have their effect, is ample confirmation of this (Giersch *et al.*, 1992). The enervating effects of excessive welfare legislation and other impediments to market adjustment to change and uncertainty are only just being realized in that country. Indeed, the *Ordo* liberals were early critics of some aspects of the social market economy. They would have little time for Müller-Armack's later claim that it would produce a new 'man' different alike from socialist man and capitalist man (Müller-Armack, 1965). For them, the features of man were pretty much universal.

If the contemporary critics of classical liberalism have the social market economy in mind as an alternative to individualism, and cite the success of (West) Germany as a confirmation of their argument, they are, in fact, mistaken. By all the measures of the reduction in liberty, e.g., rises in personal taxation, the proportion of GDP spent by the state, and the decline of personal responsibility for action brought about by compulsory welfare, Germany has become less of a free society as a result of the social market economy. Indeed, the *Ordo* liberals opposed most of these policies. Hence Gray (1992, pp. 82–3) is quite wrong (in his attack on classical liberalism) when he argues that 'the German case is the *only* one, so far, in which the role of government in the economy and in society has been radically, and seemingly irreversibly reduced'. He erroneously claims that this is a result of the social market economy. In fact, Germany is no different from other social democratic countries, public expenditure has risen from about one-third of GDP in the early 1950s to slightly less than half now (Giersch *et al.*, 1992, p. 132). This has mainly occurred through the implementation of the social market policies approved of by Gray (1992, pp. 73–89).

Note

1. These rules of industrial practice operated, apparently, without direct state enforcement.

7. Law and Constitutionalism

The explanation of the spontaneous emergence of rules and practices that sustain a market order, and which have a certain universality, whatever *particular* form they take, is only one part of the classical liberal political philosophy. We live in a world which has seen a seemingly inexorable rise of the state and the apparent inability of constitutional constraints to contain this. The claim that liberal democracy would generate a genuine public interest, i.e. the common interest that citizens have in goods which have to be supplied collectively because of market failure, is no longer plausible. Modern democracies are driven by the 'vote motive' (Tullock, 1976) which produces electoral coalitions that redistribute income to groups necessary to secure their political power. Classical liberalism is partly a normative doctrine, concerned with the necessary features of a free society, and partly explanatory; it tells us how departures from the ideal occur.

This unending politicization of social life produces outcomes of high public spending and the successive attenuation of the rights of property and contract. They were probably not directly intended by the players in this electoral competitive game yet to some extent they were predictable. What we now have is de Jasay's (1985) 'plantation state', or form of political order by which government exists as a kind of entity in its own right; it prospers from the rents obtainable from politics. The periodic validation that government personnel requires from the electorate simply drives the system rather than provides any check to it. Since re-election normally requires the satisfaction of the demands of particular groups, the conventional democratic system provides no mechanism which effectively protects the public interest from the effects of group pressure. The US constitution, which at one time provided some constraint, has long since ceased to secure a protection for the core values of a classical liberal order.

This process has not only been driven by overt political factors but also by changes in the attitudes of judicial personnel. Thus in the US the constitutional defence of liberty, contract and property was formally abandoned in 1937 (Siegan, 1980) when the Supreme Court upheld a state statute that regulated wages. From then on, it consistently refused to protect economic rights and, in a case in 1938, officially endorsed the distinction between economic and civil liberties which has become the hallmark of modern, as opposed to classical, liberalism. That economic liberty is entitled to no constitutional protection in the way that personal and civil liberty has been officially proclaimed in liberal jurisprudence (Dworkin, 1977, pp. 277–8).

The search in classical liberalism for some kind of constitutional protection for economic liberty actually derives from an inchoate theory about the relative importance of ideas and interests in the determination of social events (see Barry, 1984, 1989). In the history of individualist thought one can detect a varying emphasis on either of these two factors. One strand of thought is concerned with the overwhelming importance of ideology and stresses that in the long-run it is ideas and values and not interests that are decisive: this was a view that Keynes and Hayek shared and Dicey (1926) alluded to in his account of the rise of collectivist thought in late 19th century England. He argued that 'public opinion' had been captured by spokesmen for this value system. They were influential on social legislation partly because they had managed to redefine liberty so that it was made consistent with what was, in effect, freedom-reducing legislation. Restrictions on contract (Green, 1888) were justified on the ground that they liberated individuals from their ephemeral and self-destructive desires. We can perhaps take this argument as decisive in the reformulation of liberal doctrine since it promoted an ideal of positive liberty which is significantly different from that notion of freedom as the absence of coercive law.

If ideas explain the way the social world works, then constitutional mechanisms hardly matter since it is presupposed that an élite is always able to influence decisively opinion and policy-makers. It could be mentioned in passing that it is difficult to see how Hayek could make this view consistent with his later public-choice-influenced constitutional reform proposals (Hayek, 1979, chapter 6), or with his evolutionism (a theory that purports to explain the flow of events independently of the human will). Ideas would presumably be ineffective in the face of such overwhelming social forces.

The interests theory is clearly more deterministic (though not necessarily materialistic): since it derives from economics it is likely to emphasize the fact that certain predictions can be made about human behaviour, subject to general explanatory laws and the specification of initial conditions. It is not concerned with celebrating the virtues of liberty directly in a moral sense but rather with specifying those institutional arrangements through which individuals' choices (including their preferences for public goods) can be maximized. There is a tradition in classical liberalism which is either sceptical of, or hostile to, the claim that morality can be objectively demonstrated. James Buchanan argues that public-choice theory is designed to avoid that 'retreat into empty arguments about personal values that spells the end of rational discourse' (1977, p. 82). The normative aspect of public-choice theory is concerned with the design of those procedural rules, agreement to which precludes or makes unnecessary moral argument about outcomes or states of affairs, or even about principles.

Can there really be a neutral, objective set of rules or is the familiar distinction between procedures and end-states a mere illusion? Does not every social theorist implicitly define the rules in such a way that the preferred outcome is generated anyway? Is it really enough to point out that under democratic politics redistributive policies reward particular groups rather than establish some purer ideal of liberal equality? As we shall see below a favoured classical liberal mechanism, the common law method of adjudication, has proved to be a less effective protective device for economic liberty than its theorists once thought. In such circumstances, argument about 'ideas' becomes unavoidable even if that is confined to the design of new institutional procedures so that the otherwise irresistible push and pull of group interests might be checked.

What *has* happened, however, is a virtual revolution in the theory of law that once prevailed in Western democracies: a transformation of the legal order which had been historically characterized as a body of *private* rules to enable individuals to fulfil their self-determined purposes, with a small area reserved for necessary *public* rules, into a directed system consisting very largely of public plans and purposes. The latter is largely decided by coalitions of groups which are themselves determined by electoral pressures. In its original form the common law system was an appropriate legal mechanism for the classical liberal order. Its appositeness can be seen in at least two ways: its structural features display the properties of a spontaneous order and its mode of operation is in conformity with the (limited) moral demands of the rule of law doctrine. Its general attributes enable both an efficient use of that limited knowledge that is available in any community and an economical use of necessarily scarce *moral* capital.

It is a spontaneous order precisely because its elements do not emanate from the mind of a single (personal or institutional) law-giver but emerge in an unplanned manner from the myriad of cases that have been decided and which provide precedents, and some degree of predictability, for actors in the future. In many ways, it is a formalized expression of those informal moral rules that naturally emerge to govern processes of social interaction. Thus formalized contract law arises out of the idea of a promise; property law confirms rights of ownership derived originally perhaps from some Lockeian-type claim to first possession or from morally legitimate transfers; and tort law governs the legitimate claims that individuals have when their interests are harmed. There is thus a combination of morality and formalized legality in common law systems. It should be noted, however, that even though codified systems look as if they were designed from first principles they are better seen as coherent declarations or summaries of what had developed spontaneously (though they do preclude that judicial creativity which is a feature of common law systems). No legal order can be designed *de novo*.

It is a fundamental claim of common law theorists that the compatibility (superficially, at least) of the common law and the market system should be obvious. The security provided by contract makes it possible for an infinite number of mutually-satisfying contracts to be completed, and the compensation provided by tort law ensures that no one is made worse-off by the competitive process. In theory, market exchanges under the common law are Pareto-improvements. Of course, that provides only the minimal foundation in morality because the Pareto-principle is notoriously silent on the distribution of resources from which mutually-beneficial exchanges proceed. Indeed, this is perhaps one reason why the idea of classical liberalism looks superficially less attractive than liberal egalitarianism. In some versions, classical liberalism provides no specific theory of *original* entitlement.

The role of the judiciary is crucial in common law systems: in essence it must preserve that overall rule structure which provides some degree of predictability for transactors. The judge does not proceed solely by deductive logic but he must construct an order of events which is socially coherent in the sense of preserving a kind of continuity. This can mean that new rules may occasionally be invoked in difficult cases. As Hayek says:

> Whether a new norm fits into an existing pattern of norms will not be a
> problem solely of logic, but will usually be a problem of whether, in the

existing factual circumstances, the new norm will lead to an order of compatible actions. This follows from the fact that abstract rules of conduct determine particular actions only, together with particular circumstances. (1973, pp. 105–6)

Examples of this can be found in the original spontaneous development of environmental law, where judges had to work out procedures for dealing with external effects (see Coase, 1960). It is not that the judges have complete discretion when the rules run out, as the legal positivists seem to imply, it is rather that their creativity is limited by a duty (which ultimately must be moral) to preserve an ongoing order. According to Hayek (1973, pp. 94–7), what judges are often doing is rendering articulate rules which were hitherto inarticulate, i.e. hidden in the interstices of a legal order. However, there is clearly a subtle interplay between discovery and genuine creativity in the determination of a legal order.

It might also be objected that the process necessitates an element of retroactive law since potential litigants cannot know what the law is until the judges have determined it. This is undoubtedly true, it follows indeed from the fundamental classical liberal epistemological claim that the amount of knowledge available to any person(s) in a society is limited; no designed legal order could ever anticipate exactly all future circumstances, and changes in events, which could give rise to litigation. It is, in fact, far more likely that it is the legislature that is capricious and unpredictable in its construction of new rules and, because of the vote motive, is less reliable in the production of law which is to the benefit of essentially *anonymous* agents in the social process. Furthermore, the stress on difficult cases obscures the crucially important fact that economic and social transactions constantly take place without ever being the subject of litigation. Disputed cases constitute a minute proportion of all rule-governed phenomena.

Of paramount importance in classical liberal jurisprudence is the distinction between law and policy: a distinction between the private rules that govern individual interaction and the public legislation under which government plans, addressed to specific social purposes, are conducted. The point of private rules is that they are, in essence, purposeless (Hayek, 1973, pp. 41–6), at least in the sense that they do not embody a public end, even though they may be given an overall justification in a utilitarian sense (however, their legal and moral *validity* would hold in the absence of this rationale). They are the necessary means for individuals to realize their self-determined ends and the rights they enforce have a Kantian justification, i.e. it would be wrong to violate them on behalf of some public policy and they must be fully universalizable. Public law is supposed to emanate from public bodies charged with the responsibility of implementing plans, and these agencies are subject to democratic accountability (inadequate though that invariably is). In a country like Britain, in which legislation from a sovereign parliament takes precedence over all other claims to law, it was inevitable that public law should triumph over private law in circumstances of majority-rule democracy. Still, those countries with formal constraints on law-making power cannot be said to have fared any better in the protection of liberty or in the preservation of traditional common law procedures.

However, the problem in classical liberal jurisprudence lies not merely in the failure of constitutional constraints alone (though that is crucially important) but in the spontaneous feature of the common law itself. The theory holds that we cannot predict law's development, or even evaluate it from any external standpoint. We can only appraise it with the standard set by the internal coherence of the structure as a whole. From this perspective, it turns out to be merely a contingent fact (though clearly not fortuitous) that the development of the common law served the needs of an ideal classical liberal order. The judicial search for consistency, coherence and the universalization of rules so that they can apply to future unknown cases is by no means the same thing as the sustaining of an order of inviolable property and contract rights. For example, logically almost any rule can be universalizable so as to satisfy the Kantian requirement, and clearly not all universalizable rules are limited to the protection of property and contract. Even Hayek himself admits (1973, p. 89) that developments in English common law (especially landlord and tenant law) in the 19th century were not conducive to an orderly market society. Law here required corrective action by legislatures, or by innovative judges breaking with legal tradition.

What is more disturbing is that in the 20th century deliberate judicial intervention in common law processes has been, if anything, disruptive of its co-ordinating processes; it has not been aimed at correcting inadequacies in the legal servicing of a free order, as suggested by Hayek, but rather it has steered the legal order away from this. And this has occurred quite apart from, and in addition to, the depredations brought about by direct public intervention. The shift in the meaning of liberalism from its classical and individualistic foundations towards a social or egalitarian form has certainly been helped by a change in the judicial attitude, a phenomenon which itself is a tribute to the potency of ideas in social life.

America is the best example of this transformation since there the judiciary is to some extent constitutionally protected from politics and has the constitutional authority to resist the legislatures. For much of America's history the Supreme Court upheld the economic rights of the individual, in contract especially, against statute (formerly from the states but later from the Congress also). This protection derived from judicial interpretation, along Hayekian lines, since the Constitution does not *specifically* make contract inviolable: however, the Fourteenth Amendment's due process clause implicitly required that a special reason be produced if the economic liberty of the citizen were to be lawfully abrogated. Originally the Court demanded very special reasons for the permissibility of statutory constraints on contract.

This all ended in 1937 with the *West Coast Hotel* v. *Parrish* case. From then the Court began to uphold every economic regulation and every taking of property (Epstein, 1985). Not only that but it has extended civil liberties, notably in the areas of affirmative action (sometimes justified as a form of compensation to certain disadvantaged groups so as to make the procedural rules more neutral), expanded the rights of criminal suspects and widened the scope of civil disobedience; much of this has been achieved without the aid of legislatures. Of course, some of the Court's activity here might be made consistent with classical liberalism but what is clearly not compatible with the doctrine is the supposed asymmetry between civil and economic liberties which has now become an established feature of American law, and which was invented by the judiciary.

The irony in all this is that the turnaround in judicial behaviour has been justified by a jurisprudence that bears an uncanny resemblance to Hayek's apology for common law reasoning (and its evolutionary development). I refer here to the legal philosophy of Ronald Dworkin (1977, 1986), one of the foremost spokesmen for liberal egalitarianism. Like Hayek, Dworkin objects to a certain kind of legal positivism that reduces judicial activity to the strict reading of statutes (and other legal materials). A legal system cannot be exhaustively defined in terms of rules but must be understood as an ongoing order which must include moral principles if it is to provide some security and certainty for the participants in a social process. However, this morality is not derived from some rationalistic notion of natural law detached from actual legal practice but is embedded in the traditions of an established legal order. For Dworkin, like Hayek, interpretation of principles is required if the main elements of the rule of law are to be preserved.

In the positivist model of law, judges have strong discretion when the rules run out, and this inevitably means that a considerable amount of retroactive law, hence unpredictability, is probable since it is impossible to forecast how judges will act. In contrast, Dworkin argues that in 'hard cases', where there is some doubt about which rule to apply or where there is no rule at all, judges do not call upon considerations extraneous to the legal order but invoke principles which are a part of law, even though they are not mechanically applied, as rules customarily are. This looks very similar to Hayek's distinction between non-articulated and articulated rules; the former, though not fully expressible in formal legal propositions are essential for the judge in his endeavour to provide a more or less predictable order of events. Similarly, Dworkin argues that judges have to call upon principles if law is to retain its integrity and autonomy. For both Hayek and Dworkin, judges discover the law.

Dworkin openly concedes that judges must, to some extent, be political theorists: 'Law is deeply ... and thoroughly political. Lawyers and judges cannot avoid politics in the broad sense of political theory' (Dworkin, 1985, p. 146). However, he is careful to point out that this theorizing is constrained, not merely by written and uncontroversial law, but also by the fact that in searching for principles the judges are doing no more than bringing to the surface values which are partially submerged in the history and practice of a legal community. In a famous case, *Riggs* v. *Palmer*, decided in 1889, Dworkin shows how the principle, 'no man shall profit from his own wrongs', was used to deny inheritance to someone who had murdered his grandfather (even though the formal rules of inheritance were apparently satisfied). Later examples of the invocation of principles are much more controversial, indeed they are overtly political, but Dworkin insists that the principles which judges draw upon are not their personal values or ideologies. A system of law is to an extent neutral, and the answers it provides to difficult cases are objectively-determined by the defining elements of the order itself.

Furthermore, Dworkin makes a crucial distinction between principles and policy. In a jurisprudential division of labour (which has great philosophical significance) the legislature has the responsibility for advancing collective goals, while the judiciary protects those rights which are validated by principles. Under a written constitution, which specifies (however inarticulately) rights, the legislature is constrained only by those rights. Even in a system like Britain's, which has no formal constitutional document, Dworkin (1986, pp. 23–9) still maintains that common law adjudication must be conducted in the light of principles which underlie the system and which give correct answers in hard cases – if only the judges would see them.

Yet, from a jurisprudential position that is close to Hayek's, Dworkin has managed to produce a legal philosophy that stands opposed to the basic foundations of classical liberalism. Dworkinian judges have successively generated in America a series of decisions which have, in fact, implemented the social agenda of modern liberal egalitarianism: affirmative action (ostensibly to correct past injustices), forced integration of schools through busing arrangements, some substantive equality and in other areas where controversial decisions seem to be neither sanctioned by the Constitution nor by the non-articulated rules that underlie it. Worst of all, economic liberty apparently has no legal protection at all, since it is 'a silly proposition that true liberals must protect economic liberty as well as intellectual liberty' (Dworkin, 1977, p. 264). Or, as he insists elsewhere, the familiar civil liberties. The grounding for this (arbitrary) distinction is, presumably, that regulatory and other interventionist economic *policy* does not infringe civil rights, it does not compromise a person's right to 'equal concern and respect' (Dworkin, 1977, pp. 272–8) as discriminatory law based on race or sex does, or measures designed to curb freedom of expression do.

Of course, in Hayek's jurisprudence, the role of the judiciary is to preserve an ongoing legal order and in this activity no categorical distinction is made between economic and civil liberties. This is a more plausible understanding of a legal order for it is surely an emasculation of a predictable rule-governed process to imagine that it should only protect individual civil liberties when people's well-being is just as much a function of their economic opportunities. Those whose economic prospects are adversely affected by interferences with contract and excessive regulation, or whose property rights (as in America) are severely attenuated by public authorities' perverse use of the takings clause, surely have their rights violated just as much as those who experience arbitrary racial and sexual discrimination undoubtedly do.

The shrinkage of economic rights is perhaps even more important than the expansion of civil liberties. If there are no limits to regulation then there are clearly reduced opportunities for creativity in the market. The freedoms to experiment, to innovate and to upset existing arrangements, are vital aspects of the epistemic function of the market, i.e. its ability to co-ordinate dispersed knowledge. Even if these considerations are dismissed as being too crudely utilitarian (there are deontological strains within both liberal egalitarianism and classical liberalism which doubt that anything of specifically *moral* value can be inferred from the market's mere success in satisfying desires) it is not difficult to show that the exercise of economic rights is just as much a feature of a person's freedom as is the possession of civil liberties. Limitations on the right to contract or on the pursuit of the career of one's choice because of arbitrary licensure laws (most often passed by state legislatures at the behest of politically powerful special interests) are deprivations of liberty in the fully-fledged moral sense precisely because they put collective goals (dubious though they usually are) ahead of individual self-expression. Anyway, even Dworkin's right to equal concern and respect is vague enough to encompass economic rights, even if he has other reasons for rejecting them.

Still, it is not clear that all this involves a legal methodology which is all that far removed from Hayek's evolutionary jurisprudence. As has already been noted, the US Supreme Court's pre-1937 upholding of some economic liberties depended on a certain kind of creative judicial activity. Neither Hayek's nor Dworkin's accounts of legal procedures can be truly neutral. Both are influenced by the kind of society which they say the law should preserve. How can we possibly say which is the more authentic description of a legal system when each permits judicial innovation in order to sustain and nurture the integrity of the *law*? Once we start down the evolutionary path, and refrain from substantive evaluation of outcomes, our critical faculties are necessarily blunted and rival states of affairs and competing judicial decisions can claim fidelity to the legal process.

The twists and changes in judicial behaviour which have characterized Western legal systems in the 20th century (especially America's) are no doubt to a great extent a product of changes in ideas. Judges do seem not to want to limit their role to preserving a traditional notion of legality, or the modest replenishing of end-independent rules, but are just as anxious to shift an otherwise self-sustaining order in a particular direction. Though how far their behaviour can be understood, in a manner suggested by public choice, as a subtle response to political and electoral pressure, is an arguable point. Would the resuscitation of the classical liberal legal order require a rational reconstruction of law, via a constitutional revolution which entrenched economic liberties (and hence reduced the need for judges to play the kind of role Hayek recommended), or would it merely require a change in ideas? It is not at all clear what the classical liberal answer to this question is.

Perhaps a first step in the theoretical reformulation of classical liberal jurisprudence would be a recognition that a legal system can never be neutral between differing ways of life. Although it does permit a wide degree of liberty of choice for people to pursue their varying conceptions of the good, liberalism is itself grounded in a cultural tradition that already upholds this pluralism. This is the kernel of truth that lies in reasonable versions of communitarianism. To say this is to attenuate slightly classical liberalism's claim to universalism. But it does not eliminate it. Since much of formalized law is the codification and declaration of those rules that Hume identified as being essential for civilization and progress, its existence is a response to more or less universal needs.

None of this is meant to deny that legal systems can perfectly well exist that do not embody specifically classical liberal features, and Hayek is therefore wrong to imply that his conception of law is the only valid form and all others are aberrations, but it does suggest that the freedom and prosperity associated with them are by no means accidental. Indeed, the difficulties associated with the establishment of markets in former communist countries are largely the result of the obliteration of legality that occurred under communism. The differences between Hayek and Dworkin are not reducible to sterile linguistic arguments concerning the use of the word law. The issue is: Which of their conceptions is more supportive of a free society? Dworkin's arbitrary exclusion of economic liberty from legal protection makes his model of law inadequate for countries struggling to emerge from totally controlled economic systems.

The claims of liberal egalitarian legalism are, in fact, much more ambitious than those of classical liberalism for, in effect, they involve the universalization of what have become peculiarly American conceptions of liberty and equality under law. The very fact that such ideas are highly controversial even in the US is enough to suggest that the prospect of their exportability to communities struggling to create, or recreate, the basic elements of legality is virtually non-existent. Liberal egalitarianism takes on a definite ideological form when it presents itself as intrinsically right. It is, in fact, no more than a rationalization of a rather special form of legal order. To demand that economic liberties be given the same legal protection as civil liberties is hardly ideological: it is a recognition of necessity.

A further observation, which applies to classical liberalism and to liberal egalitarianism, is that both doctrines seem to be associated with, indeed encourage, forms of order characterized by *excessive* legalism. This phenomenon is a consequence of the fact that liberalism has historically been associated with the idea of an *abstract* society: a form of order in which essentially anonymous agents are held together by general rules. It would not be true to say that liberal society is a loose collection of strangers held together by abstract rules alone since its pluralistic structure does encourage voluntary forms of association in which more intimate social ties are given full rein. But the recourse to law to settle disputes is a feature of it that is less noticeable in other societies (such as those of south Asia), which, nevertheless, strongly feature the market, private property and competition in their social arrangements. It seems highly unlikely that the Western model (Hayek's extended order) is one to which evolution is driving all societies, as he seems to imply in *The Fatal Conceit* (1988, chapter 1).

It may be the case that excessive legalism is both costly (in straight economic terms) and socially divisive (in that it deters the emergence of non-formal dispute settling) but it cannot be wished away by idealistic communitarianism. It seems to be an inevitable feature of a certain type of open liberal society. Also, it is an especially distinctive feature of liberal egalitarian legalism which, because of its construction of more complex, substantive and contentious forms of liberty and equality, creates more opportunities for litigation. If judges could have restricted their role to one of maintaining a predictable order of events, and restricted their innovative activity to the repair and maintenance of this, it is less likely that a liberal legal order would have mutated into the complex and unpredictable morass that it has become.

8. Constitutionalism and Sovereignty

The major part of classical liberal legal theory has been addressed to the problem of containing the growth of government. The aim has been to subject it to rules. This is a crucial aspect of the rule of law but the tendency in the modern world has been for governments to evade its strictures. It has even been a claim of some classical liberal theorists that if government could be fully subject to the rule of law then there would be no need to rely on substantive, and therefore controversial, notions of natural rights, or disputable economic ideas of 'efficiency', in the evaluation of government's performance. We would simply have to question whether its activity was lawful. If the standards were strict enough considerable protection of personal liberty could be guaranteed. The criteria of lawfulness would require that rules be perfectly general, that they name no person or group, and that they be non-retrospective in application. It would be logically possible to make liberty-reducing laws consistent with these criteria, but their existence, and fidelity to them by legislatures, would constitute some constraint on government. Of course, classical liberals would also demand that a set of rights, determined by agreement, be specified in a constitution, but questions of appraisal then would not be about the intrinsic value of those rights but whether government activity had been in conformity with their requirements.

Experience has shown that constitutionalism of this type has been a rare occurrence in history. Constitutions have not only been compromised by the vagaries of judicial interpretation in more or less stable societies, but the very idea of constitutional constraint seems to be alien to all but a few countries. If a culture of constitutionalism is a definitive feature of classical liberalism it, in a curious way, damages the doctrine's claim to universalizability. For order would seem to be a product of social phenomena other than the formalized rule-following implied by liberal constitutionalism. Indeed, it would not be too far from the truth to say that societies can only make constitutions work if they already have the social attitudes that recognize the necessity for governmental restraint and which understand the meaning and value of individual rights: in which case they would not need the paraphernalia of the separation of powers, judicial review and written guarantees of liberty and equality. Britain managed to preserve economic and personal liberty for a very long time when it had, at least since the 18th century, the ideal recipe for absolutist government, i.e., a Hobbesian sovereign parliament limited by nothing other than the customs and practices of restraint which were 'internalized' by its governing class. A further irony here is that British constitutional arrangements, which include most importantly the superiority of (parliamentary) statute law over common law, were a product of spontaneous evolution; they were neither planned nor even thought of by any known person or body. That they were at one time benign but later malign is sufficient to make us at least sceptical of the argument that an explanation of social development in evolutionary terms has an automatic connection with classical liberalism. Of all the elements in classical liberal theory, constitutional order is the one most likely to need explanation by rational constructivist methods, i.e. satisfactory political rules are more easily understood and evaluated in terms of specific agreement than as the almost random products of evolution.

The claim that governmental restraint depends almost exclusively on cultural conditions and that there is little need to call upon constitutionalism is, however, misleading. The form of political rules a stable community has makes a crucial difference to the outcome of the political process; it surely wasn't simply that the US was a stable society throughout its history (with the obvious exception of the Civil War period) that guaranteed (until 1937) its market economy and private property system: it was as much to do with the particular constitutional form of the separation of powers and judicial review. Again, the slide towards collectivism in Britain, which began in earnest after 1945, was obviously hastened by parliamentary sovereignty, operating to some extent irrespective of particular movements of general opinion. A further indication of the difference that constitutions make is revealed by the fact that under sovereignty systems it is easier both to establish and to reverse collectivism, while under more complex political arrangements government intervention can be resisted and delayed to some extent but it is more difficult to undo once established.

Classical liberals have historically not been prepared to take the kind of risks that sovereignty involves: risks that have become transparent with the rise of majoritarian democracy. As Hayek observed (1978,

p. 86): 'The triumphant claim of the British Parliament to have become sovereign and so able to govern subject to no law, may prove to have been both the death-knell of both individual freedom and democracy.' Sovereignty, because it authorizes absolute legislative power, is in breach of the rule of law: a doctrine that presupposes that all agents should be subordinate to rules not of their own making. Britain could not have a formal constitution (at least prior to the country's entry into the European Community) because the rules that govern the political process are made by the actors in that process. A rule of the constitution, e.g. electoral law, has no greater significance than a routine piece of road traffic legislation. It is extraordinary to imagine that political actors would bind themselves, yet that is what the British system asks of them.

It is true, in strict jurisprudence, that parliament cannot determine the 'rule of recognition', i.e. the fundamental rule of a legal system that determines validity (Hart, 1961, chapter VI; Barry, 1993b) for it is that rule which authorizes parliament and distinguishes genuine law from bogus claims to law. But the British fundamental rule is extraordinarily permissive. Given the obvious fact that parliament does not even represent a genuine majority, let alone a wider body of opinion that would morally be required to validate changes that seriously affect people's rights and liberties, it would be odd to suppose that it would reflect the public interest, where that refers to laws or policies that concern people as members of the public rather than as members of private groups. As public-choice theory predicts, power is exercised on behalf of particular interests that can be aggregated into organized parties. Under parliamentary systems, a not very demanding electoral test is required for the exercise of sovereign power.

Despite its complex constitutional arrangements, the position of the US is little better, at least with regard to economic matters. Judicial review, which is so powerful a constraint in the area of civil liberties, is almost completely absent in the economic field so that the Congress might just as well be called sovereign here. The historical record of 'parchment' (Wagner, 1993) documents in restraining political power is dismal, certainly in the 20th century. This must largely be due to important changes in the emotive appeal that certain political concepts have undergone in the last few decades, especially democracy.

9. Liberty and Democracy

At one time in the 19th century there was a genuine fear among liberal theorists of the dangers that unrestrained majority rule posed to traditional liberties, including property rights. The naïve hopes of Bentham and James Mill that democratic institutions would maximize utility, once the 'sinister interests' of the landowners had been replaced by the common interests of everyone else, were successfully countered by the dire warnings of Lord Macauley and (to a slightly lesser extent) John Stuart Mill. But their forebodings related only to the possible overt 'tyranny of the majority', not to the insidious effects that vote-maximizing behaviour would have on the long-run structure of law and on the genuine public interest. Only Sir Henry Maine, in his *Popular Government* (1885), showed an awareness of the damage that 'wire-pullers' and parliamentary manipulators could do to the inherited structure of predictable rules. This, rather than straight tyranny, has proved to be the great threat to long-term economic order.

In the 20th century, however, the imprimatur of democracy has been sufficient to sanctify almost any act of government. The vote-maximizing process makes it rational for actors to generate policies that favour short-run redistributive activity by government, yet popular opinion validates that in the name of democracy. The market system, private property and, indeed, constitutional order itself are public goods which no one has an interest in promoting. Still, there is undoubtedly a subtle combination of the influence of ideas and interests at work here since the immense appeal of the democratic idea has underwritten the corrosive effects of more or less unrestrained group politics. One suspects that only a combination of a change in ideology and some institutional rearrangements can repair the defects in conventional democracy.

If paper-thin constitutional rules have been so ineffective in restraining politics is there any other mechanism that can perform this necessary function? One aim might be to exploit the possibility of political competition itself. Choice between competing political parties within a political regime could perhaps be extended to choice between regimes themselves. An availability of the 'exit' option for individuals dissatisfied with government might drive political authorities to keep taxation down and regulation lighter simply to avoid losing their clients. This was an idea originally suggested for local government by Charles Tiebout (1956) but it is in principle extendable to wider political authorities. If governments cannot be hemmed in by parchments then perhaps the natural process of competition could be an effective substitute. There is a nice parallel here with monetary competition, if rules cannot provide stable money then choice in currencies (Hayek, 1978) is perhaps the only alternative; though inflation will presumably have to be well-advanced in any domestic economy before a mass exit from its currency occurs.

Of course, very high costs will be incurred by individuals leaving one state to join another, more favourable one. But the idea is the essence of federalism; the existence of several states (under very simple general rules), each of which allowed free entry and exit, would provide that mechanism for a wider expression of subjective preference for various forms of government action. However, the federal idea itself has been badly damaged in the 20th century with the rise of uniform standards across a national territory. This has the effect of reducing exit opportunities. In the US it was perhaps given the final death-knell in a controversial Supreme Court decision in 1985 (*Garcia* v. *San Antonio Transit Authority*) in which it was ruled that the federal element consisted only in the fact of the states' representation in the Congress; even the paper-thin constitutional protection offered by the Tenth Amendment was judicially expunged.

The experience of the European Community (Barry, 1993) is instructive here. Originally, the practice (since 1966) was for individual states to veto proposed European-wide legislation emanating from the Council of Ministers. The requirement of unanimity undoubtedly prevented the imposition of uniformity across states. But, as public-choice theory predicts, this had efficiency costs: small states held up the implementation of otherwise desirable policies, notably the single market, the removal of trade barriers and the abolition of exchange controls. Hence the introduction of qualified majority voting in 1986 across a range of issues overcame the blocking tactics of some member states. In theory it was a fine example of normative public choice.

In practice, however, it has turned out rather differently. It has led to a growing uniformity of law across Europe in relation to social policy, the environment and labour practices. Those member states that could exploit competitive advantages by offering different standards have been bought off by inter-regional transfers. Furthermore, the European Court of Justice has tended to uphold all the important legislation from the Council of Ministers, even when that appears to be in conflict with fundamental European constitutional documents. There is a quasi-liberal constitution in Europe (primarily the original Treaty of Rome, 1957) but it has been of little avail. In any case, it is far too vague a document to function as a clear restraining instrument. Matters will only get worse with the Treaty of Maastricht (1993) since the range of issues subject to qualified majority voting has considerably widened under it. The opportunities, and incentives, for member states to exit from European law have been reduced, therefore the advantages of that strategy for individuals has been almost eliminated.[1] If political competition is to be an effective method for protecting liberty, a change in both ideas and institutional arrangements will be required.

One should not, however, completely despair of the possibilities of international political and economic competition reducing the effects of national and transnational sovereignty. The opening up of the world in the post-communist age has increased the pressure on national governments to relax their hold on their citizens. The greater mobility of capital and labour is steadily reducing the costs of exit for individuals. This is already producing the 'imitative effect' (first suggested by Hayek) of successful liberal capitalist orders: the idea of markets is spreading. In the face of a growing internationalism, even the controls introduced under sovereign constitutions might turn out to be less than decisive.

Note

1. This has led to just that kind of 'sclerosis' which was a feature of the British economy in the 1970s.

10. Liberty

To account for the emergence of a spontaneous market order and to explain the nature of the legal and constitutional rules that sustain it is only one aspect of a normative political theory. It has been a temptation for some classical liberals to avoid investigation of the moral properties of a free society, largely because these are regarded as too subjective to be admitted into rational discourse. It has been claimed that reason is incompetent to adjudicate between rival claims to virtue and must be confined to a more readily calculative role in the determination of those institutional conditions which are necessary for the maximization of whatever values individuals may hold. Even in so complex a moral theory as David Hume's, morality could be said to be only a little more than a sophisticated version of prudence. Lurking behind all this is Mandeville's cynical claim that commerce necessarily involves an abandonment of virtue. Classical liberal writers have, nevertheless, been anxious to maintain that liberty is to be valued not merely as instrumentally valuable for the production of social utility but as a necessary element in individual well-being; following Kant, it is maintained that individuals are not to be used merely as means to the ends of society. As Nozick says:

> ...there is no social entity with a good that undergoes some sacrifice for its own good. There are only individual people, with their own individual lives. Using one of these people for the benefit of others, uses him and benefits the others. (1974, pp. 32–3)[1]

This is a clear contrast with Benthamite utilitarianism where individuals disappear once their preferences are incorporated into a utilitarian calculus, in the construction of which interpersonal comparisons of utility are permitted. Freedom here depends solely on the permission of the sovereign.

It is a commonplace feature of liberal social theory that the diversity and subjective nature of human values precludes them being incorporated into some objective maximand which government is under a duty to promote. Not only does this not accord with a realistic view of how markets work (the dispersed nature of knowledge and the ever-changing nature of preferences makes it impossible for a benevolent legislator to determine such a maximand) but it also, and perhaps more importantly, drains the exchange system of intrinsic moral value.

It is to be noted that this objection is just as much addressed to authoritarian regimes that nevertheless permit free markets as it is to collectivist orders that forgo all the advantages of economic freedom (or to heavily-controlled economic orders that may nonetheless allow the conventional social liberties, rare though these are). The authoritarian examples do allow economic liberty, and this permission at least gives them some value, but it is not strictly *moral* liberty. The emerging market economies of south-east Asia, and especially China, would seem to fit this description only too well. The 'illiberal' regimes that practice this economic freedom have no doubt recognized the advantage of decentralized exchange but the driving force of this recognition of them is a simple and crude utilitarianism. The participants in such orders are, in principle, being used as means to socially-determined ends just as much as the unfortunate victims of fully-collectivized economic orders are. In the tradition of classical liberalism, liberty cannot be broken up in this way but is a principle to be used in the evaluation of all aspects of social life. Furthermore, although the tradition of liberty permits a plurality of individually-determined goals to be advanced, freedom is not simply one concept among many, that can be traded away, say, for the advancement of social justice (Barry, 1965, chapter 1), but is more properly described as part of the liberal order of procedural justice in which *fundamental* values do not compete.

The classical liberal theory of liberty involves a substantive moral claim; it is not merely a semantic analysis of the concept. If it were the latter it would have nothing to say about the obvious fact that liberty can only be enjoyed in a rule-governed context in which the liberties of some are restricted by the rights of others. If I have the liberty to accumulate property then others are under an obligation to respect it; they are forbidden from trespassing on my land or stealing my goods. This obvious fact has led some writers (Cohen, 1979) to object to a classical liberal (and broadly negative) account of liberty, i.e. one that understands freedom as absence of constraint. In Cohen's view, capitalist legal institutions which protect the property of a minority, necessarily render the proletariat, who own nothing, unfree. Any theory of liberty must therefore include an account of the permissible constraints on human action. If the law justifiably prevents others from using my property this must be because I have a *right* to freely exchange with others, to inherit, or to act on my choices in an uncoerced manner. In other words, protective laws allocate liberty rights, even though their existence does legitimately reduce the liberty of some in a formal sense.

What has to be maintained here is that a legal system that protects this right to liberty increases liberty overall. After all, the only alternative to private ownership of goods is some version of a theory of the common consumption of them; as if some fair rule could be imagined that allocated their use and which forbade exclusive possession. This is, in a sense, a feature of genuine public goods but any extension of this arrangement to ordinary goods and services on the ground that it maximized overall liberty is most implausible. All forms of ownership restrict the use of valuable objects but an examination of history reveals that a wider spread of ownership is achieved under liberal capitalism. In fact, Cohen is simply in error when he claims that law merely protects the liberty of a minority. The undoubted existence of unequal ownership is not evidence of the absence of a general liberty right. Under collective ownership the right to restrict use is simply transferred from individuals to a public agency. This is not an increase in liberty. Indeed, many classical liberals say that the existence of property is an absolute guarantee of liberty against the state. This is not historically true since there are examples of oppressive regimes preserving property rights. Still, private property is a necessary condition of liberty, if not a sufficient one.

Of course, it could be argued (Steiner, 1974) that liberty cannot be increased or decreased overall, it is only distributed in varying ways across individuals. This seems, however, to ignore the probability that a general system of law does increase liberty overall by providing that security for individuals to maximize their well-being. Though comparisons in liberty-enhancing terms between legal systems are difficult it seems rather odd to suggest that a fully-planned social system merely redistributes liberty (it is, of course, true that the planners have a great deal of liberty) rather than reduces it overall. What we look for in a legal system is how far it increases the range of available choices to individuals even if that does, as it must, reduce some choices of others. A system of general and predictable rules, which reduces direct commands to a minimum, is surely freer overall than the chaos and unpredictability of a regime subjected to ephemeral orders from the centre.

Still, we should not identify liberty with mere choice: after all a person under threat technically chooses; he prefers one alternative to another, no matter that conditions have been so manipulated that the choice is almost inevitable. It was this feature of human action that enabled Hobbes to claim that liberty and determinism are compatible. However, we do say that freedom is attenuated when the range of options available to an agent has been reduced. Threats backed by sanctions clearly reduce the range of options. This does not dispose of the problem because it is still possible to argue that market exchanges can be coercive, especially in economic depressions when available employment opportunities are narrowed, and that some intervention might be said to increase overall liberty (or, at least, redistribute it more fairly). It is true that in such circumstances the *value* of liberty is not particularly high but it still remains a controversial question as to whether state intervention, by purporting to increase opportunities, also increases liberty. It might be more proper to speak of such action as being designed to maximize a disputable conception of *welfare* (which is quite another thing). To say that people's liberty increases when their powers or capacities increase is to embark on a highly misleading course since it implies that there should be no limit on the permissibility of government activity. Almost any action can be justified on the ground that it is liberty-enhancing merely because it somehow maximizes power or capacities. A person's liberty, however, is increased if an oppressive law is relaxed, irrespective of the difference that is made to his or her powers or capacities.

Yet a full understanding of liberty requires that we take some account of the *value* of the choices that are available to people. The extent of liberty cannot be known solely by a kind of quantitative assessment of the choices available to them merely because of the absence of law. They must be important choices. In an intriguing example, Charles Taylor (1985) claims that a purely negative view of liberty is implausible. Albania, he argues, could be said to be a freer society than any in the West because it actually had fewer constraints on personal action, e.g. no traffic laws or the range of minor (and not so minor) constraints that are a feature of capitalist liberal democracies. Of course, there were severe restrictions on highly valued activities in Albania but these prohibitions were few in number.

It is, however, not at all clear that Taylor's example is especially damaging to the classical liberal conception of liberty. This doctrine does attach moral importance to liberty and does make discriminations between various liberties (though it does not accept the arbitrary distinction often offered between economic and civil liberty) in accordance to how they advance individual well-being. A lack of liberty to acquire property would be a reduction in overall liberty even if it were accompanied by fewer restrictions elsewhere. It would be absurd to deny that the market does expand liberty; it does this, not merely by satisfying people's subjective (and possibly ephemeral) desires but also by providing conditions for the formation of life-plans independently of government. And classical liberals want to assess morally the various liberties by reference to how far they enable persons to advance their own conceptions of well-being. On this criterion, laws in Albania were oppressive despite their (apparently) narrow range.

Furthermore, the argument that markets can coerce, because they sometimes do not present a wide range of choices for disadvantaged individuals, obscures the fact that freedom is normally reduced by identifiable agents: impediments to liberty are those which are the alterable and intentional actions of persons in political authority, or those who in some other way are able to determine particular outcomes. The market, although it is the product of the actions of innumerable agents, is not itself a coercive body to which we can attribute the normal notion of responsibility. It does not 'act' in any meaningful sense of the term.

This slightly modified concept of negative liberty as a right against unjustified coercion has come under attack not merely because it appears to reduce the range of coercion narrowly to political authorities but also because it is claimed to be inadequate at its foundation. It is argued that it does not properly describe what it is to be free since it makes no determinate suggestion as to what is valuable in life. We must be free for a reason and the purpose of that freedom is not revealed merely by the absence of law. Gray (1992), following Joseph Raz (1986), argues that freedom can only be understood as *autonomy*, where that seems to mean the possibility of individuals choosing from as wide a range of options as possible: 'It is patently obvious that autonomy is far more than the mere absence of coercion by others, since it is self-evident that that condition may co-exist with a complete inability to achieve any important objective or purpose' (Gray, 1992, p. 23).

It might be thought that this is simply a demand for redistribution to increase people's capacities, so that liberty becomes valuable to those hitherto unable to enjoy it, and indeed his suggestions for an enabling welfare state (ibid., chapter 5) are consistent with this project. But it is clear from his other work that Gray has a more ambitious conception in mind. In 'What is Dead and What is Living in Liberalism' (Gray, 1993, pp. 282–398) he appears to prefer a form of human flourishing which is by no means reducible to the satisfaction of subjective desire and he claims that a liberal order is deficient if it precludes the idea of 'perfectionism'. In other words, there are collective goods, quite unlike the public goods of subjectivist classical liberal theory, which have intrinsic value, i.e. they have worth even in the absence of anyone expressing a want for them. It is argued that autonomy 'presupposes as one of its constituent elements a rich public culture containing a diversity of worthwhile options' (Gray, 1992, p. 42). Raz is even more openly favourable to the idea that persons can express liberty and morality only as members of particular social groupings that embody the idea of the good: 'A person can have a comprehensive social goal only if it is based on existing social forms, i.e. forms of behaviour which are in fact widely practiced in his society' (1986, p. 308). Naturally, the specific significance of coercion diminishes in this perfectionist context; indeed Raz (1986, p. 417) subverts the standard liberal argument by suggesting that for a state not to provide the conditions for autonomy would be harmful and liberty-reducing for some people.

Gray and Raz are not adopting some kind of positivist account of liberty which would involve highly controversial concepts of rationality and the (possibly) coerced pursuit of a higher end, an approach of which Berlin (1958) was so rightly critical. Their conceptions of liberty are consistent with pluralism to the extent that they identify freedom and autonomy as the ability to choose from a variety of ends. However, the model of choice exercised in the market place would seem to be a morally inadequate understanding of freedom because it maximizes subjective choices rather than intrinsically valuable things. Though Gray does concede that the market does encourage some freedom as autonomy.

What are we to make of all this? Some would perhaps quibble a little at Gray's apparent linking of freedom with welfare in his suggestion that an uncoerced person who lacked resources would not be genuinely free. It is a commonplace in classical liberal thought that freedom is not the same as wealth. But I do not think that that is crucially important. It is true in a sense that a person's liberty can be constrained by a lack of resources and, as long as liberty is not *identified* with capacity or power, no confusion results from conceding this: although purists would still maintain that in such circumstances it is the value of liberty that is reduced rather than liberty itself. All societies, including classical liberal ones, develop a variety of ways of dealing with the victims of, say, genetic misfortune or unpredictable economic change. Indeed, Gray's critique of the contemporary welfare state's solutions to such problems is conducted in impeccably classical liberal terms (1992, chapter 6); although his own particular version of an enabling welfare system is far from classical liberalism. Also, both Raz (1986, chapter 9) and Gray (1992, chapter 6) are highly critical of conventional egalitarianism.

The real problems occur with the concept of autonomy itself and the dismissal of negative liberty as empty or meaningless. It is simply not true that the absence of coercion is not itself a value independently of a consideration of the ends and purposes that an individual may pursue. The fact that one is not coerced means that whatever is done is a product of choice, irrespective of whether it is directed to one's long-term ends, the value of which may be in dispute. There is surely some value in the fact that in a free society opportunities exist for individuals to be authors of their own actions. The demand that they should be widened is not empty or meaningless.

It is possible to say that a person acted freely even though he or she did not act autonomously in the rather rarefied sense described by Raz and Gray. It is not that absence of coercion is merely a condition for the exercise of autonomous choice. Negative liberty is not merely instrumental. People can and do protest about unjustified limitations on their liberty irrespective of the projects they wish to pursue. In fact, they may not even know them. A free society, with a vibrant market economy and a predictable legal order, is the only social arrangement in which people can come to terms with their ignorance: and lack of information here refers not just to economic knowledge but also to one's personal plans and projects. One cannot know what it is to be an autonomous agent until one has experience of freely choosing amongst alternatives. And this requires that each individual should have a sphere immune from the intrusions of coercive law. It is not that autonomy defines liberty but rather that one has to be free before one can be autonomous. To define liberty exclusively in the context of given social forms, as Raz appears to do, precludes the moral legitimacy of a person breaking out of those forms. The innovator (perhaps regrettably for a conservative) succeeds largely because he or she upsets existing social arrangements.

None of this is meant to imply that there can be human agents completely abstracted from social forms who are understood solely through the calculus of their desires (that would be to discount fool-ishly the value of spontaneously developing social rules and practices), nor is it meant to endorse the kind of mindless and deliberate non-conformism recommended by John Stuart Mill. However, it does rest on the idea that under conditions of non-constraint, individuals are the makers of their own lives, whether or not they lead them as fully autonomous agents. To accept that individuals are necessarily under-stood partly by their social natures is not to endorse the moral priority of social forms.

One can go further and challenge the importance of autonomy itself. Many people (Kukathas, 1992, pp. 101–14) lead their lives unreflectively, they follow traditional rules and practices and they make choices of a fairly trivial kind. To what extent are they unfree? Like everything else which is valuable, autonomy has an opportunity cost, the time and other resources needed to acquire it could be spent on something else. One could complain about people's foolishness in not becoming au-tonomous (they may indeed become willing victims of consumer fads and fashions in market society) but not their lack of liberty if they behave in an uncoerced manner.

The real issue in all this for classical liberalism is the enhanced role for the state in the creation of conditions for autonomy. Raz (1986, p. 161) may dismiss as unimportant the taxation (which he distin-guishes from coercion) required to preserve a common culture and things of intrinsic value, but others would not. It also involves the state, through its officials, deciding what is valuable and worth cherishing. As a matter of historical record, the efforts of purely voluntary actions in these areas is probably better than the state's. However, the matter becomes much more disputable when Raz appears to give the state not just authority in autonomy-promotion, he also imposes a *duty* on it: 'The government has an obligation to provide an environment provid-ing individuals with an adequate range of options and the opportunities to use them. The duty arises out of people's interest in having a valu-able autonomous life' (1986, pp. 417–18). Making the state responsible for the correction of low autonomy is a somewhat exotic example of its response to market failure.

Among the many difficulties with this position is the obvious fact that autonomy is an indeterminate moral ideal; it is not like rights-protection or the supply of public goods, which, although controver-sial at the edges, are capable of being formulated as reasonably coher-ent tasks for a state to perform. And although Raz is insistent that the autonomous life involves choice between alternative projects he is equally convinced that market-based individualist society is incapable of fully meeting this demand. Why not? The answer is, apparently, that this order, because it is based on subjective choice, will fail to provide objective and intrinsically valuable goods; notably the maintenance of common forms of life. But since there is likely to be considerable disagreement about what these intrinsically valuable ends are, the state, in selecting one or more out of the range of possible candidates, is likely to generate the very tensions that undermine common forms of life. Although Raz's pluralism precludes the state promoting and privileging any *particular* way of life, it is difficult to see how the authority he grants to the state would not be used in this way.

An individualistic, rule-governed social order does not preclude the development of common forms of life, indeed they are likely to emerge and be sustained spontaneously precisely because they are the unintended outcomes of individual interaction under general rules of law. Intrinsically valuable goods, such as a common culture and an artistic and scientific tradition (although they must ultimately be subjectively valued by human agents) can be treated as 'objective', rather in the way that literary works can be subject to informed discrimination, quite independently of their probably low and certainly unreliable market value, without in any way departing from the basic tenets of traditional liberal society.

A final problem with entrusting the state with too great a role in the promotion of autonomy is that this aim can and does compete with other values. Perhaps the costs in terms of taxation to pay for this is not excessive, although neither Raz nor Gray suggests any procedural device to keep this within reasonable bounds, but it does nevertheless involve a loss in negative liberty for those compelled to pay. Although Gray (1992, p. 88) argues that public spending could be reduced to 25 per cent of GDP if the welfare state were reorganized by methods that would advance his conception of liberty as autonomy, the very indeterminacy of the idea makes this wildly optimistic. He seems to think that the lessons of public choice do not have a more or less universal application and he argues that a society which develops a moral code that enjoins the open political discussion of public issues would generate more effective constraints on government spending than the cold, formal rules recommended by classical liberal theory. No evidence is produced for this proposition, which could quite properly be described as wishful thinking. To entrust the state with the responsibility of autonomy promotion while not providing formal checks on its activities here is almost certain to lead to a loss in overall liberty.

Note

1. Although Nozick (1989) has departed from his original social philosophy.

11. Contractarian Liberty

The strictures of Raz and Gray as discussed in Chapter 10 identify some difficulties with the classical liberal theory of liberty and its account of the defining features of a free society. It does sometimes involve the attempt to derive a theory of freedom from the basic propositions of economic theory, notably those concerning rational choice and subjective value, without reference to any *background* of morality. It is true that one tradition of classical liberal thought has been deeply sceptical of the truth-value of ethical statements (even of the *meaningfulness* of moral discourse itself) and has suggested that the subjective evaluation of goods in the market place is in fact the appropriate model even for normative or moral statements. All types of evaluation are rooted in individual choice. In fact, this normative individualism is not quite the same as technical ethical subjectivism or scepticism since these latter positions reject the ultimate validity of any moral claims (including individualism). However, since the important feature of classical liberal subjectivism is its denial of the existence of transcendental moral standards the difference in nomenclature is not significant. The important question is whether the value of liberty, and the institutions of a free society, are sustainable in subjectivist terms alone.

The approach is clearly linked to the contractarian tradition in social thought. This presupposes that ethical values are generated by rational individuals out of a context which is essentially non-moral. Freedom consists in the fact that the values emerge entirely from the choices of individuals: the moral and political order in which they live is a product of their actions and no person or entity has a licence to impose any form of society on them, even the conventional free society of markets and the rule of law. The institutions of a liberal order have no intrinsic value and whatever moral worth they have is solely a function of their being chosen. As we shall see, this raises serious problems for the transition to free orders from existing unfree societies, for the conditions of the status quo may be such that few would voluntarily opt for conventional liberalism. Indeed it may be irrational (in the economist's sense) for them to do so.

James Buchanan (1975, 1977) is the most sophisticated exponent of this general methodology. His meta-ethics are basically Hobbesian but he hopes to show that a limited state, and not a Leviathan, can be generated by the same motivations as those assumed by the great pessimistic philosopher of authoritarianism. In a rigorous anti-transcendental stance, Buchanan argues that all truth, be it ethical or anything else, rests entirely on *agreement*. He says that: 'Truth, in the final analysis, is tested by agreement. And if men disagree there is no truth' (1977, p. 113) and, 'Fairness, as an attribute of rules, is defined by agreement; it is not, and cannot be, defined independently of agreement, or at least of conceptual agreement' (1977, p. 130). Thus negative liberty, and the institutions that protect it, are only valuable if they are what people actually want, since any attempt to go beyond their preferences would be to 'play God'. This could, and does, lead to a kind of stultifying conservatism, although it is based on unconservative, individualistic premises.

These, then, may be thought to be unpromising propositions on which to found the idea of a free society. However, by using devices such as the state of nature and the social contract (Buchanan and Tullock, 1962; Buchanan, 1975) Buchanan shows how its main institutions would be constructed out of people's choices, unencumbered by traditional ethical trappings or communal notions. It is an entirely abstract demonstration. Notice also that his approach is purely *procedural*: there are no pre-existing ethics of fairness or justice which would be discovered if only people could be detached from their real-world predilections and temptations.

There are no limitations, derived from a supposed objective morality, on what may be agreed. On leaving an imagined (or real) Hobbesian state of nature people will construct a Protective state, an authoritative agency for validating property titles and enforcing agreed-on law, merely to economize on defence. They can make Pareto-improvements on the state of nature, because the latter involves wasteful expenditure on private protection. They will generate such a rule-structure to protect their property: but, in advance of the Protective state, both production and predation are equally valid activities as claims to property. There are, then, no exclusive Lockeian natural rights to resources. The constitutional contract must be agreed unanimously if it is to be legitimate. However, there are provisions for less-than-unanimous decision-making rules in the delivery of (subjectively-determined) public goods. These procedures are designed to overcome hold-out tactics that would be employed by minorities under unanimity. However, what makes such rules legitimate is that they would be agreed to unanimously in the original contract. It is quite likely, though, that the rules for the production of public goods would be stricter than those that prevail in contemporary majoritarian democracies.

This sort of reasoning, whatever its limitations, has at least one clear lesson for classical liberal theory. That is, institutional arrangements are a product of people's choices, they cannot be left to evolution since there is no 'invisible hand' in society, as there is in the market, to harmonize desires. All our rules, institutions and practices are capable of improvement (Buchanan, 1977, p. 38) and to submit to the blind forces of tradition would be a tame admission that people are not the makers of their own futures. The hypothetical scenarios that Buchanan constructs are devices to highlight our present predicament and to suggest alternative futures. But all recommendations must be made under the *imperium* of the rule of agreement. It would be a breach of that principle if a state of affairs (no matter how intrinsically desirable from a classical liberal perspective) were to be imposed on a status quo which contained individuals who did not subjectively value it.

It might be doubted that there is anything moral about all this. At the most, it appears to be an exercise in prudence: people adopt rules which will advance their interests, and the rules, because of the requirement of agreement, will provide universal and non-discriminatory protection. However, no conditions are laid down which ensure that they will be liberal rules. It is certainly true that Buchanan does not see morality in terms of having the right motivations: it is a matter of following rules which may, on occasions, not be in our short-term self-interests. Indeed, his whole structure is designed to overcome prisoners' dilemmas, which are endemic to all societies.

Still, one quintessentially liberal feature remains: that is the fundamental requirement of *consent*, not only to the (hypothetical) foundation of government but also to changes that may be proposed to actual forms of political authority. However, the moral force of this requirement is immediately diluted by an absence of discussion of the circumstances that accompany consent. As in Hobbes, agreements are agreements and we are not to discriminate amongst them according to the conditions in which they are made. At first sight, Buchanan appears to have added little to the Pareto principle of welfare economics, he has simply (albeit interestingly) found a new application of it. Just as the Pareto principle is silent on the distribution of resources from which trading begins, Buchanan is ethically mute about the facts that precede political agreement.

Yet the purely procedural aspects of this makes the possibility of criticism and change in existing society limited. This is because of the pivotal position of the status quo in Buchanan's thought. Although it does not have intrinsic value (as an orthodox conservative might suppose), it is where we start from and it constrains any changes we might wish to make. It is the 'whole set of rules and institutions at any point in time' (Buchanan, 1975, p. 77) and change from it has to be by agreement. Thus, whereas a moral theorist of negative liberty might wish to protest at freedom-reducing action by government (on the ground that it adversely affects individual well-being or abrogates the moral right to exchange) irrespective of questions of procedural legitimacy, Buchanan can only suggest constitutional reforms which would better protect individuals' enjoyment of valuable things already acquired. And such reforms must be unanimously agreed to.

In fact, the status quo is systematically ambiguous (Barry, 1986). It could either prohibit change, on the ground that some people would be harmed by it (which makes it Pareto-inefficient) or permit it, despite the harm, because previously agreed-on rules authorize governments to take action. The introduction of a classical liberal order to replace a collectivist status quo is both condemnable, because it would override the preferences of those who benefit from the prevailing state of affairs, and permissible because the rules of change allowed it. Either way, ethical debate has to be conducted in substantive terms and in it the value of liberty will not depend on mere agreement. In other words, morality must be *prior* to constitutional arrangements, crucially important though these are for a free society.

Buchanan implicitly recognizes (albeit reluctantly) the necessity of adding some moral notion to the conventional apparatus of economic theory. He is a firm believer in the doctrine of the moral impermissibility of using individual agents for collective ends: 'In my view, democratic values must be founded on the basic Kantian notion that individual human beings are the ultimate ethical units' (Buchanan, 1977, p. 244). And he is firmly opposed to those welfare economists who try to construct imaginary end-states of perfect co-ordination independently of the actual choices of individuals. But despite these deontological gestures it could be argued that Buchanan has only presented a purified view of economic methodology. He has saved economics from the perversions of utilitarianism but reinforced its scientific, morally neutral, integrity. This, however, would be an unjust final verdict, not only because agreement and subjective choice must feature as necessary elements in classical liberal doctrine, but also because in his stress on the importance of deontological rules there are the beginnings of a much-needed moral theory. As he says in *The Limits of Liberty*: 'Something other than the utility function employed by standard economic theory must be introduced to provide an explanatory foundation that legitimizes individuals'... claims to stocks actually produced by their own efforts independently from the interference of others' (1975, p. 63). But he gives no clear indication of what this is. It seems to me that it can only be a notion of negative liberty that focuses on individuality and rights and which has a moral force that circumscribes mere agreement. It is a morally-justifiable framework of rules and procedures designed to protect a *pre-existing* moral right to negative liberty.

12. Justice

The current dominance of liberal egalitarianism over classical liberalism is intellectually upheld by a subtle transformation of concepts that are common to both doctrines. Thus the individualistic force of classical liberal thought, its commitment to law, rights and personal liberty has been retained by egalitarians but only at the cost of giving these terms a pronounced collectivist, or at least redistributivist, twist. Examples of this exploitation of an apparently unavoidable permissiveness in political language are legion. It is justice and rights that provide perhaps the best examples of the process. That notion of moral equality which is at the basis of any liberal theory of justice has now been converted into a demand for economic equality so that the original injunction to treat people equally, under common and impartial rules, has been supplemented by the argument that they ought to be 'treated as equals' (Dworkin, 1986, pp. 295–6). And this demand can only be met by a substantial redistribution, either as justified compensation for the disadvantaged or as the rather bald demand for equality as a good thing itself.

In John Rawls's theory it is morally unacceptable that people's well-being should depend on the 'distribution of wealth and income ... determined by the natural distribution of abilities and talents' (1971, pp. 73–4) since individuals do not *deserve* these abilities and talents. They are the outcome of a 'natural lottery' which has no ethical rationale at all. Similarly, Dworkin (1981) distinguishes between inequalities which are endowment-sensitive (the product of the 'brute luck' of nature) and those that are sensitive to ambitions and efforts. Only the latter are acceptable since they are the results of actions to which the normal liberal credo about personal responsibility for action is relevant. In both Rawls and Dworkin, that income and wealth which accrues from unjustified possession of either inherited resources or from the 'luck' of natural talents constitute a kind of unowned pool which ought to be redistributed by reference to social (or philosophical) principles.

It never occurs to theorists of social justice that there may be *undeserved* entitlements, claims to assets to which neither merit, desert or need have any direct relevance. Many market exchanges produce incomes which it would be difficult to say were deserved in any conventional sense but they would still be legitimate under conventional notions of entitlement. And inheritances, of course, are the prime example of unmerited, windfall gains. Yet there are rules which establish title, whether to the products of productive labour, exchange or gifts. There is no manna from heaven available for redistribution; inherited wealth must have been created by somebody's productive efforts, and that person had a right to pass it on to whomever he or she chose. If theorists of social justice are to treat all assets as constitutive of a collectively-owned pool, to be redistributed according to principles different from those that govern the creation of these assets, they face an impossible task unless they also wish to abolish *all* accepted rules of entitlement.

However, the new doctrine of social justice is superficially subtler than old-style egalitarianism largely because it builds on (or exploits) some familiar ideas in classical liberal theory, namely the right to ownership of resources and the meaning of equality. More importantly, it could be said to have taken to extremes a popular idea in classical economics, the theory of rent. In the last century some orthodox market economists were a little disturbed by the phenomenon of rent, i.e. income derived from the lucky possession of a scarce resource that had no alternative use. What they had in mind was land. Since its earnings are conventionally not the product of entrepreneurship, it was said that they could be taxed away (or some socialized form of land ownership introduced) with no, or only a negligible, effect on productivity. Contemporary theories of social justice are based on a similar idea; that people do not own their natural talents in the way that landowners were thought to have no right to their land. Although they are not utilitarians, both Rawls and Dworkin are concerned about productivity. They have to be, since the least advantaged or the victims of brute luck must be financed (compensated?) from the 'unjust' earnings of the arbitrarily advantaged. There must therefore be incentives for individuals to create this surplus. There is, then, some justifiable inequality.

However bizarre some of the foundations of the new redistributionism may sound, they have a clear resonance for contemporary theories of justice and this has at least compelled classical liberals to flesh out their criticism of the doctrine of egalitarianism with more considered concepts of the self and of ownership. Arguments are less intense now about the adverse aggregative effects of redistribution (although it would be fatal to ignore them) and more about what a morality uncontaminated by crude utilitarianism means. Most importantly, an analysis of justice enables us to understand more clearly the differences between the ethics of liberty and those of equal liberty.

Classical liberal theories of justice are 'backward-looking' in that they are concerned with the past: how people were treated, how wealth was acquired and what actions generate what entitlements are the typical questions asked. This is perhaps why legal justice is the closest to a correct use of the concept (though this should not be identified with positive law since existing legal systems often embody injustice). In contrast, social justice is typically forward-looking. Even though it is not often utilitarian it does demand that society be reorganized so that morally better states of affairs are produced. Furthermore, classical liberal theories of justice distinguish it from whatever other virtues a society might display, such as benevolence or some notion of the good. What is distinctive about justice is its obligatory nature: it is permissible to enforce justice while the other virtues are often thought to be supererogatory (desirable but not compelling). One of the reasons redistributivist theorists use the concept of justice rather than straight egalitarianism or socialism is because they wish to capture its special urgency. We may not go as far as demanding that justice is *absolute* but we require extraordinarily good reasons to evade its dictates.

It is the backward-looking nature of justice that gives it its universal appeal. It is a minimum requirement of morality that punishment should be related to conduct, that people are entitled to equality before the law and should be given their 'due'. Of course, there can be disagreement about what some of these things may mean in practice (Aristotle insisted that like cases be treated alike, but that begs the question about what are like cases). However, if there is any kind of generic moral code it would consist almost exclusively of these features. By contrast, social justice seems a peculiarly Western concept, not universalizable but conditioned almost exclusively by developments in 20th century Anglo-American and West European political philosophy. In an important way, while being obligatory, justice makes few (positive) demands on us. As Adam Smith said: 'Mere justice is, upon most occasions, but a negative virtue, and only hinders us from hurting our neighbour' (1969, p. 160).

Closely allied to this negative conception is its moral individualism: an important argument is that we attribute the words just and unjust to the actions of identifiable persons and not to mysterious social forces. As Hayek says: 'To speak of justice always implies that some person or persons ought, or ought not, to have performed some action; and this 'ought' in turn presupposes the recognition of rules which define a set of circumstances wherein a certain kind of conduct is prohibited or required' (1976, p. 33).

Thus to complain that a distribution of income is socially unjust is to presuppose that it was determined by a human distributor whose actions can be morally appraised. Yet the distribution of income thrown up by the market is the outcome of the actions of innumerable individuals, not one of whom intended any particular pattern. The distinction between procedural justice, or the rules that govern individual action, and end-state justice, particular patterns of income and wealth, is vital here because classical liberalism holds that any attempt to freeze a pattern (irrespective of the desirability or otherwise of the chosen distribution) must involve the violation of procedural rules and the freedoms and equalities they embody (Nozick, 1974, p. 164). The market is in constant flux and to track it so as to generate and preserve social justice would make impossible demands on our knowledge, as well as increasing coercion in society. Much of contemporary social justice is powered by a quite erroneous distinction between the laws of production and distribution. This quite arbitrary distinction assumes that there is no feedback effect on production whatever distributive policy a government chooses. However, productive possibilities are not fixed but are very much influenced by how the social pie is sliced up.

It is to be noted that this account of procedural justice says nothing specifically about the role of government beyond a prohibition of its enforcement of particular end-states. A welfare state is not a priori excluded, for there may be good reasons why aid to the disadvantaged should be a legitimate state function; even though in existing welfare states the redistribution is largely a consequence of interest group pressure and has little to do with equality (Le Grand, 1982). Still, classical liberalism tends to hold that public welfare derives from benevolence rather than from the strict duty of justice.

Despite this, there may still be an argument that the state's welfare responsibilities ought to be dictated by justice rather than by benevolence or a general social duty. Raymond Plant (1991) argues that though particular outcomes of a market process are unintended they are foreseeable and that justice is as much a matter of how we respond to its victims as it is about individual behaviour under rules. In other words, justice is not entirely a backward-looking concept and injustice can occur through acts of omission as well as acts of commission. While there is obviously something to this argument, in the same way as we might say that a refusal to help someone in distress on the ground that there was no contractual obligation to do so was in a way an act of injustice, it does not affect the main thrust of the procedural theory which really objects to the *whole spread of incomes* being determined by principles, such as need and desert, which are external to the market itself. Plant's argument does not establish the case for social justice, which is normally not limited to the problem of individuals in distress, even though it might well compel classical liberals to reconsider the *duties* implied by the pure theory of procedural justice.

There are, however, some problems with the classical liberal theory of justice. For one thing, is it simply utilitarian, as Mises (1962, p. 34) certainly thought? Is the objection to social justice merely that continued interventions in the market so distort the incentive structures facing rational agents that everybody in the long-run is made worse off? Hayek, of course, claims quite rightly that he is not a utilitarian in that a firm opposition to the possibility of interpersonal comparability of utilities underlies his rejection of constructivist end-states (Hayek, 1976), but his approach is redolent of a certain kind of consequentialism. His whole endeavour is to show how the decentralized exchange system best exploits the earth's resources, and copes with a niggardly nature, so as to generate a kind of progress: no matter how abstract and indeterminate this is. There may even be a tension between his theory of the purpose-independent rules of procedural justice, which could have a Kantian foundation in their respect for persons, and his theory of the wealth-generating features of market process which has no necessary connection with abstract morality.

Since no independent source is given for the moral rights that attach to the participants in a market process there is something of a lacuna in the ethics of classical liberalism. Entrepreneurship is unquestionably an essential mechanism in the co-ordination process but does the profit, payment above marginal productivity, which it generates have any moral justification? It may be highly dangerous economically to suppose that it could be taxed away with no loss in productivity but as long as its justification is purely instrumental, the inequalities the profit motive creates will always provoke moral strictures derived from social justice.

It could be argued that the rules that govern market relationships are the rules of co-ordination rather than of justice. As already noted,

Buchanan claimed that justice is what is agreed upon. Unlike Rawls, who believes that rational individuals under certain conditions, notably including ignorance of their present circumstances and the future value of their talents, would agree on particular rules of justice (which include a specific distribution rule). Buchanan argues that *whatever* they agree on is itself just. Since Buchanan's contractors have knowledge of themselves and others, and have acquired holdings in an anarchistic equilibrium, there is little possibility that the resulting agreement will be Rawlsian. All that we can say is that to ensure predictability a set of constraints on a potentially destructive self-interest will be imposed. But are these the rules of a plausible concept of justice? Exactly the same stricture applies to the more familiar rules of justice described in the spontaneous order theory of justice in the tradition from Hume through to Hayek and Sugden. While these rules guarantee order and predictability they are not specifically about ethically decisive entitlements to property.

In Western thought, social justice theories have filled this apparent gap. Rawls[1] and Dworkin have challenged any conception of justice that allocates property titles blindly and which uncritically permits an individualistic exploitation of natural talents. In fact, it is fairly easy to show that the Rawlsian procedure is irredeemably flawed, and not merely on utilitarian grounds. Rawls's claim that individuals' natural talents constitute a common pool to be used on behalf of the least-advantaged has counter-intuitive, even bizarre implications. It clearly implies a most peculiar notion of the self and his or her moral properties. If all extraneous features, such as natural talents and inclinations, are stripped away on the ground that they are the arbitrary results of a random nature, then what is left of the person? How do we attribute moral praise or blame when all we have left is an empty shell (Nozick, 1974, pp. 183–231), drained of those features that make a description of personhood meaningful? Indeed, it is rather paradoxical that Rawls (1971, p. 27) should stress the 'separateness of persons', in his surely correct criticism of utilitarianism that it conflates individual values into a single social maximand, when his procedure itself leaves us with no genuine human beings to separate. As has often been pointed out, there is no reason in Rawls's theory why body parts should not be redistributed on grounds of justice.

From a purely economic point of view the theory is even more defective. Despite what Rawls often says about those inequalities that are justifiable in order to generate a surplus which can be distributed to the least-advantaged, there are really no incentives for entrepreneurship to operate. Yet without it there can be no capitalism. That requires profit, but since individuals are not entitled to a return on their entrepreneurial talents they are unlikely to be motivated. Apparently, they do not own these talents. In fact, the model is a version of equilibrium or market socialism in which each factor of production is paid just enough to keep it at maximum efficiency. Rawls admits as much with his claim (1971, p. 146) that his system is indifferent between capitalist ownership or socialist ownership. However, payment to entrepreneurship (which does not have a supply price) is not rent but a reward for discovery (Kirzner, 1989). It would not exist without human action so that it is impossible to imagine some mechanical substitute for it. For that reason alone we cannot be indifferent between capitalism and socialism, even if justice required a redistribution to the least-advantaged. Indeed, in Rawls's system moral hazard would be a serious problem; everybody would have an incentive to become one of the least advantaged.

I do not suggest that the classical liberal lacuna in the moral theory of justice means that some kind of Rawlsian theory becomes irresistible. The above individualist critique would be sufficient to condemn it on efficiency grounds. However, as long as property rights and ownership are ill-defined, the theory is vulnerable to those sorts of redistributive claims that cling, however precariously, to a substantive redistributive ethic supplemented by a rational choice and quasi-efficiency based explanatory model, however implausible that is. What classical liberal theories of justice have to show is not merely that the rules recommended are serviceable in the sense of guaranteeing predictability, order and efficiency but that they also establish *just* entitlements. Entrepreneurship must be shown to be not merely a mechanism for co-ordination but also the source of justice in property holdings. Only then can co-ordination rules become proper rules of justice.

The search for such a foundation has a long history in classical liberal thought. The origins perhaps lie in Locke's moral theory of accumulation by the application of labour to previously unowned objects, subject to certain provisos. In his words, 'every Man has a Property in his own Person... The Labour of his Body, and the Work of his hands, we may say are properly his. Whatsoever then he removes out of the state that nature hath provided, and Left it in, he hath mixed his Labor with, and joyned to it something that is his own, and thereby makes it his Property' (Locke, 1960, pp. 287–8). Although this formulation has provoked tremendous controversy (Hume wondered why mixing labour should, independently of a given set of rules, establish title) it has to a great extent been the starting point for exclusively moral theories of property accumulation. This is so because it provides an individualistic challenge to rules that might locate ownership rights to privileged bodies, such as the state. It might not seem to have much application to the contemporary world since what Locke was mainly talking about, land, has been unavailable for individual appropriation for a very long time. Still, property is being created all the time in other forms, where a version of Locke's rationale might very well have a place. Finally, Locke's provisos, especially the requirement that after an appropriation there should 'be enough, and as good left' for others (1960, p. 291), have been so interpreted that there would hardly be any scope for accumulation. However, appropriate constraints have been constructed which leave the basic Lockeian liberty to accumulate intact (Nozick, 1974, pp. 178–82).

The real difficulty in reconciling abstract moral theories of justice like Locke's with the results of a certain kind of Humeian spontaneity or a Buchanan-type contracting lies in the claims to rightful possession, and property rights in general, rather than in the rules governing, say, punishment and the rectification of past wrongful acts. Those features of the backward-looking elements of justice are not likely to arouse too much controversy because they seem to be parts of the generic aspect of morality; that element which, despite the claims of relativists, seems to secure almost universal support. When it comes to ownership and entitlement to goods and property, however, the rules are subject to immense cultural variation and the views of political philosophers constitute no consensus. Adam Smith pointed to the universal propensity to 'truck, barter and exchange one thing for another' (Smith, 1976b, p. 25) but he gave little guidance as to the moral entitlement of individuals to the things that were to be traded. An exchange process must, as a matter of logic, begin with things that do not emerge from exchange, and it is the rightful possession of these that is disputed as well as the entitlements that flow from them.

Locke's labour entitlement theory has the obvious disadvantage in that it implies, as socialists have noticed, that only a certain type of meritorious or desert-based activity is worthy of reward. Yet, of course, as Hayek stressed, merit is only a contingent feature of gain in a market economy. Since a market rewards according to value it is quite likely that many valued activities display little or no merit. Indeed, what might be thought of by some critics as sheer luck plays a great role in the reward structure of capitalism. Still, one cannot deny that Locke's account of first possession (of previously unowned objects), as constitutive of original entitlement, is morally significant even though it is obvious that property is created in many other ways in complex modern economies.

The way in which we can justify ownership is to look at the process by which the market system itself works. It may or may not be the case that spontaneously developing rules will accord with a theory of just rules that derives from a more abstract and purely moral justification but it is possible that in the absence of state intervention such a convergence might eventually develop. The market has to be seen as a creative process in which human action is vital: this analysis does not merely point to its efficiency properties but also to the rightful claims that the creators have to their rewards, however arbitrary they might *appear*. If it can be shown that success in the market is not the consequence of luck, then we can meaningfully use expressions such as 'deserved' in relation to reward, even though desert here may not be harmonious with the conception used by egalitarian critics of the market. Israel Kirzner (1989) has been foremost in the attempts to construct a moral theory of reward in the market.

In his theory of entrepreneurship Kirzner, building on the insights of Mises and Hayek, shows that the market is in more or less permanent disequilibrium. This means that there are always gaps to close, differences between factor prices and anticipated product prices to exploit and opportunities for creativity in the co-ordination of knowledge. Value created in this way is qualitatively different from that which is conventionally attributed to the factors of production. It is not a result of some predictable, mechanical process but is entirely a product of mental alertness to opportunities and it is rewarded not with income as such but with profit. Significantly, profit is closely related to the correction of error in a given allocation of resources. Error correction is essential precisely because real-world economies are characterized by radical uncertainty. The moral justification for this has always been difficult for orthodox neoclassical economics since that deals only with factor earnings in equilibrium: that is much easier to justify in conventional moral terms. But the concept of pure profit is, theoretically, alien to neoclassical writers: in fact, to some it is a sign of inefficiency, if not downright immorality.

The specifically moral feature of Kirzner's explanation derives from the importance he attaches to discovery in the creation of new value:

'the entrepreneurial decision to produce, is a genuine discovery; the act that implements this discovery is an act of creation. The output that the entrepreneur produces as a result of these creative acts is thus discovered output' (Kirzner, 1989, p. 13). What this means is that value-creation depends exclusively on individual insight into the uses to which resources can be put and, since it is the product of mental awareness, it does not theoretically depend on resource ownership (capital can always be borrowed). When it is said that the entrepreneurship creates something out of nothing it is meant that a thing does not have value until someone notices, or anticipates, that it will eventually command a price. In a world of uncertainty one can never know in advance what will turn out to have value.

This has a serious implication for theories of social justice because they almost always assume a given set of resources, costlessly produced and owned by no one, which can be distributed by principles which have little to do with value-creation. This applies just as much to human resources (talents) as it does to physical ones. Dworkin (1981) tries to make a distinction between natural talents, the earnings of which no one is entitled to, and the products of efforts, and ambitions, which are fully deserved. He does this to avoid the implication in Rawls that no one properly deserves anything. But there really is no distinction, for the value of those talents can only be known through efforts and ambitions. There is no value apart from that created by ambition and effort even though the skill of the entrepreneur may not always resemble what is conventionally understood as desert-worthy activity. There is no rental income here, but only the rewards that go to those who strive to create value (fortuitous though that may sometimes look).

Kirzner's argument is a subtle variant on the Lockeian thesis; the person who discovers something is morally entitled to it because it would not exist without his or her activity. No one else owns it. What we think of as valuable natural resources, e.g. oil, do not properly exist as such until someone correctly anticipates that they will have market value. Kirzner believes that it accords with our moral intuitions because it is an exemplification of the 'finders-keepers' rule. This is indeed a not uncommon ethical practice: we do regard the discoverer of something, especially a scientific or medical innovation, as being entitled to its rewards. However, Kirzner's theory would apply to much more controversial areas. For example, the corporate raider who notices that certain assets are undervalued on the stock market, buys them up with borrowed money and organizes them in profitable ways, no doubt creates new value but one questions whether his activity is worthy of the same moral approbation as that of a person who profits from the discovery of a cure for a serious disease. Conventional morality does not regard the two types of discovery as morally similar, especially as the raider is often accused of causing unemployment.

Regardless of this point, which reflects a common moral prejudice that yearns for objective measures of value, there are further difficulties in the application of the finders-keepers principle. Does it not rest on the exploitation of people's ignorance? Can a distinction be drawn between genuine discovery and fraud? The second point is perhaps ethically more serious since there may be well-founded doubts about ownership: especially in stock market transactions (Barry, 1991, chapter 3) where information is at a premium. On the assumption that entrepreneurship takes place within the firm it is quite unclear whether employees, who actually make discoveries, are entitled to all the rewards (perhaps by trading on undisclosed information on the stock market) or whether the owners are. Even Kirzner (1989, pp. 172–3) admits that there may be doubts concerning ownership, about what the act of discovery actually consists of. Particular circumstances may make it impossible to apply directly the finders-keepers principle. We apparently have to rely on tradition and conventional legal interpretations with regard to ownership. Attention to these practices may, however, involve a dilution of the principle.

This point brings us back to the original problem: the connection between rules of justice derived from convention and those (like Kirzner's) that emanate from more abstract and universal notions of morality. A classical liberal theory of justice runs into difficulties when these two approaches collide, as potentially they can. Direct and uncontroversial applications of finders-keepers may be rarer than Kirzner supposes. It is quite likely that conventions, which may not always accord with the abstract morality of individualism, will, nevertheless, have a greater claim on people's intuitions as they gradually become internalized in a Humeian manner.

In certain cases, communal rights of ownership (especially of scarce natural resources, such as water) may develop which will put strict limits on the possibilities of discovery alone creating private property rights. There is nothing to stop the determined classical liberal theorists of justice maintaining that ownership must always inhere in individuals, and that this is validated by a rationalistic natural law, despite what convention might imply. However, this rationalistic approach may not always cohere with our moral intuitions, which are often inspired by a broader conception of desert than that permitted by classical liberalism. Still, such an approach provides a much-needed supplement to a Hayekian theory which is curiously silent on those distributive problems and disputes about ownership that are not catered for by pure procedural rules. Something like Kirzner's theory is required if the traditional Lockeian justification for ownership is to be given a modern application and the morality of capitalism demonstrated.

Note

1. Rawls (1993) has altered the theoretical foundations of his theory of social justice but its egalitarian thrust remains the same.

13. Classical Liberalism and Civil Society

It might have been thought that, with the spread of market capitalism and the growing distaste for the state, classical liberalism would have experienced something of an intellectual renaissance. It is clear that this is not taking place. Various forms of interventionism still retain their grip on the imagination of social theorists and political philosophers. The intellectual debate has certainly shifted from arguments between proponents of capitalism and advocates of central planning to issues about the different types of market capitalism, but the distinctive features of classical liberalism have become somewhat blurred in this intellectual reorientation. It is even said that the doctrine only had relevance to the historic battle against Marxism: and now that the latter has little relevance to the modern world the central tenets of individualism are likewise of limited application.

One reason for this might be the fact that, as mentioned earlier, classical liberalism has certain ideological overtones. To some extent it presents itself as a doctrine of universal applicability and for that reason seems to be incapable of accounting for the nuances of the differing social and economic forms that might be encompassed under the broad heading of market capitalism. Evidence of this is readily apparent in the varieties of corporate organization that are revealed by the most cursory examination of existing market societies. The Anglo-American style of business, with its 'loosely-held' form of corporate government in which anonymous shareholders, concerned only with immediate gratification, drive the economy, is often contrasted unfavourably with the more intimate style of corporate organization practiced, say, in Germany (Barry, 1993a), where owners are more closely linked with management and apparently concerned with the social effects of business activity.

This has not only efficiency implications (indeed it is a fundamental claim of classical liberal epistemics that it is impossible to know a priori which type of economic management will be successful) but also moral ones. For Anglo-American capitalism has come under increasing critical fire precisely because of its anonymity; its alleged Mandevillian, amoral motivations are said to be corrosive of those communal bonds that are thought to be essential for the maintenance of civility. If classical liberalism does embody these features (which may be doubted) it is thought to be irrelevant for communities whose history and traditions make them quite unsuitable for an easy transplant of individualism. It is to some extent true that classical liberals have presented a vision of the good society as one in which anonymous agents are held together by very general rules and these individuals tend to be identified independently of discrete communal affiliations. It is also the case that some writers have naïvely held that spontaneous processes and competition between rival political and social forms would somehow lead to the triumph of specifically liberal orders, characterized in the above way.

Against the ambitious geopolitical claims of some, but by no means all, classical liberals a rival theory has emerged in recent decades: the idea of 'civil society' (Gray, 1993, pp. 283–328). Although many of the features of individualism are embedded in this doctrine, significant departures have been made from it to justify the claim that civil society represents a new and superior normative goal. It is true that some of the dissenters in Eastern Europe used the idea, in their struggle against communism, as representative of something different from Western liberalism, and more akin to a European tradition of civility that had been obliterated by communism.

Civil society recognizes an essential pluralism in human values, that there is no one way of life that has a unique hold on our reason and that the good society cannot be identified with an unsullied individualism or collectivism. Differing forms of social organization can coexist under the rule of law as long as the state is precluded from exclusive control of all aspects of life. The state is viewed, almost in a Hegelian manner, as a kind of neutral arbiter of disputes, an impartial guarantor of stability charged with the responsibility of preventing one subset of society predominating over all others. Of course, in an obvious tribute to classical liberal jurisprudence, theorists of civil society insist that the state itself should be bound by law, as in the idea of the *Rechtsstaat*.

Furthermore, civil society does not accept that the relentless operation of market forces alone is sufficient to meet with the idea of order and humanity. That is why in the theory of the social market economy the state was given the responsibility of preventing an unaided market disintegrating into monopolies and cartels and therefore spontaneously destroying the order of freedom. Though it should be pointed out here (Tumlir, 1989) that some writers in the tradition held that a strengthened civil law was a more effective device for maintaining market freedom than was the state.

Again, theorists of civil society are not against the state having a welfare role (though it is vastly different from that in Western democracies). It is mandated not merely by a morality of benevolence but also by the desire to preserve a special kind of ordered liberty: the victims of relentless market process are not merely in need in a tangible sense but they are also disabled from participation in civil society as full citizens. A theory of citizenship is now being developed which maintains that capitalism is unstable if it fails to integrate everyone fully into its economic and social structure.

One is entitled to ask whether all this represents a radical departure from classical liberalism. Of course, the slightly more benign attitude towards the state that civil-society theory evinces is vulnerable to the severe criticism of public-choice theory. This has successfully demonstrated that its officials in a democracy can be as predatory as any market trader driven by self-interest. But the idea of proper constitutionalism is common to both doctrines, though the excessive legalism of anonymous market orders has led theorists of civil society to favour more communal modes of dispute-settling and less individualistic types of adjustment to change. If classical liberalism is presented as an ideology, whose features never change and which is appropriate to all social circumstances, then the theorists of civil society would undoubtedly have a point. But this is a caricature of the doctrine.

Classical liberalism is not an ideology in this crude sense. Since its central tenet is liberty the doctrine necessarily allows for differing forms of social organization, operating within the rule of law, to develop. Its stress on voluntarism means that communal and non-market associations, e.g. churches, welfare associations and private educational foundations, can flourish under the aegis of common rules of just conduct. If anything, liberal egalitarianism, with its goal of shifting the social order towards an end-state of substantive equality, is far more ideological. The existence of classical liberal orders, however imperfect, and forms of civil society, is in fact a threat to liberal egalitarianism. This is because the pluralism they encourage and the variety of institutional arrangements they generate constitute potential sources of inequality which the liberal egalitarian will want to eliminate by use of the state's power. Although theorists of civil society have a more favourable attitude to the welfare state than do classical liberals they are hostile to the kind of welfarism that has developed in contemporary social democracies.

Classical liberal theories of procedural justice are necessary, if not quite sufficient, for the preservation of most of the values of civil society. The main features of this order are surely reproducible without the help of social justice. That may be a type of universalism but it is certainly a very modest one. If there are generic moral principles for mankind, as most people would agree, then classical liberalism has contributed much to their articulation, both practically and philosophically. This holds true independently of the obvious discoveries that the doctrine has made in economic theory and organization.

References

Axelrod, R. (1984), *The Evolution of Co-operation*, New York: Basic Books.

Barry, B. (1965), *Political Argument*, London: Routledge and Kegan Paul.

Barry, N.P. (1984), 'Ideas Versus Interests: The Classical Liberal Dilemma', in N. P. Barry, *et al.*, *Hayek's 'Serfdom' Revisited*, London: Institute of Economic Affairs.

Barry, N.P. (1986), *On Classical Liberalism and Libertarianism*, London: Macmillan.

Barry, N.P. (1989), 'Ideas and Interests: The Problem Reconsidered', in A. Gamble, *et al.*, *Ideas, Interests and Consequences*, London: Institute of Economic Affairs.

Barry, N.P. (1991), *The Morality of Business Enterprise*, Aberdeen: Aberdeen University Press.

Barry, N.P. (1993a), 'The Social Market Economy', *Social Philosophy and Policy*, **10**, 1–25.

Barry, N.P. (1993b), 'Sovereignty, the Rule of Recognition and Constitutional Stability in Britain', *Journal des Economistes et des Etudes Humaines*, **4**, 159–76.

Benson, B. (1990), *The Enterprise of Law*, San Francisco: Pacific Research Institute for Public Policy.

Berlin, I. (1958), *Two Concepts of Liberty*, London: Oxford University Press.

Böhm, F. (1960), *Reden und Schriften*, Karlsruhe: C.F. Müller.

Böhm, F. (1989), 'The Rule of Law', in A. Peacock and H. Willgerodt (eds), *Germany's Social Market Economy*, London: Macmillan.

Buchanan, J.M. (1975), *The Limits of Liberty. Between Anarchy and Leviathan*, Chicago: University of Chicago Press.

Buchanan, J.M. (1977), *Freedom in Constitutional Contract*, Austin, Texas: A. & M. University Press.

Buchanan, J.M. and Tullock, G. (1962), *The Calculus of Consent*, Ann Arbor: University of Michigan Press.

Coase, R.H. (1960), 'The Problem of Social Cost', *Journal of Law and Economics*, **3**, 1–44.

Cohen, G. (1979), 'Capitalism, Freedom and the Proletariat', in A. Ryan (ed.), *The Idea of Freedom*, Oxford: Clarendon Press.

De Jasay, A. (1985), *The State*, Oxford: Basil Blackwell.

De Jasay, A. (1991), *Choice, Contract, Consent*, London: Institute of Economic Affairs.

Dicey, A.V. (1926), *Law and Opinion in England*, 2nd ed., London: Macmillan.

Dworkin, R. (1977), *Taking Rights Seriously*, London: Duckworth.

Dworkin, R. (1981), 'Equality of Resources', *Philosophy and Public Affairs*, **10**, 283–345.

Dworkin, R. (1985), *A Matter of Principle*, Cambridge: Harvard University Press.

Dworkin, R. (1986), *Law's Empire*, London: Fontana.

Epstein, R.A. (1985), *Takings: Private Property and the Power of Eminent Domain*, Cambridge: Harvard University Press.

Eucken, W. (1950), *The Foundations of Economics*, Edinburgh: William Hodge.

Eucken, W. (1951), *This Unsuccessful Age*, Edinburgh: William Hodge.

Giersch, H., Paque, K. and Schmieding, H. (1992), *The Fading Miracle*, Cambridge: Cambridge University Press.

Gray, J. (1989), *Liberalisms: Essays in Political Philosophy*, London: Routledge.

Gray, J. (1992), *The Moral Foundations of Market Institutions*, London: Institute of Economic Affairs.

Gray, J. (1993), *Post-Liberalism: Studies in Political Thought*, London: Routledge.

Green, T.H. (1888), *Works*, edited by R. Nettleship, London: Oxford University Press.

Hamm, W. (1989), 'The Welfare State at its Limit', in A. Peacock and H. Willgerodt, *Germany Neo-Liberals and the Social Market Economy*, London: Macmillan.

Hart, H.L.A. (1961), *The Concept of Law*, London: Oxford University Press.

Hayek, F.A. (1948), *Individualism and Economic Order*, London: Routledge and Kegan Paul.

Hayek, F.A. (1960), *The Constitution of Liberty*, London: Routledge and Kegan Paul.

Hayek, F.A. (1967), *Studies in Philosophy, Politics and Economics*, London: Routledge and Kegan Paul.

Hayek, F.A. (1973), *Rules and Order*, London: Routledge and Kegan Paul.

Hayek, F.A. (1976), *The Mirage of Social Justice*, London: Routledge and Kegan Paul.

Hayek, F.A. (1978), *The Denationalisation of Money*, 2nd edition, London: Institute of Economic Affairs.

Hayek, F.A. (1979), *The Political Order of a Free People*, London: Routledge and Kegan Paul.

Hayek, F.A. (1988), *The Fatal Conceit*, London: Routledge.

Hume, D. (1953), *Hume's Political Essays*, edited by C. Hendel, New York: Liberal Arts Press. Originally published 1748.

Hume, D. (1972), *A Treatise of Human Nature*, London: Fontana. Originally published 1739.

Kirzner, I. (1973), *Competition and Entrepreneurship*, Chicago: University of Chicago Press.

Kirzner, I. (1979), *Perception, Opportunity and Profit*, Chicago: University of Chicago Press.

Kirzner, I. (1989), *Discovery, Capitalism and Distributive Justice*, Oxford: Basil Blackwell.

Kukathas, C. (1992), 'Freedom versus Autonomy', in J. Gray, *The Moral Foundations of Market Institutions*, London: Institute of Economic Affairs.

Le Grand, J. (1982), *The Strategy of Equality*, London: Allen and Unwin.

Lenel, H. (1989), 'Evolution of the Social Market Economy', in A. Peacock and H. Willgerodt, *German Neo-Liberals and the Social Market Economy*, London: Macmillan.

Locke, J. (1960), *Two Treatises of Government*, edited by P. Laslett, Cambridge: Cambridge University Press. Originally published in 1690.

MacIntyre, A. (1981), *After Virtue*, London: Duckworth.

Maine, H. (1885), *Popular Government*, London: John Murray.

Mandeville, B. (1924), *The Fable of the Bees*, edited by F.B. Kaye, London: Oxford University Press. Originally published 1705.

Manne, H. (21965), 'Mergers and the Market for Corporate Control', *Journal of Political Economy*, **73**, 110–20.

Mills, J.S. (1848), *Principles of Political Economy*, London: J.W. Parker.

Mises, L. (1949), *Human Action*, Chicago: Henry Regnery.

Mises, L. (1962), *Liberalism*, Kansas: Sheed, Andrews and McMeel.

Mulhall, S. and Swift, A. (1992), *Liberals and Communitarians*, Oxford: Basil Blackwell.

Müller-Armack, A. (1965), 'The Principles of the Social Market Economy', *German Economic Review*, **3**, 80–96.

Müller-Armack, A. (1979), 'Economic Systems from a Social Point of View', in J. Thesing (ed.), *Economy and Development*, Mainz: Konrad Adenauer-Stiftung.

Nozick, R. (1974), *Anarchy, State and Utopia*, New York: Basic Books.

Nozick, R. (1990), *The Examined Life: Philosophical Meditations*, New York: Simon and Schuster.

Plant, R. (1991), *Modern Political Thought*, Oxford: Basil Blackwell.

Popper, K. (1957), *The Poverty of Historicism*, London: Routledge and Kegan Paul.

Rawls, J. (1971), *A Theory of Justice*, Cambridge: Harvard University Press.

Rawls, J. (1993), *Political Liberalism*, New York: Columbia University Press.

Raz, J. (1986), *The Morality of Freedom*, London: Oxford University Press.

Robbins, L. (1935), *The Nature and Significance of Economic Science*, 2nd edition, London: Routledge and Kegan Paul.

Röpke, W. (1950), *The Social Crisis of Our Time*, Edinburgh: William Hodge.

Röpke, W. (1960), *A Humane Economy*, London: Wolf.

Sandel, M. (1982), *Liberalism and the Limits of Justice*, Cambridge: Cambridge University Press.

Siegan, B. (1980), *Economic Liberties and the Constitution*, Chicago: University of Chicago Press.

Smith, A. (1969), *The Theory of Moral Sentiments*, edited by E. West, Indianapolis: Liberty Press. Originally published 1759.

Smith, A. (1976a), *The Theory of Moral Sentiments*, edited by D.D. Raphael and A.L. Macfie, Oxford: Clarendon Press. Originally published 1759.

Smith, A. (1976b), *An Enquiry into the Nature and Causes of the Wealth of Nations*, edited by R.H. Campbell and A.S. Skinner, Oxford: Clarendon Press. Originally published 1776.

Steiner, A. (1974), 'Individual Liberty', *Proceedings of the Aristotelian Society*, Oxford: Basil Blackwell.

Sugden, R. (1986), *The Economics of Rights, Co-operation and Welfare*, Oxford: Basil Blackwell.

Taylor, C. (1985), *Philosophical Papers*, Cambridge: Cambridge University Press.

Tiebout, C. (1956, 'A Pure Theory of Local Expenditure', *Journal of Political Economy*, **64**, 416–24.

Trakman, L. (1983), *The Law Merchant*, Littleton: Rothman.

Tullock, G. (1976), *The Vote Motive*, London: Institute of Economic Affairs.

Tumlir, J. (1989), 'Franz Böhm and the Development of Economic-Constitutional Analysis', in A. Peacock and H. Willgerodt, *German Neo-Liberals and the Social Market Economy*, London: Macmillan.

Wagner, R. (1993), 'Parchment, Guns and Constitutional Order', in C. Rowley, (ed.), *Property Rights and the Limits of Democracy*, Aldershot: Edward Elgar, for the Locke Institute.

Wallich, H. (1955), *Mainsprings of the German Revival*, New Haven: Yale University Press.

Walzer, M. (1983), *Spheres of Justice*, New York: Basic Books.

Index

Adam Smith into the Twenty-First Century

Adam Smith into the Twenty-First Century

Edwin G. West

Professor Emeritus
Carleton University

The Shaftesbury Papers, 7
Series Editor: Charles K. Rowley

Edward Elgar
Cheltenham, UK • Brookfield, US

Published by
Edward Elgar Publishing Limited
8 Lansdown Place
Cheltenham
Glos GL50 2HU
UK

Edward Elgar Publishing Company
Old Post Road
Brookfield
Vermont 05036
US

British Library Cataloguing in Publication Data
West, E.G. (Edwin George)
    Adam Smith into the twenty-first century. – (The
Shaftesbury papers; 7)
    1. Economics   2. Classical school of economics   3. Economic
forecasting
    I.Title   II.Series
    330.1'53

Library of Congress Cataloguing in Publication Data
West, E. G.
    Adam Smith into the twenty-first century / Edwin G. West.
    (The Shaftesbury papers; 7)
    1. Free enterprise   2. Smith, Adam, 1723–1790   3. Economics–
–History. 4. Economic history—1990–   5. Liberalism. 6. Economic
development. I. Title. II. Series.
    HB95.W45   1996
    330.15'3—dc20   95–40190
                                                                          CIP

ISBN 1 85898 197 2

Printed in Great Britain at the University Press, Cambridge

Contents

Preface

I am especially grateful to Charles Rowley for his many good suggestions. I also wish to acknowledge constructive discussion with Charlotte Twight, Ronald Bodkin and Brian Erard. I benefited considerably from the Liberty Fund Conference '"Life, Liberty and Property" and the Limits of Democracy' in Charleston, S.C., December 1991, and from the colloquium on 'Ethics, Liberty and Markets', Boston, June 1993, which was also sponsored by the Liberty Fund. Finally, and as always, I am grateful to the continuing friendship and intellectual support of my economist colleagues at Carleton University.

1. Introduction

It is no secret in the present post-communistic era that the works of Adam Smith are being consulted and scrutinized with new vigour. After the collapse of their centrally directed economies, Eastern European countries are being told that the only route to survival is that of the free market and democracy. It is not surprising that they are now seeking advice from the West. They will be disappointed with Adam Smith, however, if they expect his *Wealth of Nations* (1976a) to be a simple 'users guide' to the instant setting up of a free enterprise system from scratch. Smith's work, in fact, contains an impressive amount of history and scrupulous attention to the many different versions of slowly evolving legal frameworks and constitutions that have provided varying degrees of encouragement to workable free market exchange systems. And while 'natural liberty' emerged from Smith's worldwide survey as a key ingredient for prosperous and law abiding societies, he shows that the 'culture of liberty' has taken many forms.

Having recently written about newly found relationships between Smith's writing and emerging modern *economic* concepts and theories (West, 1990), the focus of this book is upon the broad institutional approach and vision of Smith. Among the aspects that will be considered are philosophic issues such as the role of virtue, citizenship and civic humanism, and questions pertaining to jurisprudence and political science. One purpose is to try to determine the degree to which Smith's writings can be interpreted only in the special historical circumstances of his time. This, of course, is a useful endeavour in its own right, and one that Winch (1978, p. 5) describes as an experiment in 'recovery rather than recruitment'. Beyond this, however, Winch gives the impression that he believes there is not much of a 'useable past' in Smith. But even if he has sound reasons for this disposition, this is no reason for others to stop the search and discourage members of the ex-communist countries from looking for inspiration from Smith's vast wisdom.

This book assumes that Smith does have a 'usable past' and will demonstrate that there is much more in his work to stimulate and challenge the modern reader than is usually supposed. In this period of political upheaval and economic challenges there is much new political, philosophical, and economic debate afoot. Could it be that bringing Smith, as it were, into the fellowship of modern philosophers, economists and political analysts, might trigger new insights relevant to current circumstances? We shall maintain that the answer is substantially in the affirmative. The reader, however, will of course judge for himself.

It is exciting to note that Smith's economic conclusions can now be tested by empirical work that is going on in the social sciences, work that is not directly provoked by reading *The Wealth of Nations*. The book will begin by reviewing such new research on the following hypotheses or propositions:

1.   that democracy is conducive to economic growth;
2.   that government improves with the expansion of trade or commerce;
3.   that on any plausible definition of 'liberty' it too is associated with growing prosperity.

We shall show that hypotheses (2) and (3) are the most clearly stated by Smith. Hypothesis (1) reflects the popular political language of Western advice to Eastern Europe and countries of the USSR. It will be shown that it is likely that Smith would be much less enthusiastic about this hypothesis.

The book will next 'engage' both Adam Smith and John Locke in a current debate about whether and in what circumstances authoritarian leaders would behave in the interests of others in society. Chapter 3 investigates the classical Greek connection with Smith in the context of the roles of virtue, citizenship and 'civilized monarchies' in promoting social harmony. Very close to these matters, also, is the recent discussion attempting to associate Smith with what has become known as 'civic humanism'. It will be concluded that there seems, undoubtedly, to be some connection, but not so much as is often claimed.

Chapter 4 concerns the writings of two or three contemporary authors who are inclined to emphasize what has been called the 'dark side' of Smith. This line of thought attributes to him serious second thoughts about the 'virtues' of the invisible hand, together with a list recognizing what we now call 'market failures'. Our own verdict will be that much of this interpretation is based on a misreading or misunderstanding of Smith.

Finally, Chapter 5 will address the issue of classical liberalism and the question whether recent literature has contained uninformed attempts 'to force an 18th century man [Smith] into a 19th century mold' (Letwin, 1988, p. 79). Our conclusion will be that the attempt has indeed taken place despite the fact that the liberalism of J.S. Mill of the 19th century is vastly different from Smith's. Finally, it will be argued that it is Smith's liberalism that is the more proper subject for consideration for application to the 20th and 21st centuries.

2. Institutional Structure as a Key to Growth

After over two centuries since Adam Smith's *Inquiry into the Nature and Causes of the Wealth of Nations* it is instructive to compare his central conclusions with those of today's investigators of the very same topic. Although the modern economist prefers to address the subject in terms of, say, 'contemporary factors that account for differential growth across economies', the quest is, after all, approximately the same as Smith's search for 'nature and causes'. It is interesting, moreover, that the newer literature is increasingly attentive to legal, political and generally institutional variables that might affect growth in ways that are beginning to echo several components of the Smithian agenda.

What has been happening for several years in economics is a strong departure from the neo-classical preoccupations with the abstract, static and 'institutionally sterile' neo-classical models. In the Walrasian construction, prices alone were sufficient for efficient allocation while institutions of all kinds were presumed to be superfluous; firms, clubs, families could not, under such reasoning, enhance efficiency. And no interest was expressed in the possible differential effects of political constitutions and legal frameworks, subjects always uppermost in the mind of Smith. But all that indifference seems to be eroding now. Economists today take seriously the proposition that different constitutional designs can explain substantial differences in economic performance.

According to a student's notes of his lectures delivered in Glasgow in the 1760s, Smith, influenced undoubtedly by Montesquieu, welcomed especially the element of separation of powers that had developed in the British constitution of his day. Monetary affairs had to be dealt with in the Commons; the judges were independent of the king; the Habeas Corpus Act was further security to individual freedom, while the jury system was also a 'friend of liberty'. And, of course, it was natural liberty, first propounded by the 17th-century natural law social scientists and jurists Grotius and Pufendorf, that was to him the chief end of the well-constructed state. Such liberty implied freedom of contracts, freedom from invasion of private property together with the predictability and stability of the economic environment. All these conditions contributed to a continuous economic growth that benefited 'all ranks of society'.

Smith and Democracy

Consider now the recent empirical work by economists that has been looking for a correlation between democratic governments and economic prosperity. This would, at first sight, appear to be following in Smith's footsteps. And Western political leaders, after all, are encouraging the ex-communist countries to establish democracy as well as free markets, the emphasis on each being about equal. Is this the empirical test that Smith would have demanded? It is first important to keep in mind Donald Winch's question in Thweatt (1988): 'How much can now be learned from Smith by treating him from a Whig-Historical perspective within which the main issue is one of deciding in what respects he anticipated or foreshadowed, or failed by a large or small margin to foreshadow, what later generations of economists regard as significant?' One must certainly be constantly aware, as Winch emphasizes, that Smith worked with concepts, language, and outlook that were peculiar to the 18th century. But although special care must be taken to avoid anachronistic interpretations, we should surely not be inhibited from searching for ideas and arguments in Smith that may be of some use or inspiration in the late 20th century. True scholarship surely demands a judicious approach that searches Smith's writings in order to separate the potentially enduring from the more time bound material.

Those who today are not too sensitive to the peculiarities of historical context may see in Smith an enthusiastic democrat. If so they will be interested in the results of recent empirical investigations that have set out, in effect, to determine whether the introduction of democracy around the world can indeed tell us anything about 'the nature and causes' of 20th-century changes in the wealth of different nations. Przeworski and Limongi (1993) have examined 18 studies since 1966 that have generated 21 findings. Among them, eight found in favour of democracy, eight in favour of authoritarianism, and five discovered no difference. Przeworski and Limongi conclude that it is difficult to attach much significance to these results one way or the other.

Does such lack of firm evidence then throw doubt upon Adam Smith's reasoning? To find an answer to this question we must first enquire more closely how much Smith was, in reality, a champion of democracy and how far his preoccupations on this subject were shaped by special 18th-century circumstances. His writing shows, in fact, that he was very sceptical of many aspects of democratic government. In one place, indeed, he refers to 'the thoughtless extravagance that democracies are apt to fall into' (V.ii.a.5.) Consider next the fact that most democratic governments are based on simple majority voting. In Smith's view, the use of this rule was particularly conducive to statutory protectionism. In effect the vote was a property right that, to Smith, could violate other, more legitimate, property rights. The evidence for this view is his reference to statutory regulations that enabled members of the same trade to tax themselves to provide sickness and welfare funds. By giving them a common interest to manage, Smith observed, the regulation 'renders such assemblies necessary'. After that, a simple majority vote is given statutory respect, and this in turn is followed by a severe setback to the Smithian system since it takes away the liberty of the minority that is at the 'spearhead' of competition – the cost-cutters. In his words:

> An incorporation not only renders them [the assemblies] necessary, but makes the act of the majority binding upon the whole. In a free trade an effectual combination cannot last longer than every single trader continues of the same mind. The majority of a corporation can enact a by-law with proper penalties, which will limit the competition more effectually and more durably than any voluntary combination whatever.[1]

The implication is that in a full democracy, with active governments operating on simple majority rules, one can predict rent-seeking by special interest groups resulting in legislation such as tariffs, bounties, and price-fixing laws that Smith abhorred. In these circumstances, indeed, organized pressure for legislation itself becomes a commercial undertaking.

It is this scenario that today impresses what Rowley (1992) calls the Virginia Political Economy school (VPE). Members of this school have for some time challenged the assumption of the vote motive as the basis of majoritarian democracy. The reason offered is that individual citizens have no rational incentive to register their vote because the probability of their changing an electoral outcome is almost negligible. This is offered as one explanation of substantial vote abstentions in the real world by 'rationally ignorant' citizens. Meanwhile, even if civic duty compels the vote it may not induce the informed vote, since rational ignorance will be widespread among the electorate. In such circumstances, voters may vote their superficial preferences, 'while operating elsewhere among the interest groups to pursue their underlying political objectives' (Rowley, 1992, p. 81). The field is thus left open largely for the interest (pressure) groups. Any given group will, of course, engage in political action to secure legislatively bestowed special interest, such as licence, tariff or quota, which, although imposing a small individual cost on a large number of other voters, generates substantial benefits for the relatively small number of interest group members.

The problem with such interest group activity is that (a) it causes considerable waste in resources devoted to obtaining, or defending against, rent-seeking, (b) it results in serious distortion in the allocation of resources. The distortion is caused primarily by the large variation across industries in the transaction costs of collective political action. The trade that stands the greatest chance of securing for itself monopoly privileges via legislation is the one that faces the smallest cost of political organization. Adam Smith clearly recognized this phenomenon in his own day:

> Country gentlemen and farmers, dispersed in different parts of the country, cannot so easily combine as merchants and manufacturers, who being collected into towns, and accustomed to that exclusive corporation spirit which prevails in them, naturally endeavour to obtain against all their countrymen, the same exclusive privilege which they generally possess against the inhabitants of their respective towns. They accordingly seem to have been the original inventors of those restraints upon the importation of foreign goods which secure to them the monopoly of the home market. (1976a, p. 462)

Because of this asymmetry also 'the law gave a monopoly to our bootmakers and shoe-makers, not only against our graziers, but against our tanners' (ibid., p. 654–5).

There is implicit recognition too, in Smith, of the observation by Gordon Tullock (1967), that the excess costs of monopoly also take the form of defensive lobbying by its potential *victims* who are opposed to existing monopolies or proposals (petitions) for new ones. Tanners, for instance, who were less dispersed than graziers, began to retaliate politically and were eventually successful.

> By subsequent statutes, our tanners have got themselves exempted from this monopoly, upon paying a small tax of only one shilling on the hundred

weight of tanned leather...Our graziers still continue subject to the old monopoly. (1976a, p. 653)

With respect to the possibility of purchasers of products taking the offensive and lobbying to obtain monopsony power, Smith reports one conspicuous example. The woollen manufacturers had successfully lobbied parliament to legislate severe restrictions against the export of wool. The ostensible reason was based on the mercantilist argument that universally recognized fine cloth could be made with the use of English wool only. If, therefore, the export of it could be totally prevented, England could monopolize almost the whole woollen trade of the world. Even if the advocates of this reasoning were correct in their assumption that English wool was the best (which Smith denied), the benefits of the export restriction would accrue not to all citizens in England, but to the wool manufacturers exclusively; for the consequence of the export restrictions was a lower (quasi-monopsonistic) price of wool to the manufacturer buyers.

> Our woollen manufacturers have been more successful than any other class of workmen, in persuading the legislature that the prosperity of the nation depended upon the success and extension of their particular business. They have not only obtained a monopoly against the consumers by an absolute prohibition of importing woollen cloths from any foreign country; but they have likewise obtained another monopoly against the sheep farmers and growers of wool, by a similar prohibition of the exportation of live sheep and wool...The effect of these regulations has been to depress the price of English wool, not only below what it would naturally be in the present times, but very much below what it actually was in the time of Edward III ... To depress the price of this commodity below what may be called its natural and proper price, was the avowed purpose of those regulations; and there seems no doubt of their having produced the effect that was expected of them. (1976a, pp. 647, 651–2)

There has been considerable debate concerning the current size of the waste involved in rent-seeking. Empirical analysis in 1988, however, demonstrated that the dissipation of wealth as a consequence of rent-seeking is several orders of magnitude larger than any losses through allocative inefficiency (Laband and Sophocleus, 1988; Gwartney and Wagner, 1988). Arguably, therefore, Adam Smith's intuition that economic growth was significantly checked by the costs of rent-seeking seems to have been reasonably founded.

Not all schools of thought agree with that of Virginia Political Economy. Its most vocal opponent is the Chicago Political Economy group (Rowley, 1992, pp. 69–76). One member of this school indeed recently argued that 'democratic political markets are organized to promote wealth-maximizing outcomes' (Wittman, 1989, pp. 1395–6). Paradoxically, while Wittman's work was entirely non-empirical, it was accepted for publication in the most highly regarded journal of the Chicago school, which contains the world's most empirically-oriented economists (Rowley 1992, p. 72).

One distinguished older member of the Chicago school, Milton Friedman, seems to be an exception in this context. He has recently pointed to the example of one Asian country which apparently comes closer to his ideal market economy than does modern America. Hong Kong, Friedman observes, has had considerably more economic freedom than the US since the 1950s. There have been no tariffs and no import or export quotas except those such as textile export quotas forced upon Hong Kong by US protectionists. Taxes in Hong Kong have ranged between 10 and 20 per cent of the national income, which is very much lower than in the US where government spending is now about 44 per cent of the national income. Besides this there has been an absence of price controls, and Hong Kong has not had America's minimum wage laws. Meanwhile there has been little evidence of the suppression of human freedoms such as freedom of speech and the press. All this has happened despite the absence of democratic political representation. And most impressive of all, the level of per capita income in Hong Kong has quadrupled since the 1950s despite a tenfold increase of population and the absence of anything in the way of foreign aid (Friedman, 1992).

Friedman finds a remarkable contrast over this period between Hong Kong and India. The latter country, he says, received political freedom from the British but subsequently witnessed little in the way of economic freedom. The democracy established in India was used subsequently to churn out legislation that imposed extensive controls over imports, exports, foreign exchange, prices and wages. The result, Friedman argues, is that the standard of life for the great bulk of the Indians has hardly risen compared with 40 years ago. The Friedman disposition to look at events in this way is surely closer to Adam Smith than to the current Chicago Political Economy group.

Jacob Viner (1958, p. 85) once observed that Smith believed in some degree of representation in the law-making authority, although his criteria of representation were not fully democratic ones. The fact is that Smith was not opposed to constitutional democracy altogether, but he was more concerned with the establishment of general laws that laid down the permanent limits to the coercive powers of government than with the precise voting rules within them. He was convinced, nevertheless, that the other extreme of arbitrary monarchical despotism had to be ruled out. To some extent, Smith seems to have had much in common with the Founding Fathers of the American constitution, which was a preference for a blend of republicanism and democracy. In a 'full democracy' the will of the people, or 'popular passion', as 18th-century writers like Smith were apt to call it, unfortunately reigns supreme. What the Founding Fathers were seeking was a constitution wherein it is not the will of the people that predominates but a *rational consensus*. And it is this which is implicit in the term 'consent'. Such a republic, if ruled by wise men, could enjoy a liberty that is not threatened by tyrannical majorities. Meanwhile, in 18th-century Europe, Smith saw residual advantages occurring in some prevailing monarchies, especially those that contained a blend of limited democracy or republicanism.

Some writers believe that what matters to Smith is not so much the form of government as the presence of justice and the degree of civilization (Forbes, 1975, p. 198). Smith maintained that several contemporary monarchies provided what he called 'good government', and the key to this was the guarantee of liberty and security of individuals and their property. At the same time, Smith is on record as saying that some development of representative institutions is a necessary security for free government. The 'representatives' he had in mind, however, were the country's most distinguished individuals or what he called 'the leading men of society' (1976a, p. 621). The combination of a wise monarch and selected eminent members of society provided the best chance of political stability and consequently economic progress. Smith did not look for his 'leading men', in a favoured hereditary nobility. The privileged aristocracy, as in Scotland, was always oppressive, whereas 'No oppressive aristocracy has ever prevailed in the colonies' (1976a, p. 944). The colonies of New England, Smith repeatedly observed, were particularly well governed.

Ultimately then, Smith appears to have adopted the Blackstonian opinion of the British constitution as a 'happy mixture of all the different forms of government properly restrained'. In practice, according to Forbes (1975), it was largely a question of maintaining the balance between 'the influence of the crown' and the 'force of the democracy', between the 'monarchical and democratic parts of the constitution' (1976a, p. 625). In *The Wealth of Nations* there is recognition of a gradation of freedom (despotism) applying to any real world government. The gradation was high in New England but less so in Britain. 'Even in Britain it is but a very figurative consent we have [to taxation], for the number of voters is nothing to that of the people' (Smith, 1977, p. 94). But even without an extended franchise, the degree of liberty in Britain was tolerable. The implication is that any positive degree of discretion available to the constitutional monarchy has to be employed with justice and restraint. As further examples of the gradation of freedom across different countries, Smith observes that the French government, 'though arbitrary and violent in comparison with that of Great Britain, is legal and free in comparison with those of Spain and Portugal' (1976a, p. 586).

This survey of the setting in which Smith considered the different types of government obviously shows the importance of the 18th-century context in which he wrote. It will be maintained, nevertheless, that there are threads of reasoning that can be described as being consistent with some of the findings of the late 20th century discipline of economics and public choice. And this despite the potential criticisms of the Whig-Historical perspective that has already been described and against which this chapter is trying to guard.

As already shown, there is a 'modern' flavour in Smith in his drawing the connection between majority voting and what we now call 'rent-seeking'. His stressing, meanwhile, of the importance of a well-designed constitution or legal framework to underpin individual liberty and freedom of contract is consistent with modern 'public choice' literature such as Buchanan and Tullock's *Calculus of Consent* (1962). But consider, too, the modern argument of some economists that democracy unleashes excessive pressures for immediate consumption (Huntingdon and Dominguez, 1975). Such 'explosion of consumption', they insist, reduces investment demand and thereby retards growth. Smith may well have had this sequence of thoughts in his mind when he associated democracies with 'thoughtless extravagance'. But what are the alternatives? It will be argued by other economists that the non-democratic countries in the 20th century have had even worse consequences for growth; witness the recent failures of several Latin American authoritarian regimes and those of the Eastern European communist countries. The evidence here, nevertheless, remains mixed. One is obliged, after all, to include the 'Asian miracles', such as Singapore, Taiwan, South Korea and Hong Kong in any review of the recent record of authoritarianism.

We have to reiterate that Smith appears to have preferred neither full democracy nor despotic monarchy. Instead he envisaged stable societies that were most conducive to growth as having a 'happy mixture' of democracy and monarchy. The element of democracy would encourage liberty or 'utility' while that of mature monarchy would provide what Smith called 'authority' or order and justice.[2] The latter point has a bearing on the proposition that an element of authoritarianism or 'command' in society can usefully act as some check on the 'excessive' pressure by the populace for present over future consumption. Przeworski and Limongi (1993) insist, however, that this argument is incomplete because it fails to answer why the authoritarian leaders would behave in the interests, long-run or short-term ones, of anyone else. Smith had an answer which, although no doubt more relevant to his own time, seems at least to be consistent. The mature 'dynastic' monarchy, Smith appears to be saying, would operate in its long-term interests and these include growth of the national product and the consequent happiness of the people. In the competitive and dynamic economy the benefits of 'universal opulence' and growth would (and had done so in recent history) 'extend itself to the lowest ranks of the people' (1976a, p. 22). The 'game' being played between the king and his subjects was cooperative, not competitive. This was largely the French model of monarchy in which 'The sovereign himself can never have either interest or inclination to pervert the order of justice, or to oppress the great body of people' (1976a, p. 586).

Smith versus Locke

Like Hume, Smith objected to John Locke's theory of political obligation which uncompromisingly excluded the 'civilized' monarchies of modern Europe. Smith and Hume took the European monarchies as they found them and concluded that typically they had a relatively high degree or 'gradation' of liberty and respect for law and order. It is Locke who would have been sympathetic with Przeworski and Limongi's question in 1993 (above) as to why authoritarian leaders would behave in the interests of others in society, 'As if when men quitting the State of Nature entered into Society, they agreed that all of them but one, should be under the restraint of Laws, but that he should still retain all the Liberty of the State of Nature, increased with Power, and made licentious by Impunity' (Locke, 1988, p. 93).

But even assuming that self-interest is universal, Smith would have contended that a monarch who made a credible commitment to the support of liberty and respect for contracts would soon see that this stable environment increased the wealth of his nation to the *mutual* benefit of king and subjects. Compare this with Locke who argued that 'Greatness may...keep those Animals [subjects] from hurting or destroying one another who labor and drudge only for his Pleasure and Advantage, and so are taken care of, not out of any Love the Master has for them, but Love of himself, and the Profit they bring him' (1988, p. 93). Smith would deny that the 'animals' (subjects), laboured *only* for the monarch's pleasure. The monarch would grant the true liberty that views individuals as ends in themselves. He would know that only positive-sum cooperative behaviour could bring lasting benefits for each participant, the royal leader bringing 'profits' to his subjects as well as vice versa.

The ultimate choice between these contrasting positions is not the simplest of tasks, especially if we confine ourselves to the a priori nature of the arguments. The least that can be said is that a systematic appeal to evidence is necessary before further progress can be made. For their part, both Smith and Hume regarded the evidence of their day on the whole supportive of their reasoning. They conceded that real world monarchies were not perfect and that they certainly contained substantial elements of authoritarianism. But in effect their habit was to ask about any criticisms of monarchies, 'compared with what?'.

Locke was no doubt less thorough and wide-ranging in his empiricism than Hume, the later historian and 'European'. But even Hume's empirics and sources of evidence leave much to be desired for today's standards. So ultimately one must conclude with a call for still more evidence and for continuing research both historical and contemporary. Meanwhile, however, Locke on the one hand, and Smith/Hume on the other, deserve the credit for at least stating their (testable) hypotheses in fairly clear terms.

Government Improves with the Expansion of Commerce

Another testable hypothesis in Smith is his proposition that 'order and good government' increase with the growth of commerce and economic output generally. In *The Wealth of Nations* Hume is said to have been 'the only writer' so far to have noticed this connection. And while Hume's conclusion was simply based on his wide-ranging historical survey, Smith followed up with a sociological explanation of the phenomenon. The power of both the barons and the clergy was gradually eroded with economic progress. This unintended effect is explained by Smith to have been the result simply of these previously dominant individuals slowly bargaining away their power so as to purchase more and more of the novel and often ostentatious goods that the dynamic free enterprise system was producing:

> The gradual improvements of arts, manufacturers, and commerce, the same causes which destroyed the power of the great barons, destroyed in the same manner, through the greater part of Europe, the whole temporal power of the clergy. In the produce of arts, manufactures, and commerce, the clergy, like the great barons, found something for which they could exchange their rude produce, and thereby discovered the means of spending their whole revenues upon their own persons, without giving any considerable share of them to other people. Their charity became gradually less extensive, their hospitality less liberal or less profuse. Their retainers became consequently less numerous, and by degrees dwindled away altogether. The clergy, too, like the great barons, wished to get a better rent from their landed estates, in order to spend it, in the same manner, upon the gratification of their own private vanity and folly. But this increase of rent could be got only by granting leases to their tenants, who thereby became in a great measure independent of them. (1976a, p. 803)

But whether or not Smith's explanation of the phenomenon is persuasive, the proposition that he and Hume present of a correlation between economic growth and order-plus-good-government seems, at least at first sight, to lend itself more readily to empirical tests. In this respect it is interesting that in their 1993 survey Przeworski and Limongi conclude that their statistical studies invariably show that the level of economic development, measured by a variety of indicators, is indeed positively related to the incidence of stable democratic regimes: 'The *prima facie* evidence in support of this hypothesis is overwhelming: all developed countries in the world constitute stable democracies while stable democracies in the less developed countries remain exceptional (p. 62).

One can, of course, debate whether this finding unambiguously supports Smith's position since, as described previously, he was dubious about several aspects of democracy. Nevertheless, since the above empirical conclusions relate to *stable* democracies, there could well be some connection at least with Smith's prediction that economic progress brings *order* as well as 'good government' to countries.

Wealth via Liberty: The Crucial Smithian Factor

The modern evidence referred to so far relates to Smith's central pronouncements only indirectly. This is partly due to the fact that he was absorbed and preoccupied with the institutions that were peculiar to his late 18th century. It would certainly be difficult and not very meaningful today to find any substantial data pertaining to Smith's ideal polities featuring his optimal balance of monarchy and democracy.

There remains, however, the most important, but as yet largely unexplored, avenue. If we focus on the ultimate social ingredient of Smith's economically progressive states, we must proceed immediately, not to an examination of different regimes (republicism, democracy, monarchy), but directly to the reputation and record of *liberty* in each country. The overwhelming and prior importance of liberty was expressed by Smith as follows:

> All systems either of preference or of restraint, therefore, being thus completely taken away, the obvious and simple system of natural liberty establishes itself of its own accord. Every man, as long as he does not violate the laws of justice, is left perfectly free to pursue his own interest in his own way, and to bring both his industry and capital into competition with those of any other man, or order of men. The sovereign is completely discharged from a duty, in the attempting to perform which he must always be exposed to innumerable delusions and for the proper performance of which no human wisdom or knowledge could ever be sufficient; the duty of superintending the industry of private people, and of directing it towards the employments most suitable to the interest of the society. (1976a, p. 687)

Many suggested interpretations have been made about Smith's adjective 'natural' that describes liberty. A closer reading of the last quotation suggests, nevertheless, that it is *economic* liberty that is of leading importance. And to test formally for its presence one needs data for as many countries and as many dimensions of economic liberty as possible. In their recent article, Scully and Slottje (1991) selected a total of 15 attributes of economic freedom. These included freedoms of property, international financial transactions, movement, information, peaceful assembly, and communication through the print media. A special feature of the analysis was the weighting of the attributes in their construction of an index of economic liberty.[3] After proceeding to construct a number of summary indexes of economic liberty, using weighting methods, Scully and Slottje found each of them to be robust. All the rankings indicated that economic growth and real domestic product per capita are positively correlated with economic liberty. This empirical work, completed almost exactly two centuries after Smith's demise, appears then to demonstrate that *the* central proposition in *The Wealth of Nations* not only lends itself to empirical refutation (and can therefore be classified as scientific), but has so far withstood the test.

Notes

1. It is interesting that John Rawls (1971) concedes (p. 356, n.15) that majority rule violates liberty.
2. Smith, the ultra advocate of the benefits of the division of labour was consistent in emphasizing that the task of government itself was to a large extent better done by 'specialists in the trade' such as royal personages who had been brought up to it. The scandalous story of the British East India Company was used to drive home his point. Referring to the company's courts of directors, Smith concluded: 'But it seems impossible...to render those courts in any respect, fit to govern, or even to share in the government of a great empire; because the greater part of their members must always have too little interest in the prosperity of that empire, to give any attention to what may promote it' (1976a, p. 752). 'No two characters seem more inconsistent than those of trader and sovereign' (1976a, p. 819).
3. One method used was weighting by the variance in the attributes of liberty or principle component analysis. A second method used an instrumental variable (hedonic) approach and weighted by the regression coefficient.

3. Virtue, Citizenship and Civilized Monarchies

Several analysts (see especially Winch, 1978) might argue that the picture of Smith, so far presented here, appears to have neglected 'politics' in the Aristotleian sense, or as normally defined, and has overemphasized the economic to the detriment of moral themes in Smith. Is it really true, such writers will ask, that Smith's work meant that for the first time in the history of political philosophy, economy came to completely dominate, if not displace, polity? The preoccupation with the self-interest of *The Wealth of Nations* might have caused us to forget the strong role of sympathy in his *The Theory of Moral Sentiments*. Surely there is something more in Smith than a simple recommendation of the nightwatchman state enjoying a strong legal framework wherein the invisible hand has the 'run of the house'. We should not forget that an important part of his literary plans that Smith left unfulfilled (see the penultimate sentence in *Moral Sentiments*[1]) was his intended presentation of a science of jurisprudence in the form of an account of the general principles of law and government and their evolution through time. And we should take every opportunity to follow up clues on this missing work from the newly discovered student notes of his Glasgow lectures.

One can readily agree with much of this commentary. It is certainly important not to confine one's attention exclusively to *The Wealth of Nations* if the objective is to obtain a comprehensive and well-balanced interpretation of its author. But at least one attempt has already been made in this book to place Smith in some substantial historical context. His emphasis on reliance of the 'leading men' of society outside a privileged heredity nobility has already been referred to. Such leaders are prompted by something more than narrow self-interest, and that additional something could, indeed, be partly rooted in the classical renaissance role of 'political virtue'.

In his study of classical renaissance republicanism or civic humanism, Pocock (1971 and 1975) describes an 18th-century tension be-

tween 'Court' and 'Country' whereby the former comprises participants in corruption and influence-peddling in parliament, while the
latter consisted of the opposing 'Whigs' who were usually independent
men of landed property. The latter were attempting to combat the
asymmetric power of the Court by insisting on a constitution resting on
the true separation of powers and guarantees of liberty. While Smith
was well aware of the current tension, he apparently tried to distance
himself somewhat from the prevailing 'factions'. It was his endeavour,
after all, to conduct a dispassionate, arm's length, or scientific study of
social and political phenomena, hence the title of 'Sceptical Whig' that
some writers, following Forbes (1975), think fit to apply.

This detached and reflective Smith appears not content to leave the
construction of the constitution entirely to the unintended effects of an
invisible hand. From Smith's review of history he could distil *some* role
to be played by virtue, patriotism and citizenship in any successful
society. Smith's two psychological principles of political obligation
were utility and authority. In his monarchy–republic dualism, the latter
represented utility and the former represented authority. Smith always
spoke approvingly of 'civilized monarchies' and from his historical
surveys he was convinced that the risk of absolutism becoming uncivi-
lized despotism usually occurred when discretionary powers were con-
ferred on subordinate bodies. The growth of commerce was associated
with the emergence of *royal*, not delegated, absolutism and this, in turn,
was initially the best relative protector of liberty. The simultaneous
emergence of the separation of powers, Smith believed (with
Montesquieu), was, of course, another great advantage which modern
times had over ancient.

Detaching himself from his tutor, Hutcheson, on the issue of Locke's
theory of voluntary contract and tacit consent, Smith proceeded to
search for his own account of the emergence of political systems with
the progress of society. And he wanted to do this by systematically
recording the causal connections between precise historical facts sur-
rounding the same evolution. The emphasis, in other words, was more
on positive than normative analysis, although these terms themselves,
as Winch reminds us, are post-18th century.

Smith's study of the effects of liberty on economic prosperity has
been well discussed in the literature, and we have shown that modern
empirical work offers substantial support to the idea. According to
Winch (1978), however, Smith's grasp of the equally significant effects
of commerce on liberty have been neglected. This theme, which had

already been delineated by Smith's predecessors Montesquieu, Hume, and other Scottish historians of civil society such as Kames, Ferguson, and Millar, was given a particularly Smithian 'twist'. The focus in *The Wealth of Nations* is upon unintended consequences of individual actions in the past. Thus the commercial revolution was an unexpected consequence of the pursuit of vanity by the barons (see chapter 2). It was favourable to liberty because it destroyed a source of arbitrary power. But once Smith envisioned the final flourishing of commerce, was this really the ultimate fulfilment of things? Before answering this question it will be helpful to look closer at the suggestion of close connections with Smith's work and the tradition of civic humanism.

Civic Humanism

At this point it will be convenient to discuss in a little detail the proposition of some writers that the concept of civic humanism in Smith has been neglected by modern interpreters while the dominant attention has been placed on *homo oeconomicus*. A reading of the *Theory of Moral Sentiments* leaves no doubt about the presence of 'humanism' in Smith. Somewhat more debatable, however, is the use of the adjective 'civic' to describe it. The definition of 'civic' is that which pertains to citizens or citizenship. This leads us to enquire how much of the average low-income individual's time did Smith consider to be ideally devoted to being a citizen in the sense of attending public meetings, participating in council chamber voting, and generally debating in the Aristotleian fashion. If we read Smith himself on the subject of citizenship he certainly sees it as important, but not so much in the way just described. Smith's good citizen is typically at his place of work and outside the council chamber. 'Good citizenship' can still be practised in one's workplace and neighbourhood. It consists largely in being orderly, respectful and helpful to others: 'He is not a citizen who is not disposed to respect the laws and to obey the civil magistrate; and he is certainly not a good citizen who does not wish to promote, by every means in his power, the welfare of the whole society of his fellow-citizens' (1976b, p. 231). The 'whole society', of which Smith speaks, is very widespread indeed:

> Man, according to the Stoics, ought to regard himself, not as something separated and detached, but as a citizen of the world, a member of the vast commonwealth of nature ... We should view ourselves, not in the light in

which our own selfish passions are apt to place us, but in the light in which any other citizen of the world would view us. (1976b, p. 140)

In this perspective, Smithian 'civic' or 'citizen' virtue consists largely of a positive disposition or outlook. And it is one that can indeed be described as virtuous in the Greek sense. But how far is this citizenship dimension completely detachable from Smith's 'economistic' individual of the market place? One example shows that such detachability is not possible. Citizens of the world are not as closely tied to each other as are individuals within the immediate circle of family and friends. If unknown persons across the seas had to rely on our benevolence for what they received, Smith argued, they would never be supplied. In most cases the market, operating via the pursuit of self-interest, is the only way to secure the global cooperations of individuals in the production of goods and services. Government provision, at least of private goods, is not the answer. Even when motivated by benevolence, the politician's actions will tend to favour his immediate supporters and will not result in the *general* good. The invisible hand of the market sees to it that the unknown and unimportant will have their wants served along with those of others. Citizenship of the world and market participation thus converge.

It would be improper, however, to conclude that *world* citizenship was the only outlet for 'public spirit' in Smith. The world consists of several countries and each one requires a constitution that guarantees the rule of law and individual freedom. Those with the greatest public spirit are the intellectuals who volunteered their creative genius to the construction of an appropriate set of general rules for the benefit of all their fellow citizens. The leader of a successful political party, Smith tells us, may sometimes be of service to his country in a much more important way than achieving foreign conquests: 'He may re-establish and improve the constitution, and from the very doubtful and ambiguous character of the leader of a party, he may assume the greatest and noblest of all characters, that of the reformer and legislator of a great state: and, by the wisdom of his institutions, secure the internal tranquillity and happiness of his fellow-citizens for many succeeding generations' (1976b, p. 232). It is clear that in Smith's view the ideal legislator should be strongly endowed with beneficence, or what he calls in the political context, a 'public spirit'.

The danger is, however, that public spirit often becomes swamped by other dispositions. Man's natural obsession with the niceties of mechanical contrivances and his love of mechanisms for their own sake, for instance, will frustrate or side-track his public spirit. The 'spirit of system' was apt to compete with public spirit, which *par excellence* was founded 'upon the love of humanity, upon a real fellow feeling...'. The 'spirit of system' was the insatiable desire of the planner to construct society like a machine.

> This spirit of system commonly takes the direction of that more gentle public spirit, always animates it, and often inflames it, even to the madness of fanaticism...The great body of the party are commonly intoxicated with the imaginary beauty of this ideal system, of which they have no experience, but which has been represented to them in all the most dazzling colours in which the eloquence of their leaders could paint it. Those leaders themselves, though they originally may have meant nothing but their own aggrandisement, become, many of them in time, the dupes of their own sophistry, and are as eager for this great reformation as the weakest and foolest of their followers. Even though the leaders should have preserved their own heads, as, indeed, they commonly do, free from this fanaticism, yet they dare not always disappoint the expectation of their followers, but are often obliged, though contrary to their principle and their conscience, to act as if they were under the common delusion. (1976b, p. 232)

Thus while it is relatively easy to discuss and aspire to classical republicanism, it faces serious problems of implementation which perhaps were not sufficiently analysed before Smith. Not only were there stubborn public prejudices standing in the way, there was also the competition of would-be constitution-makers who believed that they too were practising the highest civic or public virtue when in fact their public spirit was somewhat tainted with excessive enthusiasm and dogma. The man whose public spirit was not so tainted, but was prompted by true benevolence, would act with tactful diplomacy and go along with some of the imperfect constructions of society, 'moderating what he often cannot annihilate without great violence'. 'He will accommodate, as well as he can, his public arrangements to the confirmed habits and prejudices of the people, and will remedy, as well as he can, the inconveniences which may flow from the want of those regulations which the people are averse to submit to' (1976b, V1. ii. 2. 16).

The 'man of system', in contrast, was 'wise in his own conceit':

> he seems to imagine that he can arrange the different members of a great society with as much ease as the hand arranges the different pieces upon a

> chess-board; he does not consider that the pieces upon the chess-board have no other principle of motion besides that which the hand impresses upon them; but that, in the great chess-board of human society, every single piece has a principle of motion of its own, altogether different from that which the legislator might choose to impress upon it. (1976b, p. 233, 234)

Some planning, some erection of rules of justice, was of course necessary. And some element of vision of perfect policy and law was helpful. But to make impatient clamour to establish it all at once was to display the highest degree of arrogance:

> It is to erect his own judgement into the supreme standard of right and wrong. It is to fancy himself the only wise and worthy man in the commonwealth, and that his fellow-citizens should accommodate themselves to him, and not he to them. (1976b, p. 234)

Smith was no believer in the inevitability of progress. The pieces of the chess-board moved according to the principle of self-direction and also the principle of the pressure of the planner's hand. Things could go either way:

> if those two principles coincide and act in the same direction, the game of human society will go on easily and harmoniously, and is very likely to be happy and successful. If they are opposite or different, the game will go on miserably, and the society must be at all times in the highest degree of disorder. (1976b, p. 234)

As further evidence that Smith was urging calm and dispassionate reflection as necessary qualities in the constitution-making task, we find him appealing to the public spirit of the 'leading men' of philosophy:

> Nothing tends so much to promote public spirit as the study of politics, of the several systems of civil government, their advantages and disadvantages, of the constitution of our own country, its situation, and interest with regard to foreign nations, its commerce, its defence, the disadvantages it labours under, the dangers to which it is exposed, how to remove the one, and guard against the other. Upon this account political disquisitions, if just, and reasonable, and practicable, are of all the works of speculation the most useful. Even the weakest and worst of them are not altogether without their utility. They serve at least to animate the public passions of men, and rouse them to seek out the means of promoting the happiness of the society. (1976b, p. 186)

A reasonable conclusion from all these quotations is that Smith starts out in the classical republican tradition and with some emphasis on the Greek virtues, but pioneers his way through to his own social science approach. From an initial suggestion as to what the good society *should* look like he begins to concentrate on what is practical, expedient and viable in an imperfect society. His knowledge of the world's shortcomings, meanwhile, was derived from his and Hume's wide survey of history. And it was largely from the same source that he arrived at judgements as to what will work in practice. Civilized monarchies were one example. John Locke's complete dismissal of monarchies was too hasty and too 'rational'. The independent line of thought which seems to have been breaking through here goes under the heading of political theory. As we have seen, the developing focus was upon devising a set of rules, a 'system of justice', upon which mankind could live in concord. Men could not passively rely on some invisible hand to do this, they had to do it consciously for themselves. Smith did not entertain that kind of conservative political philosophy which believes that constitutions appear by some mystical process. True, we often respect those constitutions that we inherit; but the respect is directed not so much at Nature as at the accumulated wisdom of our predecessors.

It was this aspect of Smith that provoked disagreement from Carl Menger in the 19th century. To him the state, like language, law, money and markets, was not typically the intended legislative product of society's common will, but instead was 'the unintended result of social development' (1985, p. 147). A search for reasons to explain such important, but unintended, results was, for Menger, as for Friedrich Hayek (1945, p. 527) and Karl Popper (1965, p. 342), the central challenge facing social science. More recent discussion, however, questions whether intentional and unintentional phenomena justify complete separation. Selective intentional (constructivist) behaviour, it is now explicitly argued, can *support* spontaneous (unintentional) order. (Williamson, 1994, pp. 323, 325; Buchanan, 1975, p. 183, fn.13). It is these latter writers who appear to be following closest in Smith's footsteps.

In examining this process of constitution-building, Smith almost stumbles upon important positive, as distinct from normative, propositions. For instance, in part II, section II of *Moral Sentiments* he starts with the Greek-like assertion that man can subsist happily only in society and that this will flourish where love, friendship and gratitude prevail. Smith then leads himself into the consideration of whether a society could subsist even without these positive virtues and concludes that it could: 'Society may subsist among *different* men as among different merchants, from a sense of its utility, without any mutual love or affection; and though no man in it should owe any obligation, or be bound in gratitude to any other, it may still be upheld by a mercenary exchange of good offices according to an agreed valuation' (emphasis added).[2] Smith was not saying that society can subsist among those who are ready to hurt each other; only that positive mutual affection is not a necessary condition: 'If there is any society among robbers and murderers, they must at least, according to the trite observation, abstain from robbery and murdering one another' (ibid.).

This peculiarly Smithian departure from his inherited Greek traditions of thought is the emerging political analogue of his mutual-benefit-by-exchange theme of his 'self-interest' economics. By such 'calculus of consent' argument Smith reveals his grasp of a truth which is not theological or even scientific, but essentially political.[3] Politics, in the functional or constitutional sense, as distinct from the Greek idealist sense, is about consensus, not about visions of the 'complete jigsaw' of a virtuously perfect and comprehensive state (Buchanan, 1967). A constitution can be expected to emerge, Smith now argues, whose function it is simply to allow the coexistence of heterogeneous people. In the 'great chess-board of human society', Smith tells us, 'every single piece *has a principle motion of its own*' (1976b, p. 234, emphasis added).

The interesting fact, meanwhile, is that the sceptical Whig and other sceptics can accept the proposition as it stands shorn of any Deistic or other implications. For they will acknowledge as many 'worlds' in a given legal constitution as there are individual members in it; such a constitution, in other words, is seen by the sceptic not as *the* good society but simply as a mechanism for tolerant interaction of almost as many 'good societies' as there are individuals or groups within it.

Although certainly somewhat spasmodic, the above quotations of Smith do suggest that his thought was moving in this politically individualistic direction, a direction which was in some conflict with the earlier classical Greek influences on him. Smith, the believer in 'natural liberty', was clearly beginning to acknowledge a kind of pragmatic negative liberty which sees politics, in the constitution-making sense, as an attempt to reach compromise between individuals with admittedly different values. He had arrived, in other words, at the threshold of the open society. But to travel further there was yet *some* surviving need of classical ethics. The world, after all, still needed the 'public spirit' that could motivate the most reliable architects of required changes in the constitution.

Notes

1. Smith's sentence reads as follows:

    I shall in another discourse endeavour to give an account of the general principles of law and government, and of the different revolutions they have undergone in the different ages and periods of society, not only in what concerns justice, but in what concerns police, revenue, and arms, and whatever else is the object of law. (1976b, p. 342)
2. This whole argument is contained in *The Theory of Moral Sentiments* in the opening three paragraphs of part II, section II, chapter III (1976b, p. 86).
3. Buchanan and Tullock in their *Calculus of Consent* (1962) have developed in much stimulating detail this strand of Smithian thought.

4. Smith's Reservations about the Age of Commerce: The Question of Alienation

Once the commercial revolution eliminated gross forms of dependency on the barons and the clergy, were there any remaining barriers to the flourishing of individuals? Are we really to believe the idea that Smith was content, without any qualifications, to look forward to a simple harmony of egoisms through *laissez-faire* and the invisible hand? Most observers agree that Smith had several reservations. Disagreement remains, however, as to their *degree* of importance in his overall final judgement.

One Smithian reservation relates to the adverse effects of the division of labour. Winch (1978) quotes from Smith's *Lectures*: 'The minds of men are contracted and rendered incapable of elevation. Education is despised, or at least neglected, and heroic spirit is almost utterly extinguished' (1977, pp. 255–9, 261). Although Winch maintains that the modern word 'alienation' is not entirely appropriate to such diagnosis, it was his mentor Jacob Viner who pioneered the application to Smith and most current writers seem comfortable with the term.[1]

Smith's prescription for intervention in education starts out being based, among other things, on a desire to encourage a martial spirit. And in addition to his concern for the deleterious effect of the factory environment on morals, he was just as disturbed by the spread of urbanization that accompanied the division of labour. Since a worker in large towns was less under the eye of the 'impartial spectator' of social opinion than was his counterpart in the village, the need for education here was the greatest of all.

Alienation implies a deviation from some 'true' path or 'human fulfilment'. The concept therefore calls for each writer's view, or theory, of *the state of not being alienated*. To represent the 'norm' we need a phrase such as 'normal alienation' or 'neutral alienation'. But even this must be a relative term comparing 'alienation' with what we can call the 'non-alienated state'.

Since we do not, and apparently cannot, live in conditions of abundance, we must choose our social organization from the lesser of the evils or 'imperfections'. For example, it was too often assumed in the past that the 'socialist society', as distinct from Smith's 'commercial society', has no such 'imperfections' and is certainly not marred by alienation. This 'theory' implies that only in a world without what Marx called the commodity mode of production and exchange (i.e. the socialist society) does alienation completely disappear. Yet this is unsupported by empirical evidence (West, 1969, p. 17). Marxists, moreover, have failed to offer any clear practical solution to the 'alienation problem', a problem that is allegedly one of the main justifications for the socialist revolution. Factories, with identical industrial processes continue to feature in both socialist and capitalist worlds. Each therefore provides a similar potential at least for technological alienation.

Because Adam Smith acknowledged technological alienation as a 'blemish' in his system, does not imply that he was making a *socialist* (Marxian) criticism. Marx urged the 'cure' of the virtual abolition of private property. Smith's anti-alienation plan, in contrast, was aimed at the *protection* of private property. The policy was expressed via Smith's proposals for publicly supported education. Contending that 'gross ignorance and stupidity' could result from the division of labour and benumb the understandings of all inferior ranks of the people, Smith advocated intervention against 'alienation' in the first place to *protect the state*. Smith urged an education to encourage order, decency, a military spirit, and a respect for government, all of which certainly seems to have the overtones of civic humanism.

> An instructed and intelligent people besides, are always more decent and orderly than an ignorant and stupid one. They feel themselves each individually, more respectable, and more likely to obtain the respect of their lawful superiors, and they are therefore more disposed to respect those superiors. They are more disposed to examine and more capable of seeing through, the interested complaints of faction and sedition, and they are, upon that account, less apt to be misled into any wanton or unnecessary opposition to the measures of government. (1976a, p. 788)

While in Marx's view, government, as an instrument of the ruling class, was a reactionary factor in itself, Smith initially sees government (or the law) as a key instrument for removing 'basic imperfections'. A socialist revolution would presumably have been regarded by him as one of the 'dreadful disorders' or 'enthusiasms' he wanted to educate the public to avoid.

It is interesting also to compare Smith's with Rousseau's idea of alienation. The two writers clearly had opposite notions of the 'non-alienated state'. In Smith it is a social state wherein it is possible to pursue 'art, beauty, and refinement'; in a society that is based on Justice, Prudence, and Benevolence; and populated with individuals who cannot live without 'Wonder, Surprise, and Admiration' (West, 1964). The most important industry of human life is employed 'not in procuring the supply of our three humble necessities, food, clothes, and lodging, but in procuring the conveniences of it according to the nicety and delicacy of our taste' (Smith, 1977, p. 48). The procuring of conveniences, moreover, is best done with the specialist help of one's fellows.

Rousseau's non-alienated man, in contrast, is not much interested in arts and sciences, nor in the assistance of his fellows. The reason is:

> His few wants are so readily supplied, and he is so far from having the knowledge which is needful to make him want more, that he can have neither foresight nor curiosity. (Rousseau, 1968, p. 33)

Whereas Smith's naturally happy and 'unalienated' individual is a social being who needs the sympathy of his fellows, these same qualities to Rousseau are symptomatic of alienation:

> the savage lives in himself; a man of society always out of himself cannot live but in the opinion of others; and it is, if I may say so, from their judgement alone that he derives the sentiment of his own existence.[2]

The disposition to seek the approval of others inevitably produces 'real indifference for good and evil'. Men become deceitful, calculating, and vain: 'everything becomes factitious and acted, honour, friendship, virtue, and often vice itself, of which, we have at last found out the secret of being vain'. Rousseau's 'noble savage', in contrast, experiences real liberty and repose. For the root of alienation in Rousseau, as in Marx, is economic interdependence and exchange based on private property:

> But from the instant in which one man had occasion for the assistance of another, from the moment that he perceived that it could be advantageous to a single person to have provisions for two, equality disappeared, property

was introduced, labour became necessary, and the vast forests of nature were changed into agreeable plains, which must be watered with the sweat of mankind, and in which the world beheld slavery and wretchedness begin to grow up and blossom with the harvest.[3]

In Adam Smith the primitive condition is completely inimicable to *his* 'non-alienated', i.e. social, state:

> Before we can feel much for others, we must in some measure be at ease ourselves. If our own misery pinches us very severely, we have no leisure to attend to that of our neighbour; and all savages are too much occupied with their wants and necessities to give much attention to those of another person. (1976b, p. 205)

Some writers believe that alienation in Smith comes especially in the form of isolation and powerlessness. But the entry into a commercial state (which Smith often equates with 'civilization') fulfilled a necessary condition for a *decrease* in isolation. For it abolished widespread poverty and hunger, and this was necessary (see the last quotation) before an individual could give attention to others.

To Smith, then, unlike Rousseau and Marx, property, wealth, and 'commodity production' are all preconditions for the 'non-alienated state'. And in this state individuals pursue refinement and art:

> I do not mean that improvement of arts and refinement of manners are the necessary consequences of commerce...only that it is a necessary requisite. (1977, p. 132)

Certainly Smith acknowledges that there can be 'excessive' ambition and lust for material gain. Nevertheless, considerable production above subsistence *did* contribute further to happiness and fulfilment in the Smithian philosophy; for production often became a creative activity in itself (West, 1969, p. 22).

Several years ago I drew attention to the fact that in Book I of *The Wealth of Nations* Smith maintains that in the division of labour, by exclusive concentration on one object, workers are 'much more likely to discover easier and readier methods of attaining that object'. Yet, in contrast, in Book V, he argues his 'second view', that when a man performs only a few operations he has *not* occasion 'to exercise his invention in finding out expedients' (West, 1964). Robert Lamb (1973) and Donald Winch (1978) accept Nathan Rosenberg's 1965 reply to this 'paradox', a reply which makes use of Smith's 'historical stages of progress' thesis. According to Rosenberg, when Smith's ultimate stage of the division of labour is reached, the job of inventing falls exclusively into the hands of a few scientific specialists. Rosenberg's argument, however, has its own inconsistency. He does not quarrel with Smith's first view – that the earlier capitalist division of labour encouraged the worker creatively to participate in inventing. So at this stage there must have been a kind of optimum degree of capitalist factory division of labour; and under *it* at least the worker was *non-alienated* (in Smith's sense). But this is not compatible with the 'socialist critique' with which Rosenberg eventually attempts to associate Smith. For, in the opinion of Marx, capitalism, even under an optimum (non-'extreme') division of labour, is still objectionable. The root of this 'critique', to repeat, is commodity production for exchange. In this scenario workers will be alienated under *any degree* of the division of labour.

Smith did recognize that invention might one day become somewhat concentrated in the hands of scientists. It is important, nevertheless, to recognize that to him a commercial society would still be preferable to the alternatives. In the 'rude' society every man has some knowledge, ingenuity, and invention, 'but *scarce any man has a great degree*'.

[In a civilized (commercial) society] ... though there is little variety in the occupations of the greater part of individuals, there is an almost infinite variety in those of the whole society. These varied occupations present an almost infinite variety of objects to the contemplation of those few, who, being attached to no particular occupation themselves have leisure and inclination to examine the occupations of other people. The contemplation of so greater variety of objects necessarily exercises their minds in endless comparisons and combinations, and renders their understandings, in an extraordinary degree, both acute and comprehensive. (1976a, p. 783)

Smith believed it possible that this great prize of scientific excitement in the society as a whole, could and should be shared by the mass of mankind, especially through education. It is certainly erroneous to believe simply that Smith advocated education almost entirely as a means to economic growth. The real end was an active, creative, and absorbed populace. Smith argued that, after education was publicly encouraged, the application in their places of work of the principles of geometry and mechanics would exercise and improve the common people in those principles which were 'the necessary introduction to the most *sublime as well as* to the most useful sciences' (1976a, p. 785, 786).

Despite our above interpretation of Smith's treatment of the aliena-tion problem, some writers remain convinced that it reveals an unre-lenting 'dark side' of his commercial society. Following Heilbroner (1975), Pack (1991) argues that capitalism is for Smith only one level or stage of human development. Capitalism must eventually give way to something else because of its 'downside' in terms of its deleterious effect on character formation. Not only do workers become brutalized and ignorant, but capitalists become 'greedy, devious and manipulative' (p. 159). Pack, however, does not explain that Smith never used the (Marxian) term 'capitalism'.

Similarly Heilbroner (1975) concludes that Smith is admitting that his system of natural liberty, when turned into a *laissez-faire* capitalist economy, eventually leads to moral and economic decay and must be replaced. The Heilbroner of 17 years later, however, is at a considerable loss to recommend any viable alternatives. Noting that Sweden has gained the reputation of being 'capitalism with a human face', never-theless he sadly observes 'its momentum has come to a halt, and it is very difficult to envisage how it can go beyond its present none-too-difficult situation' (Heilbroner, 1992, p. 116).

There follows a tentative exploration of the possibility of going 'beyond Sweden' into a still newer society whose integrating principle would be *participation*:

> The engagement of all citizens in the mutual determination of *every phase* of their economic lives through discussion and voting...[where] widely shared decision-making by discussion and vote displaces decision-making by self-interest alone. ...It assumes that social and economic equality has replaced social and economic inequality as the widely endorsed norm of the society, because equality seems best suited to enable individuals to lead the most rewarding lives they can. (Heilbroner, 1992, p. 117, emphasis added)

It is difficult, however, to take seriously any proposal to make every economic decision a subject for voting. The transaction costs would be enormous. The economy would surely grind to a halt if *every* choice of each individual's clothing, diet, and occupation, for instance, were to be the subject of a 50 per cent majority approval, and this following extended deliberation. With so much human energy and time devoted to defensive and offensive politicking, the growth of the GNP could very soon become negative. And we would then end up with the opposite of Smith's vision of the prosperous and growing society that brings happi-ness to everybody including those in the 'lowest ranks'.

As for equality, even if more of it resulted from Heilbroner's society it could well be in the form of 'the equality of misery'. But there is no guarantee that equality *would* result; for it is naïve to suppose that voting can emasculate self-interest. The use of the political process by well-organized coalitions typically results, as Smith warns us, in costly redistribution to favoured groups and the expense of the rest of society, which usually includes the poor. Meanwhile the 'tyranny of the majority' in such a world constitutes a perpetual threat to liberty. And it was liberty that Smith championed most as the only avenue for individual independence, self-respect and human dignity.

After outlining his preferred 'post-capitalist' social order, Heilbroner, nevertheless, continues:

> Do I therefore think it will be the direction of things during the twenty-first century? I do not. The transition is too difficult, the rearrangements too complex...Participatory economics will not become the social order in the twenty-first century no matter what, catastrophes included. (1992, p. 118)

From this assessment then, it looks as if we shall go into the 21st century with Adam Smith! While ex-socialist countries are returning to his counsel, intellectuals such as Heilbroner are evidently hard put to offer any particular alternative.

Heilbroner's verdict on the alienation problem in *The Wealth of Nations* is accompanied by the assumption that Smith had no solution to it. This is not true. The most conspicuous offered 'cure' of the problem, of course, was Smith's proposal for public education. But if we search and reflect further we shall see that Smith's whole project of a dynamic and growing commercial society contains automatic remedies through time.[4] Recall that Smith stresses that alienation only affects the 'common people'. Those of some rank or fortune 'generally have a good deal of leisure, during which they may perfect themselves in every branch either of useful or ornamental knowledge'. In addition such individuals have the money to afford education. 'It is otherwise with the common people. They have little time to spare for education. Their parents can scarce afford to maintain them even in infancy' (1976a, p. 784). This explanation seems to be at odds with the earlier statement in Smith's *Lectures* that education was 'despised'. Before it can be asserted that individuals are irresponsible in the sense of not choosing education, it must be demonstrated that it is in their power to afford it and to have the necessary leisure for it. The last quotation from Smith, however, denies this.

Since Smith's system of natural liberty foresees steady growth of real income for all classes, it predicts that the ability to obtain education in terms of income and leisure will grow through time. This will at least ensure the necessary condition for private purchases of education. And since, on Smith's argument, alienation will weaken as education increases, one solution to his problem is largely 'built in'. Subsequent evidence in fact unambiguously reveals the steady decline in weekly hours of work (or the increase of leisure) since Smith wrote (Zeisel, 1958). Meanwhile the general conclusion of economic historians is that in Britain in 1850 real wages were about double what they had been in the period 1801–1804 which was a decade after Smith's death (Neale, 1975, p. 173).

Did the increase in individual income and leisure of the 'common people' lead them to purchase education in Britain after Smith's demise in 1790? Henry Brougham's Select Committee reported (in 1820) that in 1818 about 1 in 17 of the population of England and Wales was being schooled. This schooling was paid for largely by working parents. If education is a normal good, we would expect this measure of schooling to increase with the rise in incomes. Brougham's Committee reported that the figures for 1818 were a considerable improvement on 1800 when the earliest estimate was made. In 1828, Brougham in his private capacity followed up the report for 1818 with a 5 per cent sample survey of his own, using the same sources (the parochial clergy) as before. His findings suggested that the number of children in schools had doubled in ten years.

Such evidence alone would challenge the view that tastes for education need to be *imposed*. If education consumption begins to appear and to rise with income, then the most appropriate government strategy might be one or more of the following: (a) redistribution of income, (b) more patience at a time of steady income growth, and (c) concentration on removal of barriers to such growth.

The rising income explanation of education growth implies that, as per capita income increased in the 19th century, schooling grew 'naturally' in response. Table 4.1 demonstrates the growth of schooling in England and Wales prior to it being made free, compulsory and supplied by government.

It is shown that the annual growth of scholars over the period exceeded the annual growth of population. During the compilation of the 1851 educational census, it was reported that the average attendance at school of working-class children was nearly five years. The Newcastle

Table 4.1   Growth in private schooling, 1818–58

Year	Population	Average annual growth rate of population	Number of day scholars	Average annual growth rate of day scholars
1818	11,642,683 ⎤	1.40	674,883 ⎤	3.6
1833	14,386,415 ⎤		1,276,947 ⎤	
1851	17,927,609 ⎦	1.47	2,144,378 ⎦	3.16
1858	19,523,103 ⎦	1.21	2,525,462 ⎦	2.35

Sources: The 1851 census and the 1861 Newcastle Commission.

Commission reported that by 1858 it had risen to nearly six years (see West, 1975, p. 27). And the attainment of a threshold for most people was reported in the 1861 Newcastle Commission's conclusion that 'almost everyone receives some amount of schooling at some period or another'.[5]

It is true that government subsidies to schools were introduced in 1833, but their aggregate value was very low (only £20,000 in 1833). By 1841, they were still so small that they amounted to a sum considerably less than that collected from parents for schooling in the City of Bristol alone. The major 19th-century legislation, of course, came in 1870 when the Forster Act introduced government schools for the first time. Yet by 1869 most people in England and Wales were literate, most children were receiving a schooling and most parents, working class included, were paying fees for it (West, 1970, p. xvii.).

Adam Smith's 'policy recommendations' on education included the suggestion of copying the Scottish parochial school system dating from the Act of 1696. This laid down that a school should be erected in every parish and that teachers' salaries be met by a tax on local heritors and tenants. This schooling, however, was not made compulsory by law; and neither was it made free. The parental fees made up a big part of the teachers' salaries and were paid by every social class. The Scots did not have 'free' and compulsory schooling indeed until about the same time as England did (in the 1880s). Moreover, in 1818 it was the fee-paying private schools that were bearing the main burden of Scottish education in terms of the number of scholars. For every one Scottish parochial school pupil in 1818 there were two non-parochial school pupils. And the latter outnumbered the former by much more than 2 to

1 in the growing industrial areas such as Glasgow – the very areas where Smith argued there was greater need for schooling (West, 1975, chapter 6).

Werhane (1991) argues that Smith's list of failures of *laissez-faire* are not 'acknowledged exceptions' but, rather, failures of the ideal to be realized. 'Smith is neither a Utopian nor a pessimist about his ideal of a political economy' (p. 172). It is well known that Smith was somewhat suspicious of joint-stock companies, yet, Werhane argues, it is unlikely that he could have imagined proletariat ownership and management of an economy: 'He had no confidence in the political or economic judgment of most human beings, either singly or in collective organizations in which responsibility was separated from ownership' (Werhane, 1991, p. 173). In the private schools that catered to the demands of the 'common people' in Scotland at the beginning of the 19th century, responsibility was typically *not* separated from ownership, and their growth, Smith might well have argued, was in no small part due to the natural liberty that (a) allowed them to exist and (b) created the (growing) incomes that helped create the demand for them.[6] It is true that private schools often received private endowments (subsidies) and that Smith was highly critical of them. But the substantial growth of schooling in the Industrial Revolution towns of Scotland such as Greenock, Paisley and Glasgow, was accomplished largely by the so-called 'adventure' (for profit) establishments. The practice of endowing schools was much more prevalent south of the border.

The penultimate paragraph of Smith's long section on public works (1976a, V.ii) deserves more attention than it usually receives. It shows a final balancing of all the arguments reviewed earlier in the same chapter. Although expenditure on institutions for education and religious instruction is no doubt beneficial to the whole society, he concludes, and while it may be defrayed by the general contribution of the whole society, it 'might perhaps with *equal propriety, and even with some advantage, be defrayed altogether* by those who receive the immediate benefit of such education and instruction, or by the *voluntary contribution* of those who think they have occasion for either one or the other' (emphasis added). Smith always wants the parents to pay; and if there is to be some non-parent support Smith relies on *voluntary* contributions from the 'neighbours'. This is *not* therefore an argument in favour of *state* education as so many writers tend to believe.

To conclude this fairly extensive discussion of the issue of alienation, despite the fact that some writers describe Smith's admission of it to be 'one of the strongest indictments of modern capitalist society ever made' (Pack, 1991, p. 144), such criticism, if valid, applies at least as much to socialism and communism as we know it. But as Archibald (1992) has emphasized, there is an important distinction between technologically induced and institutionally induced alienation. The former, which is Smith's version, is simply a product of the division of labour which is to be found in non-capitalist as well as capitalist societies. Institutionally induced alienation is the main complaint of Marx. For him capitalism alienates because it estranges (separates) the worker from his own labour and is therefore fundamentally doomed, whatever the degree of the division of labour. In Smith, in stark contrast, the very ability to separate the workers' productivity and sell it gives them control of their labour and enables them at last to be independent (Werhane, 1991, p. 147).

It is interesting to note, finally, that Smithian (technologically induced) alienation has now been substantially eroded since technological advance has lightened tasks, reduced hours, and improved working conditions; 'few tasks in advanced countries can now be brutalizing in the sense of Smith' (Archibald, 1992, p. 65). But Smith could say that this 'self-correcting' consequence is predictable in his system of natural liberty that improves welfare in all its aspects.

Other Smithian Reservations

Of the list of Smithian failures of *laissez-faire*, the concentration here has been deliberately on the alienation issue because it appears to create the greatest attention, if not excitement. There is no need to pursue the other alleged deficiencies of capitalism that Smith is said to recognize because I have assessed them in detail elsewhere (West, 1990, chapter 7). The remaining examples refer to such subjects as roads, canals, the post-office, the public mints and some aspects of building regulations and banking practices. And it is debateable whether, as Werhane argues, one should treat these as exceptions rather than failures of the ideal to be realized.

What appears to the present author to be undeniable is that 'failures' receive disproportionate attention by several of the critics so that due perspective is often lost. Pack (1991), for instance, is angry with President Reagan for having introduced his policies in the 1980s using the authority of *The Wealth of Nations*. Pack's argument in effect says that because of Smith's numerous and weighty qualifications to the virtues of the invisible hand, he was far less *laissez-faire* than Reagan; and the latter must have known this. Yet to be minimally consistent with the recommended political economy in *The Wealth of Nations*, Reagan would have had to abolish all of the following: minimum wages, export subsidies, marketing boards, capital gains taxes, 'free' education, and the whole US system of central banking. Had Reagan done so he would then indeed have invited the description of an 'extreme advocate of laissez-faire'. But since he didn't, it is difficult to accept Pack's view of Reagan as being more 'extreme' than Smith.

Notes

1. See, for instance, Archibald (1992), Forbes (1975), and Werhane (1991).
2. From Smith's translation in his review of the *Discourse* in *The Edinburgh Review*, 1755, p. 124.
3. Smith's translation, ibid., note 2, p. 132.
4. The ideas in this paragraph are developed much further in West (1996), in which I maintain that because Smith himself had not fully thought through his total position, he involved himself with some contradictions.
5. R.S. Schofield notes that it was '...the opinion of an educator of the time' (the master in charge of the Borough Road School in London pre-1800) that 'it took twelve months to teach a child to read and between three and four years to teach him to write well with some simple arithmetic' (1973).
6. The Scottish lowlands gained the reputation of reaching relatively high levels of literacy at the end of the 18th and beginning of the 19th centuries. The Scottish parochial school system usually receives the main credit for this, yet this is not easily justified when they were so outnumbered by the private schools.

5. Adam Smith and Liberalism

On the question of how far Smith can be considered to be a liberal, Winch (1978, p. 5) rightly urges that one of the primary responsibilities of the historian is 'to be concerned with what it would be conceivable for Smith, or someone fairly like him, to maintain, rather than with what later generations would like him to have maintained'. After his own essay in 'recovery rather than recruitment', Winch strongly rejects the characterization of Smith's politics as that associated with the 'English tradition of liberal individualism' reaching back to Hobbes and Locke and going through to John Stuart Mill. This book has certainly demonstrated differences between Smith and Locke, although these can easily be exaggerated. What will next be argued is that the contrasts between Mill's and Smith's 'liberalisms' are probably much more substantial, although the main differences we detect here are separate from those that Winch emphasizes.

From the many faceted term 'liberal' we can recognize, at least, three general categories: classical liberals, social liberals, and neo-liberals. The central idea in the classical liberalism of Smith and Hume was liberty under the law. People should be free to follow their own interests and be constrained only by rules that prevent them encroaching on the liberty of others. It is in this way that the scene is set for the operation of the free market and the maximization of welfare via the workings of the invisible hand.

The ideas of 19th- and 20th-century social liberals feature an enthusiasm for democracy and legislative restrictions on the operation of markets. Such intervention is justified on the grounds that markets are not always neutral and often lead to the systematic disadvantage of some groups. John Maynard Keynes and William Beveridge declared themselves to be liberals and clearly fall into the category of social liberals.

Neo-liberals include modern thinkers who are critical, especially of what they see to be the costly bureaucratization of democracy and the eventual failure of governments to reduce rent-seeking, chronic unemployment, and 'stagflation'. The economist Milton Friedman now argues that the actions of government are usually against the interests of the people in general. Similarly, the political philosopher Robert Nozick urges a 'minimal state'. Meanwhile James Buchanan's writings signify perhaps more than any other the work of a neo-liberal who revives much of the classical liberalist spirit via the careful redesign of constitutions.

With regard to J.S. Mill, it seems clear that he was one of the first of the social liberals and a writer who failed to foresee the potential extent of the bureaucracy problem and other expensive government failures. During his lifetime Mill espoused several political causes, including his support for democratic institutions, for the emerging feminist movement and for the protection of individuals from the tyranny both of political majorities and of public opinion. Given these credentials, Gray (1988, p. 119) observes, it seems natural to ask: 'If Mill is not a liberal, who is?' Obviously it is a matter of which definition one has in mind. We can see already one important contrast between Mill's social liberalism and Smith's classical liberalism in the instance of Smith's lack of enthusiasm for democracy described earlier. But there are many other contrasts and some of them will be illustrated below. Meanwhile there is no denying that there are some elements of 18th-century Scottish Enlightenment thinking in Mill's writings. His frequent defence of the individual against 'despotism' or 'tyranny' of all kinds, for instance, is clear evidence of this. But the *dominant* theme in Mill, it will be argued, is the 19th-century's increasing need to develop, through innovative government, social policies that meliorate, if not obviate, market solutions.

To the casual reader, the one contribution of J.S. Mill that qualifies him as the truest of liberals is his famous essay *On Liberty*. This work emphasizes 'one very simple principle', the Principle of Liberty (Mill, 1962). An agent's liberty, Mill argues, should be constrained only if harm to others is thereby prevented. In practice, however, judgements about whether harm has been done are complex and difficult. To meet this problem Mill himself proceeds to apply the Principle of Utility, or at least that of indirect utility. To be in a position to make judgements about the presence or absence of harm, involves the constraining authority in making disciplined judgements about aggregate social welfare. One is reminded of Smith's warning that the sovereign should make no such attempts. By allowing individuals to make their own decisions, he urged, the sovereign would be freed from a duty, 'in the attempting to perform which he must always be exposed to innumerable delusions and for the performance of which no human wisdom or knowledge could ever be sufficient (1976a, p. 687).

The criterion of utility that Mill applies in his test of aggregate welfare is more complex than appears at first sight because it has to be translated into terms of happiness which is the only thing that has intrinsic utility (Gray, 1988, p. 123). But how can Mill trade off what he calls his 'higher pleasures' against the 'lower' when both are related to happiness? The conclusion is that generally Mill's utilitarianism is centrally flawed because it is ultimately unable to make comparative judgements about aggregate welfare.

Another element of Mill's ultra rationalistic liberalism is his emphasis on the assumption that each person comes into the world with unique individuality or 'essence'. This should be compared with Smith's belief that it is nurture rather than nature that is the biggest determinant of individuals' future career development (*The Wealth of Nations*, 1977, p. 572). And it was Mill's playing down the role of inherited cultural tradition in determining individuality that led Hayek (1976, pp. 1–32) to declare Mill's position to be one of false individualism.

Mill's focus on the individual to the relative neglect of institutional and constitutional matters can be seen best in his theory of progress. To him, society progresses primarily by innovations generated by the individual human mind. For Mill the wealths of different nations vary mainly because of differences in the tastes or attitudes or mental makeups of individuals within them. It is interesting, for instance, to compare Mill's main reason for the 'stationariness' of China with Smith's explanation. Mill concludes that the fact that the increase of capital in China has come to a stand while the returns are still so large 'denotes a much less degree of the effective desire [by individual Chinese] of accumulation, in other words a much lower estimate of the future relatively to the present, than that of [individuals in] European nations' (Mill, 1969, p. 173).

In Smith's discussion of China the emphasis, in contrast, is on the institutional and legal background. Thus a defect in the law, Smith observes, can raise the rate of interest substantially:

> When the law does not enforce the performance of contracts, it puts nearly all borrowers nearly upon the same footing as bankrupts…The uncertainty of recovering his money makes the lender exact the same usurious interest which is usually required from bankrupts. (1976a, p. 112)

Smith's reason why the increase in capital in China 'has come to a stand' (Mill's words) is thus quite different. Moreover, Smith continues,

> In a country too, where, though the rich or owners of large capitals enjoy a good deal of security, the poor or the owners of small capitals enjoy scarce any, but are liable, under the pretence of justice, to be pillaged and plundered at any time by the inferior mandarins, the quantity of stock employed in all the different branches of business transacted within it, can never the equal to what the nature and extent of that business might admit. (1976a, p. 112)[1]

Interventionist Policies

There is no doubt that Mill and colleagues such as Nassau Senior were confident that proper judgements about government intervention to determine the highest aggregate welfare could easily be made. Marion Bowley (1949) maintains that the attitude of Senior and Mill marked an important breach with the preceding generation of political economists:

> It is one thing to maintain, as a principle, that the duty of Government is to keep out except in special cases, however literally that phrase is interpreted. It is quite another to assert the right, duty and possibility of intervention for the common good, and that the only limit to the duty of Government is its power, without any first principal limiting that power. This is what Senior and effectually J.S. Mill were asserting in 1847. (p. 276)

In other words, following Mill's Principle of Liberty, government could intervene anywhere simply by announcing that a harm to someone in society needed correcting, the definition of harm being left to government. When professor of economics at Oxford in 1847, Senior wrote down some revealing personal thoughts on the relation of economic analysis to policy. In the first of three lectures on the subject he asserted that the business of government extends beyond the provision of protection and the punishment of internal or external violence or fraud:

> The only rational foundation of government, the only foundation of a right to govern and of a correlative duty to obey, is expediency – the general benefit of the community. It is the duty of a government to do whatever is conducive to the welfare of the governed. The only limit to this duty is its power. (Bowley, 1949, p. 265)

In Bowley's opinion this quotation implied that the sacred and respected rule of non-interference was thrown overboard. The departure from Smith could not have been clearer.

In the final book of his *Principles*, first published in 1848, Mill argued openly about the inadequacy of the *laissez-faire* school which limited the province of government to the protection of person and property against force and fraud. Mill apparently wanted a clear break from this tradition. First he distinguished undesirable or *authoritative* interference which referred to intervention that controlled the free agency of individuals. The other kind of intervention he described as *non-authoritative*. An example of it would be intervention that, while leaving individuals free to use their own means of pursuing any object of general interest, 'the government, not meddling with them, but not trusting the object solely to their care, establishes, side by side with their arrangement, an agency of its own for a like purpose' (Mill, 1969, p. 942). Under this rubric, Mill argued the legitimacy of government participating in their business *as a general principle*, but in a way that he believed avoided any degree of 'meddling'. He offered the following illustrations: 'There might be a national bank, or a government manufactory, without any monopoly against private banks and manufactories. There might be a post-office, without penalties against the conveyance of letters by other means...There may be public hospitals, without any restriction upon private medical or surgical practice' (p. 942). With respect to education Mill argued: 'Though a government, therefore, may, and in many cases ought to, establish schools and colleges, it must neither compel nor bribe any person to come to them' (ibid., p. 956). A public (government) school should exist: 'as one among many competing experiments, carried on for the purpose of example and stimulus, to keep the others up to a certain standard of excellence'. What is interesting here is Mill's a priori confidence that the government schools would always be the superior pacemakers (Mill, 1981, p. 240).

With benefit of hindsight, such propositions today seem highly contestable, and Smith could undoubtedly have challenged them. Experience has shown that when a government enters a particular profession or industry there are automatic and apparently unavoidable restrictions placed on the private competitors. The public enterprise has the extra advantage of having the reliance on government tax revenue and access to loans that rest on the public credit. The individuals connected with the public supply, moreover, often become a political constituency in their own right and are able to press successfully for further degrees of protection. A post office that exists 'without penalties against the conveyance of letters by other means' does not conform to reality. The penalties are both economic, for the reasons of special financial advantage just mentioned, and political, since usually post offices have also secured *legal* sanctions against mail delivery by third parties.

Adam Smith's vision was of quite a different nature to Mill's in these respects. Smith argued, for instance, that unsubsidized private schools were in an unfortunate minority because the salaries of the public school teachers

> put the private teachers who would pretend to come into competition with them, in the same state with the merchant, who attempts to trade without a bounty in competition with those who trade with a considerable one. (Smith, 1976a, p. 780)

Smith, it seems, had grasped the phenomenon of what modern economic literature calls the 'crowding out' of the private by the public institutions and was anxious to avoid its dangers at all costs.

The above interpretation of J.S. Mill may appear somewhat severe to some readers. This is probably because he always gives the impression of making a careful examination of two sides of any question. His chapter XI 'Of the grounds and limits of the laissez-faire or non-interference principle' (1969, pp. 941–79) is a case in question. He sets out the pros and cons in a way that will appeal to most reasonable men. For the 19th-century 'orthodox economist', for instance, Mill was very reassuring when he readily acknowledged that the non-interference principle, that is, *laissez-faire*, should be the general principle, departures from which must be justified by the claim of overriding expediency: 'Laissez-faire, in short, should be the general practice: every departure from it, *unless required by some great good*, is a certain evil' (1969, p. 950, emphasis added).

Writers such as Ellen Paul (1979) regard the words in italics in the previous quotation as the operative ones. For here was the *implicit* advocacy of the utilitarian standard. Paul concludes that:

> In the final analysis, Mill really has one standard, expediency, not two as would appear from the way in which his argument unfolded. By the end of his argument, the expediency standard reigned supreme, and the laissez-faire principle is almost completely discarded. Mill declared finally, that the government can do anything important to the general interest. (1979, p. 194)

The fact is that ultimately Mill was substantially distrustful of Smith's invisible hand. Each individual, Mill repeatedly insists, by pursuing his own interest, would not necessarily be led by the invisible hand to take the course that would be most beneficial to society. For Mill questioned, time and again, whether the individual could be the best judge of his/her own interests, especially if he or she belonged to the poorer classes.

Mill versus Smith on Education

In his *Principles of Political Economy* (1969), John Stuart Mill confronted the question whether the buyer is always qualified to judge of the commodity and concluded that: 'If not, the presumption in favour of the competition of the market does not apply in this case'. Medicine was an obvious example of this sort of market failure. Even if the patient could be relied upon to purchase some minimum amount at his own expense, and from his own free will, this would not necessarily imply that the patient would select the right medicine without assistance. Similarly with education: 'The uncultivated cannot be competent judges of cultivation'.

It is interesting that, in contrast, Adam Smith had maintained that, with respect to medicine, people were not such children in the choice of their doctors, as the would-be paternalists were fond of believing: 'That doctors are sometimes fools as well as other people, is not, in the present time, one of those profound secrets which is known only to the learned'.

Adam Smith obviously had a far different understanding of institutional realities. Whereas the utilitarians believed that government educational enterprises could do things more efficiently than the market, it was Adam Smith's view that:

> Those parts of education, it is to be observed, for the teaching of which there are no public institutions, are generally the best taught ... the three most essential parts of literary education, to read, write and account, it still continues to be more common to acquire in private than in public schools; and it very seldom happens that anybody fails of acquiring them to the degree in which it is necessary to acquire them. (1976a, p. 764)

By 'public institutions' Adam Smith meant generally those establishments that received subsidies with the result that their employees were not fully dependent on their incomes from their customers. Such establishments included the endowed private schools, that is schools receiving private subsidies largely from bequests. There is no reason to believe, however, that Smith would have had different views about institutions receiving subsidies from government.

Mill's opinion was striking in contrast:

> Now any well-intentioned and tolerably civilized government may think, without presumption, that it does or ought to possess a degree of cultivation above the average of the community which it rules, and that it should therefore be capable of offering better education and better instruction to the people, than the great number of them would spontaneously demand. Education, therefore, is one of those things which it is admissible in principle that a government should provide for the people. (1969, p. 953)

It should be noticed that the words 'well-intentioned' and 'tolerably civilized' to describe government is illustrative of the innocent and optimistic faith in the reformed democracy that Mill hoped was arriving by the mid 19th century. While Smith had his doubts about democracy, he was not against some intervention in education. But he confined it to the provision of finance and to a proposal for licensing entry into the mechanical trades on the basis of passing basic examinations in literacy and numeracy. But always he relied on consumer choice to secure efficiency in the delivery of education. Mill, in contrast, opposed free choice in education and in the Essay 'Endowments' in 1869, explicitly rejected Smith's analysis because he believed the common-man-education-consumer did not know what was good for him. From Smith's classical liberal position, however, he would respond that the experience of making choices in education is itself an education (Blaug, 1975, p. 589). Smith, in other words, implicitly had faith that the 'uncultivated' *could* one day become 'cultivated', and largely from their own efforts and resources.

Mill's Production/Distribution Distinction

The most fundamental change in political economy that appeared in Mill's *Principles* was his separation of production from distribution (Part I of his book is devoted to Production and Part II to Distribution). According to Ellen Paul this was a complete change from the perspective of Adam Smith: 'By treating production as a primary, almost a given, Mill was able later in his discussion of distribution to treat the products of industrial society as almost pre-existing entities, there to be distributed by those in authority' (1979, p. 160). The result of this was to 'sever the connection between the laws of economics and the political prescriptions associated with the laissez-faire doctrine'.

Mill tells us in his *Autobiography* (Mill, 1960) that he believed that the production distribution distinction was the original element in his *Principles*. The laws of production, he argued therein, have the properties of natural laws and the laws of distribution are subject to human invention and institutions. And if the laws of distribution are man-made then existing property relations can be interfered with on the principle of equity. It was in this way that Mill introduced the search for practical means of redistribution as a crucial part of the political economist's task. Another justification, in Mill's view, for departing from *laissez-faire* was thus introduced. The practical problem, in his words, was to determine which 'institutions of property would be established by an unprejudiced legislature, absolutely impartial between the possessors of property and the nonpossessors' (Paul, 1979, p. 160). Adam Smith would seriously question Mill's confidence in finding a legislature that is 'unprejudiced' and 'absolutely impartial' concerning the redistribution of property. But more important he would point to the reduced incentives to create property once such redistribution was decreed.

Gray (1988) observes that this part of Mill's writing reveals 'the central distributionist heresy of revisionary liberalism'. The realization that the free market had production and distributive dimensions simultaneously, which was pervasive in Scottish Enlightenment thinking, becomes forgotten under Mill's social liberalism:

> A 'manna from heaven' view of how goods came into the world is insinuated and the systemic impact of distributive arrangements on productive life is evaded. This disastrous dissociation of production from distribution licenses the contemporary delusion that productive and distributive institutions may be promiscuously mixed so as to secure some ideal pattern of justice in society. (Gray, 1988, p. 130)

This central example of Mill's economic philosophy again illustrates crucial differences between Mill and Smith. Mill's ultra rationalism once more leads him to neglect real world practices and institutions that are strong potential constraints on his egalitarian plans, plans that required substantial taxation of the owner's wealth. Smith, in contrast, points to 'the greater part of merchants and manufactures' transferring their capitals out of their home country after being 'continually exposed to the [excessive] mortifying and vexatious visits of the tax-gatherers' (1976a, p. 927). Mill's abstract intellectualism forgets or severely underestimates also the potential of ordinary citizen resistance to taxation. And it has been his approach and influence, no doubt, that has led to the neglect by many economists, until recently, of the real dimensions of the growth of the underground economy. In Smith's day this economy largely took the form of smuggling. Outright legal prohibitions of imports of certain commodities, Smith observed, did not stop importation, they only raised the import costs. As for general taxation, his review of history and knowledge of his own times, led to his own estimate that ordinary people will rebel when as much as half their property is taxed away from them.

The Population

The labouring classes were openly and strongly criticized by Mill for failing to hold their numbers in check. Indeed we have here an example of what Mill believed to be a justified intervention to prevent harm to others. In Mill's view, the decision of a low-income worker to increase the size of his family had what we now call adverse external effects on society. Unable to prevent other low-income workers from doing the same, cumulative individual actions would lead to an expansion of the population relative to a fixed wages fund, and therefore to a decline in average wages and to one step closer to the subsistence level economy.

One intervention that Mill advocated to meet this problem was the official encouragement of labour monopolies in the form of trade unions. Mill openly faced the fact that union activity would inevitably impose the harm of a fall of wages or loss of employment on non-unionized labourers:

> For...there is no keeping up wages without limiting the numbers of competitors for employment. And all such limitations inflict distinct evil upon those whom it excludes – upon that great mass of labouring population which is outside the Unions; an evil not trifling, for if the system were rigorously enforced it would prevent unskilled labourers or their children from ever rising to the condition of the skilled. (1967, vol. 5, p. 663)

But despite this 'evil' Mill championed the unions because he believed they represented the more responsible sections of the population, sections of individuals who were more farsighted and less likely to have large families. Whether this kind of redistribution, and attempt at balancing harms, is acceptable on any principle of equity today is surely doubtful. But the fact that Mill was reconciled to imposing a serious institutional restriction on many members of the poorer classes, a restriction or harm imposed by unions on their ability to sell their labour, is again in striking contrast to Adam Smith who denounced such a barrier as 'a plain violation of the most sacred property' (1976a, p. 138).

The pessimism of Mill on the subject of population reflects quite a different economic vision of the world than that of Adam Smith. In Mill, as in Malthus and Ricardo, an increase in national production leads to an increase in population that eventually cannot be sustained at an above-subsistence wage. The reason was the operation of diminishing returns in the production of food on a fixed quantity of land. It was Malthus who had pioneered the belief, or strong probability, that the ultimate outcome of the struggle between procreation and the growth of food supply would be an overpopulated society with individuals existing at a depressed subsistence level.

So much for the 'dismal science' members of the classical school. To Adam Smith an increasing population was certainly the effect of an accumulation of capital. But the increase of population takes time and lags behind the capital expansion. This expansion, meanwhile, automatically generates a growth in the demand for labour. And capital, which Smith called 'stock', is to a large extent an accumulation of consumer goods which are advanced to workers for the next period of production:

> If this demand is continually increasing, the reward of labour must necessarily encourage...the marriage and multiplication of labourers, as may enable them to supply that continually increasing demand by a continually increasing population. ...it is in this manner that the demand for men, like that for any other commodity, necessarily regulates the production of men. (1976a, p. 98)

It is important to grasp, however, the dynamic nature of Smith's system compared with that of his successors. Increasing divisions of labour encourage expansions of capital which, in turn, induce increases in population which feed the new requirements of new divisions of labour and so on. The growth of the incomes of families in this process is stronger than their propensity to reproduce:

> It deserves to be remarked, perhaps, that it is in the progressive state, while the society is advancing to the further acquisition...that the condition of the labouring poor, of the great body of the people, seems to be the happiest and most comfortable. (1976a, p. 99)

Real historical events, no doubt, influenced the different dispositions of Smith and Mill. In Smith's time the growth rate of population was 3.5 per cent per decade. In the later period, 1810 to 1820, the population growth rate reached the astonishing figure of 16.9 per cent. But an appeal to such historical evidence helps to test each writer's theory. Despite the unprecedented population increase, the gross national income per head increased by greater than 1 per cent per annum in the years 1801–1871. Historians appear to believe that wages improved significantly especially from 1840 onwards. There does remain controversy whether wages rose appreciably in the early part of the century and especially between 1800 and 1820. But few would argue that wages actually fell on average over this period, a situation that would be necessary to confirm the prediction of Malthus and Mill. Many resources, during the early 1800s, moreover, were dissipated in the war against Napoleon.

The Stationary State

John Stuart Mill not only predicted the imminence of the stationary state but also was ready to welcome it. The reason was there would be 'much room for improving the Art of Living, and much more likelihood of its being improved, when minds ceased to be engrossed by the art of getting on' (Mill, 1969, p. 751). Here again we have Mill expressing his own values and in a way that is consistent with his belief that progress in civilization called primarily for an environment that allowed each individual to pursue his/her inner individuality or 'essence'. Such pursuits would go beyond concern with the further progress of industry which was, in any case, concerned with mere material things. The 'Utopian' stationary state that Mill desired, meanwhile, would be one where the problem of overpopulation had been resolved, probably, no doubt, after the success of his policy of elevating the power of labour unions (described above). In addition, and because of what Mill believed to be the feasible separation of distribution from production, a new era of social justice would prevail following a policy of appropriate redistribution that Mill personally, and pure democracy implicitly, approved of:

> Only when, in addition to just institutions, the increase of mankind shall be under the deliberate guidance of judicious foresight, can the conquests made from the powers of nature by the intellect and energy of scientific discoverers become the common property of the species, and the means of improving and elevating the universal lot. (Mill, 1969, p. 751)

Although some writers have detected in Smith's work also a march to some ultimate stationary state, the fact is that once economic growth is started via the establishment of Smith's natural liberty there is no stopping it. Growth through successive applications of the division of labour brings capital accumulation and this in turn produces technological improvement *ad infinitum*:

> As the accumulation of stock is previously necessary for carrying on the greater improvement in the productive powers of labour, so that accumulation naturally leads to this improvement. (1976a, p. 277)

In opposition to Mill's scenario, individuals in Smith's world flourish mentally and culturally in a dynamic rather than a stationary state. For Smith, economic productivity is always seen as an art in the aesthetic sense as well as in the sense of an applied skill. And individuals participate in an art when they are consumers as well as when they are workers. Consumers are restless searchers and are always goading manufacturers to improve their products:

> Such is the delicacy of man alone, that no object is produced to his liking. He finds that in everything there is need for improvement. (Cannan, 1896, p. 158)

> The whole industry of human life is employed not in procuring the supply of our three humble necessities, food, clothes and lodging, but in procuring the conveniences of it according to the nicety and delicacy of our tastes. (Ibid., p. 160)

The theme persists throughout Smith's works. In his essay, 'The History of Astronomy' (1795), he again presents man as a creature who cannot live in an excessively routinized or stagnant society. Man could not live without Wonder, Surprise, and Admiration: 'What is new and singular excites that sentiment which, in strict propriety, is called Wonder; what is unexpected, Surprise, and what is great or beautiful, Admiration.'

For Smith, in other words, wealth is the potential expression not merely of natural power but also of the emerging human personality. When wealth increases, men will indeed liberate and fulfil themselves. The pursuit of the wealth of *nations* provided the necessary dynamic condition conducive to the happiness of *individuals*.

It may be argued that all the contrasts between Smith and Mill outlined above amount merely to a difference in economic interpretation of events or a difference in economic analysis and therefore are not relevant to an enquiry into crucial differences in their ideas of liberalism or political philosophy. I do not agree. Suppose, for example, the real world reflected that of the Mill/Ricardian model with its stationary state, because of diminishing returns and population growth in an environment of technological stagnation. Even if Smith had to adopt this verdict, would he adopt Mill's normative disposition? The answer is surely in the negative. Smith could never agree to Mill's advocacy of labour monopolies to control population because this would interfere with the rights of workers who were frozen out. Smith appealed here to the requirements, not of utility, but of natural law. Deliberate hindrances to some individuals from offering the property of their labour to others on mutually acceptable terms is condemned as being 'a plain violation of this most sacred property' (1976a, p. 138). As for Mill's demand for a socially just redistribution, this again would be completely alien to Smith. The determination of Millian 'social justice' requires comparative judgements about aggregate welfare that Smith would dismiss as impossible. But even if they were possible, he would not trust democratic government with the responsibility.

Smith's concept of liberty was not Mill's. The latter's *Principle of Liberty*, contained in his famous essay (1962), to reiterate, justified government intervention to prevent harm. The requirement of utilitarianism in some cases was a trade-off between harms so that the least social harm would ensue. The harms to excluded workers under a government sanctioned labour monopoly would be offset by a long-run reduction in the harm to society via reductions in family size. Smith would condemn this kind of social calculus because the necessary interference with free market determined wages by itself infringes Smithian (natural) liberty without exception.

> It is a manifest encroachment upon the just liberty both of the workman, and of those who might be disposed to employ him. (1976a, p. 138)

From what has been argued one can indeed agree with Winch (1978) that it is wrong to claim Smith to be a paradigmatic liberal in the sense of J.S. Mill and his 19th-century associates. But Winch argues that the main difference is that Smith is speaking a different, 18th-century language with its overtones of civic humanism. That language, moreover, reveals a certain philosophic disposition to substitute the civic arena for the amoral if not immoral market place, at least at the margin. Yet Winch is disappointed that his argument has not done well against those who dogmatically place Smith in the English tradition of liberal individualism that began with Locke and ended with J.S. Mill: 'Pointing out, as must and has been done, that Smith was by no means a doctrinaire advocate of laissez-faire has not succeeded in shifting the debate outside the confines of the liberal capitalist framework' (Winch, 1978, p. 14).

In emphasizing Smith's so-called exceptions to *laissez-faire*, Winch is of course following in the steps of his distinguished teacher, Jacob Viner, whose influential essay, 'Adam Smith and Laissez-Faire', first appeared over 50 years ago (see Viner, 1958, pp. 213–45). But we have expressed elsewhere several objections to Viner's position (see West, 1990, chapter 7). And, to use the words of Werhane (1991), Smithian exceptions to *laissez-faire* might better be regarded at most as failures of the ideal to be realized. The precise subject for discussion here, however, is whether J.S. Mill's liberalism can be placed in direct ancestry with the writings of Adam Smith. I answer in the negative, as does Winch, but for largely different if not opposite reasoning. On my interpretation, J.S. Mill claimed much more serious and extensive exceptions to *laissez-faire* than did Smith. And in looking for a non-market agency to correct the failures Mill relied on 'democracy' to a degree that Smith would have surely questioned.

Adam Smith's long-run analysis is based on a search for the best practical procedures and expedients in the context of liberty. The problem of a lack of education in the populace, for example, was for Smith gradually best solvable through time by the people themselves without any help from government-run schools.[2] As well, the problem of poverty was in part due to the actions of government in supplying favours to special interest rent-seekers that usually raised the price of goods for the poor. Since governments aggravated the poverty problem from Smith's perspective, they could not be relied on to redistribute in the manner so confidently claimed by Mill. Meanwhile the problem of low incomes would for Smith be eased with the growth of the wealth of nations which benefited all ranks despite the many negative influences of governments. And as for Mill's proposed government agencies to exist side by side with private ones so as hopefully to provide an example of the best practice, nothing surely could have been further from the mind of Smith because he mistrusted any reliance on responsibility that was separated from ownership (Werhane, 1991).

No doubt there are many difficulties in defining or understanding the term 'liberal' but it seems reasonable to assert that a liberal is at least someone who, on most issues, prefers individual actions to collective action. Adam Smith believed that the main shortcoming of collective action was its frequent connection with lobbying for favours by interest groups, a process which 'retards, instead of accelerating, the progress of the society towards real wealth and greatness' (1976a, IV.ix.50). Smith's main objective, at least in *The Wealth of Nations*, was to remove or at minimum to stop the expansion of this costly type of government intervention. And in his opinion it accounted, indeed, for *most* intervention. It was in this sense that he typically preferred the freedom of individual action. If only the 'systems of preference' that collective action had created could be swept away, society could be in a vastly improved situation. On this it is necessary to reiterate some words from a Smithian passage quoted earlier:

> All systems either of preference or of restraint, therefore, being thus completely taken away, the obvious and simple system of natural liberty establishes itself of its own accord. Every man, as long as he does not violate the laws of justice, is left perfectly free to pursue his own interest his own way, and to bring both his industry and capital into competition with those of any other man, or order of men. (1950, IV.ix.51)

We return to the comparison of Smith's condition that a person's freedom to do anything should be allowed provided he/she 'does not violate the laws of justice', with J.S. Mill's condition that liberty should be allowed *except* where 'harm to others' may thereby be prevented. The wording of Smith's condition is clearly the tighter and less likely to provide loopholes for ambitious, arrogant and ideological legislators. The comparison here is thus between the classical liberalism of the 18th century with the ambivalent, if not flawed, J.S. Mill liberalism of the 19th century. One can agree with Winch that the two are not compatible, but obviously for reasons different from his.[3]

According to John Gray (1993), liberalism 'as a doctrine with aspirations for universal prescriptive authority' is dead (p. 314). But liberalism survives independently of the fundamentalist or comprehensive theory such as that of the utilitarians, which latter we must now discard. The fault of the 'single theory' concept is that it does not allow comfortably for value-pluralism: 'If there is an ultimate diversity of forms of human flourishing, embodied in ways of life only some of which can be accommodated within a liberal regime, then liberal orders have no general superiority over orders that are not liberal' (ibid., p. 314).

The 'liberalism' that Gray rejects is that which is 'a doctrine with aspirations for universal prescriptive authority'. If by 'universal prescriptive authority' he means the predetermination by the state of the end results of the competitive 'race', most readers will agree. What this position does is to reject Millian liberalism from the outset. The question remains, however, whether 'true' liberalism requires any universal authority at all. Classical liberalism surely does require one, at least, and that is the institution of the law and the rule of law. The competitive 'race' requires rules of the game that all contestants will respect. To penalize those who violate them requires a set of predicted penalties that can be imposed; and this calls for none other than one minimum universal authority: the law itself. More generally, a successful liberal society requires certain government services which can be placed under the Smithian heading: Justice, Defense, and, with certain qualifications, selected Public Works. Classical liberalism surely demands this central institutional base and this can then be presented in terms of a 'fundamentalist' theory, ideology or philosophy.

Gray, in other words, may be going too far in stripping away from true liberalism in rejecting anything that can be seen as one single or fundamentalist theory, or ideology. True liberalism, Gray maintains, should allow for 'value pluralism'. But again it depends on the meaning of this phrase. 'An objective pluralist', Gray maintains, 'will have good reason to favour a variety of regimes, communal and political, in which a diversity of uncombinable excellences may flourish' (Gray, 1988, pp. 295–6). This may well be true. But for classical liberals such as Smith, it was necessary also to *reject* another variety of regimes. These included at least, slavery, despotism and anarchy. And such consensus among classical liberals about what it is they are against, begins to constitute a common ideology. And this itself approaches fundamentalism of sorts. In decrying fundamentalism altogether, Gray seems exclusively to have one version in mind, that of J.S. Mill. One can certainly disagree with Mill's reasoning. But it is not necessary also to close the door altogether to other attempts at foundational ideology.

Gray proceeds to argue that even if its philosophic foundations have collapsed, what is still living in liberalism is the historic inheritance of civil society: 'It is civil society that should be the object of theorizing, not "liberalism" or any abstract conception of liberty' (ibid., p. 314). Civil society is then described by Gray as one that is tolerant of diverse views, religious and political and in which the state does not attempt to impose one comprehensive doctrine. The true liberals in the end are the theorists of liberty, those who make a serious study of the *practice of liberty*. In this mood Gray recommends us to return to the thoughts of the 18th-century Scottish school which included Hume, Smith, Ferguson, Millar, and Kames. The feature that Gray likes is the empirical exploration that such schools conducted in their review of real-life institutions recorded in history. But having used inductive methods of study, the Scottish writers proceeded to their judgements, implicit or explicit, as to what works best in view of the historical record. What emerged then was the beginnings of a fundamentalist classical liberalism. Gray, himself, seems to come close to this in his 1988 essay where he concludes:

> The dominant Millian paradigm of contemporary liberalism is radically defective and ought to be abandoned. We are wise, I believe, if we return to the classical liberals, for whom liberalism was a search for principles of political justice that could command assent among persons with divergent preferences, values and views of the world. (p.138)

Such a statement seems quite acceptable provided we qualify the reference to agreement among persons with divergent values and views of the world. For liberalism to have meaning there must also be some minimum *convergence* of views of the world, or some common ideology concerning, say the need, at least, for a rule of law and a respect for the negative liberty that we do indeed find among the writers of the Scottish school.

The Wealth of Nations is typical of this tradition in its wide survey of different forms and societies including Greek republics, federal governments, governments of mercantile companies, the constitution of American colonies, and church/state relationships. Gray maintains that civil society among other things, is tolerant of a diversity of religious views. On this one can find agreement in a reading of Book V of *The Wealth of Nations*, where Smith makes probably the most eloquent attack on government-established religions.[4] A second feature of civil society that Gray observes is limited government. Smith again is in full agreement as we have already shown. A third feature of Gray's civil society is the institution of private property. Smithian support here is found in Part II of Chapter 1 of Book V of *The Wealth of Nations*. Next Gray argues that civil societies need not have the complete political and economic institutions of liberal democracy. Smith again would apparently agree. Finally, civil society, according to Gray, respects the rule of law, voluntary association, and mobility. Again all of these features are to be found recommended in *The Wealth of Nations*.

But there is an important aspect of Smith that needs to be added to Gray's description of his traditional civil society as it relates to England. He refers (1988, p. 276) to the belief of MacFarlane (1976) that England was an individualist society immemorably. This apparently implies the individualism that finds expression in common law. But how much individualism in reality reached the light of day from the 15th to the 18th century? The common law failed to protect the individualist rights of the ordinary man against the onslaught of mercantilist regulation. The infamous Elizabeth Statute of Apprentices forbade mobility between parishes, regulated wages, hours of work and occupational entry. There was surely not much room for individualism here. And widespread protectionism by way of statute law had severe implications for freedom to do and to make. Smith, the enemy of mercantilism and rent-seeking, would take kindly to many of the aspects of civil society described by Gray but he would speak more urgently of the need to protect it from the incursions of governments.

Adam Smith's 'liberalism in practice' did civil society a favour by condemning the serious assaults of statute law on freedom and prosperity. And these assaults are by no means over. Smith's liberalism is not dead. It has been there all along. And in the 1990s it appears to be enjoying such fresh life as to carry it well into the 21st century.

Notes

1. It is interesting that over two centuries after Smith wrote, nothing much has changed. According to one recent report, China 'lacks an independent legal system, a code of private-property rights, developed financial markets, a banking system and bankruptcy laws' (*The Economist*, editorial, 5 March 1994).
2. It is true that Mill made the famous objection that: 'A general state education is a mere contrivance for moulding people to be exactly like one another...' (1962, p. 239). His objection, however, is not that free consumer choice is eroded but that the state would abuse its monopoly power. Moreover, Mill was agreeable to some state-provided education through special government schools that would provide 'example and stimulus'.
3. Smith obviously meant by respect for the 'laws of justice' something more than simply the existing body of legal rules (Letwin, 1988, p. 66).
4. William Letwin (1988, p. 75) argues that Smith made an exception in the case of the established Presbyterian Church of Scotland, but this is open to debate.

References

Archibald, G.C. (1992), 'Three classical economists on trouble, strife, and the 'alienation of labour', *Canadian Journal of Economics*, **XXV**, 1, February.

Blaug, M. (1975), 'The Economics of Education in English Classical Political Economy: A Re-examination', in A. Skinner and T. Wilson (eds), *Essays on Adam Smith*, Oxford: Clarendon Press.

Bowley, M. (1949), *Nassau Senior and Classical Economists*, New York: Augustin Kelly.

Buchanan, J.M. (1967), 'Politics and Science: Reflections on Knight's Critique of Polanyi', *Ethics*, **77**.

Buchanan, J.M. (1972), 'Review of Rawls' *Theory of Justice*', *Public Choice*, **13**, 123.

Buchanan, J.M. (1975), *The Limits of Liberty: Between Anarchy and Leviathan*, Chicago: University of Chicago Press.

Buchanan, J.M. and Tullock, G. (1962), *The Calculus of Consent*, Ann Arbor: University of Michigan Press.

Cannan, E. (ed.) (1896), *Lectures on, Justice, Policy, Revenue and Arms, by Adam Smith*, Oxford: Clarendon Press.

Ekelund, R.E. (Jr) and Hebert, R.T. (1990), *A History of Economic Theory and Method*, New York: McGraw-Hill.

Forbes, D. (1975), 'Sceptical Whiggism, Commerce and Liberty', in A. Skinner and T. Wilson (eds), *Essays on Adam Smith*, Oxford: Clarendon Press.

Friedman, M. (1992), 'Economic Freedom, Human Freedom, Political Freedom', California: The Smith Center for Private Enterprise Studies, California State University, Harvard.

Gastil, R.D. (1982), *Freedom in the World*, Westport, Conn.: Greenwood.

Gay, John (1993), *Post Liberalism*, New York: Routledge.

Gray, John (1988), 'Mill's and Other Liberalisms', in K. Haakonssen (ed.), *Traditions of Liberalism*, St Leonards, NSW: The Centre for Independent Studies.

Gwartney, J. and Wagner, R.E. (eds) (1988), *Public Choice and Constitutional Economics*, Greenwich, Conn.: JAI Press Inc.

Haakonssen, K. (ed.) (1988), *Traditions of Liberalism*, St Leonards, NSW: The Centre for Independent Studies.

Hayek, F.A. (1945), 'The Use of Knowledge in Society', *American Economic Review*, **35** (4), September.

Hayek, F.A. (1948), *Individualism and Economic Order*, Chicago: University of Chicago Press.

Hayek, F.A. (1976), *The Mirage of Social Justice*, London: Routledge and Kegan Paul.

Heilbroner, R. (1975), 'Paradox of Progress: Decline and Decay', in A.S. Skinner and T. Wilson (1975).

Heilbroner, R. (1992), *Twenty-First Century Capitalism*, Concord, Ontario: Anansi Press.

Hume, D. (1888), *A Treatise of Human Nature*. First published 1739.

Huntingdon, S.P. and Dominguez, J.I. (1975), 'Political Development', in F.I. Greenstein and N.W. Polsby (eds), *Handbook of Political Science*, vol. 3, Reading: Addison-Wesley.

Krueger, A. (1974), 'The Political Economy of the Rent Seeking Society', *American Economic Review*, **64**, June.

Laband, D.N. and Sophocleus, J.P. (1988), 'The Social Cost of Rent-Seeking: First Estimates', *Public Choice*, **58** (3), 269–76.

Lamb, R. (1973), 'Adam Smith's Concept of Alienation', *Oxford Economic Papers*, **XXV**, 275–85.

Letwin, W. (1988), 'Was Adam Smith a Liberal?', in K. Haakonssen (ed.), *Traditions of Liberalism*, St Leonards, NSW: The Centre for Independent Studies.

Locke, J. (1988), *Two Treatises of Government*, edited by Peter Laslett, Cambridge: Cambridge University Press.

MacFarlane, Alan (1976), *Origins of English Individualism*, Cambridge: Cambridge University Press.

Menger, C. (1985), *Investigations into the Method of the Social Sciences with Special Reference to Economics*, New York: New York University Press.

Mill, J.S. (1960), *Autobiography*, New York: Columbia University Press.

Mill, J.S. (1962), *On Liberty*, 4th ed., London: Collins Fontana.

Mill, J.S. (1967), 'Essays on Economics and Society', in J.M. Robson (ed.), *Collected Works*, vols 4 and 5, Toronto: University of Toronto Press.

Mill, J.S. (1969), *Principles of Political Economy*, New York: Augustin Kelley reprint. Originally published 1848.

Neale, R.S. (1975), 'The Standard of Living, 1780–1844: A Regional and Class Study', in Arthur J. Taylor (1975).

Pack, S.J. (1991), *Capitalism as Moral System*, Aldershot: Edward Elgar.

Paul, E.F. (1979), *Moral Revolution and Economic Science: The Demise of Laissez-Faire in Nineteenth Century British Political Economy*, Westport, Conn. and London: Greenwood Press.

Pocock, J.G.A. (1971), *Politics, Language and Time*, New York: Princeton University Press.

Pocock, J.G.A. (1975), *The Machiavellian Moment*, Princeton: Princeton University Press.

Popper, K. (1965), *Conjectures and Refutation*, New York: Harper.

Przeworski, A. and Limongi, F. (1993), 'Political Regimes and Economic Growth', *Journal of Economic Perspectives*, **7** (3), 179–201.

Rawls, J. (1971), *A Theory of Justice*, Cambridge, Mass.: Harvard University Press.

Rosenberg, N. (1960), 'Some Institutional Aspects of *The Wealth of Nations*', *Journal of Political Economy*, December.

Rosenberg, N. (1965), 'Adam Smith and the Division of Labour: Two Views or One?', *Economica*, February.

Rousseau, J.J. (1968), *The Social Contract*, edited by N. Cranston, Harmondsworth: Penguin Books.

Rowley, C.K. (1992), *The Right to Justice*, Brookfield, Vermont: Edward Elgar.

Schofield, P.S. (1973), 'Dimensions of Illiteracy, 1750–1850', *Explorations in Economic History*, **X** (437–50).

Scully, G.W. (1988), 'The Institutional Framework and Economic Development', *Journal of Political Economy*, **96** (3), June.

Scully, G.W. and Slottje, D. (1991), 'Ranking Economic Liberty across Countries', *Public Choice*, **69**.

Skinner, A. and Wilson, T. (1975), *Essays on Adam Smith*, Oxford: Clarendon Press.

Smith, A. (1795), 'The History of Astronomy', in *Essays on Philosophic Subjects by the Late Adam Smith*, London: T. Cadell.

Smith, A. (1896), *Lectures on Policy, Justice, Revenue and Arms*, edited by E. Cannan, Oxford: Clarendon Press.

Smith, A. (1976a), *An Inquiry into the Nature and Causes of the Wealth of Nations*, reprinted in two volumes, edited by R.H. Campbell, A.S.

Skinner and W.B. Todd, Oxford: Clarendon Press. Originally published 1776.

Smith, A. (1976b), *The Theory of Moral Sentiments*, edited by D.D. Raphael and A.L. Macfie, Oxford; Clarendon Press. Originally published 1759.

Smith, A. (1977), *Lectures on Jurisprudence*, Report of 1762–3 (LJ(A), dated 1766 LJ(B), edited by R.L. Meek, D.D. Raphael and P.G. Stein, Oxford: Clarendon Press.

Stigler, G. (1971), 'Smith's Travels on the Ship of State', *History of Political Economy*, **3**.

Taylor, Arthur J. (1975), *The Standard of Living in Britain in the Industrial Revolution*, London: Methuen.

Thweatt, W.O. (1988), *Classical Political Economy: A Survey of Recent Literature*, Boston: Kluwer.

Tullock, G. (1967), 'The Welfare Costs of Tariffs, Monopolies and Theft', *Western Economic Journal*, **5**, June.

Viner, J. (1928), 'Adam Smith and Laissez Faire', in *Adam Smith 1776–1926*, Chicago: University of Chicago Press.

Viner, J. (1958), 'Adam Smith and Laissez-Faire', in *The Long View and the Short*, Illinois: Glenco.

Werhane, Patricia H. (1991), *Adam Smith and his Legacy for Modern Capitalism*, Oxford: Oxford University Press.

West, E.G. (1964), 'Adam Smith's Two Views on the Division of Labour', *Economica*, February.

West, E.G. (1969), 'The Political Economy of Alienation: Karl Marx and Adam Smith', *Oxford Economic Papers*, **27**, July.

West, E.G. (1970), *Education and the State*, London: IEA, second edition.

West, E.G. (1975), 'Adam Smith and Alienation: A Rejoinder', *Oxford Economic Papers*, **27**, July.

West, E.G. (1975), *Education and the Industrial Revolution*, London: Batsford.

West, E.G. (1976), *Adam Smith: The Man and His Works*, Indianapolis: Liberty Press.

West, E.G. (1990), *Adam Smith and Modern Economics: From Market Behaviour to Public Choice*, Aldershot: Edward Elgar.

West, E.G. (1996), 'Adam Smith on the Cultural Effects of Specialization: Splenetics versus Economics', *History of Political Economy*, **28** (1), Spring.

Williamson, O. (1994), 'Visible and Invisible Governance', *American Economic Review*, **84** (2), May.

Winch, D. (1978), *Adam Smith's Politics*, Cambridge: Cambridge University Press.

Wittman, D. (1989), 'Why Democracies Produce Efficient Results', *Journal of Political Economy*, **97**, December.

Zeisel, J.S. (1958), 'The Workweek in American Industry 1850–1956', *Monthly Labor Review*, **81**, January.

Index

voting and Swedish model 31–2

wages and population 47, 49
Wagner, R.E. 8
wealth
  creation of
    and good government 13–14
    and liberty 13, 15–16
  and liberty 50
welfare
  and government intervention 41

  social 39–40
Werhane, P.H. 35, 36, 37n, 52
West, E.G. 1, 27, 29, 34, 37n
Whigs 18
Williamson, O. 23
Winch, D. 1, 5, 17, 18, 26, 29, 38, 51–2
Wittman, D. 9

Zeisel, J.S. 33

Economic Policy in a Liberal Democracy

Economic Policy in a Liberal Democracy

Richard E. Wagner

Professor of Economics
George Mason University

The Shaftesbury Papers, 8
Series Editor: Charles K. Rowley

Edward Elgar
Cheltenham, UK • Brookfield, US

Published by
Edward Elgar Publishing Limited
8 Lansdown Place
Cheltenham
Glos GL50 2HU
UK

Edward Elgar Publishing Company
Old Post Road
Brookfield
Vermont 05036
US

British Library Cataloguing in Publication Data
Wagner, Richard E.
  Economic policy in a liberal democracy. – (The Shaftesbury papers; 8)
  1. Economic policy   2. Liberalism – Economic aspects
  3. Democracy – Economic aspects
  I. Title   II. Series
  330.9

Library of Congress Cataloguing in Publication Data
  Economic policy in a liberal democracy / Richard E. Wagner.
  — (Shaftesbury papers; 8)
  1. Welfare economics.   2. Pressure groups.   3. Liberalism.
  4. Economic policy.   I. Title.   II. Series.
  HB846.W33   1996
  338.9—dc20   95–40191
                                                              CIP

ISBN 1 85898 401 7

Printed in Great Britain at the University Press, Cambridge

Contents

Preface

The break up of the Soviet empire has been widely greeted throughout the Western world as indicating the triumph of liberal democracy over despotic socialism. Indeed, Francis Fukuyama, in *The End of History and the Last Man* (1992), asserted the very end of Hegelian history in arguing that we have seen the universal and eternal triumph of liberal democracy. This may be a comforting thesis, but the evidence about its accuracy necessarily remains in the future. What seems currently to be reigning triumphant could be the ultimate historical peak, but also it could be merely an inflection point.

Moreover, regardless of what it is that may be currently in the ascendancy, it is far from clear that it is properly called liberal democracy. Socialism of the despotic, Soviet-type seems clearly to be in retreat, not least through its inability to serve as an effective means for organizing economic activities in complex societies. To cite this retreat as testimony for the triumph of liberal democracy, however, is to adopt an unduly narrow, bifurcated view of historical options. For there is a third, robust contender: social democracy, as a kinder and gentler, though still authoritarian form of the socialism that characterized the Soviet empire. There is good reason to think that economic policy in the West is following the path of social democracy. Moreover, this path is easy to follow and hard to avoid.

This book contains a three-part examination of the theory and practice of economic policy for a liberal society. The first part (Chapters 1–2) explains how welfare economics represents an effort by economists systematically to bring intelligence and wisdom to bear on the problem of achieving good government, and to do so in a way that generally supports a liberal democracy. It has sought to do this by offering principles of navigational guidance for the conduct of economic policy in a liberal society.

The second part (Chapters 3–5) explains why welfare economics has been unable to fulfill the aspirations of its developers. Much of this inability is due to inadequate intellectual foundations. Welfare economics generally treats the economy as a simple organization and not as a complex order. It has given inadequate attention to the severe limitations on competence under which actual states must operate, as contrasted with the idealized states portrayed in formalized blackboard exercises.

The third part (Chapters 6–8) seeks to characterize an alternative approach to the subject matter of welfare economics, which can articulate reasonable guidance for the conduct of economic policy in a way that is appropriate for a liberal society. This alternative approach focuses more on the constitutional framework within which state policies are enacted than on particular policies themselves, and in so doing is related to some German-language scholarship on *Ordnungstheorie* and *Ordnungspolitik*. In this case the central concern is not whether the state is larger or smaller *per se*, but whether its activities operate to maintain and support the framework of the liberal order within which people organize their activities.

I am grateful to Charles K. Rowley, Viktor J. Vanberg, and Karen I. Vaughn for valuable advice on many of the issues addressed here, and to the Lynde and Harry Bradley Foundation for its continuing support of my scholarly efforts.

1. Intelligence, Fate, and Good Government

In *Federalist*, No. 1 Alexander Hamilton asked 'whether societies of men are really capable or not of establishing good government from reflection and choice, or whether they are forever destined to depend for their political constitutions on accident and force'. Hamilton argued that we are not prisoners of whatever it is that fate brings us, but that reflection and choice can be brought to bear on the task of achieving good government. That task was construed, in effect, as a form of social agriculture.[1]

As a problem of social agriculture, the attainment of good governance entails both normative and positive elements. Normatively, there must be some standard of desirability. Agriculture attempts to improve upon what Mother Nature offers, by imposing reflection and choice upon what otherwise would be the vagaries of fate. Among other things, it must be possible to distinguish between desirable and undesirable forms of plant life. Vegetables may be put into the category of desired plant life while weeds are not, though even here the growth of knowledge may reveal useful features or properties of what were previously viewed simply as undesirable weeds.

All of the normative wishes in the world are useless, however, without some idea of how to achieve those wishes. Squash may be preferred to ragweed, and squash in people's stomachs may be preferred to squash devoured by bugs. Without knowledge of how to restrain the bugs and weeds, however, the yield of squash for human consumption will be left to fate and chance. It is the same for social agriculture, as Hamilton noted in *Federalist*, No. 1. We may recognize that people would generally prefer to go through their lives free from fear of being preyed upon by others, whether in the form of local bandits or thugs or in the form of invasions by foreign hordes. We may likewise recognize that people may prefer to see their children grow up in prosperous, free, and peaceful environments, and not be plagued by poverty, enslavement, or war.

Mere recognition of these preferences does nothing to satisfy them. Mother Nature may herself give us islands of peace and periods of prosperity, but to move beyond her offerings and limitations requires more than wishful thinking. It requires the application of intelligence concerning the social equivalents of the principles of soil chemistry and plant genetics, so as to allow the social equivalents of the flowers and the vegetables to flourish while restraining the weeds and bugs.

This book accepts the basic normative foundations encapsulated by the general principles of liberal democracy. In so doing it affirms the central value of personal liberties, including those expressed by principles of property and contract as providing a framework for the organization of economic activity. As such, it acknowledges the normative desirability of a market economy, which is simply the abstract noun we use to characterize the network of economic relationships that arises when people relate to one another within the framework provided by the principles of property and contract.

A market economy, however, does not mean the absence of government as a locus of coercion in human affairs. There is no natural harmony among people. The potential for conflict is always latent, and the extent to which that latency remains dormant or erupts will depend on numerous things, many of them not well understood or easily controlled. In any case, governments are generally acknowledged as important institutions for maintaining social peace; however, they can also serve as instruments of repression and violence.

Government has been described well by Vincent Ostrom (1984) as representing a type of Faustian bargain. Government involves the injection of evil, the use of force over people, into human affairs. The use of this instrument of evil is countenanced because of the belief that such goods as peace and prosperity will be promoted. However fervently we may wish that the evil of force over people may be used to promote the good, we must acknowledge that it can also be used to promote the bad. The hope is that government will serve as an instrument of just war within a civil society. As with the doctrine of just war generally, government's use of force would be justified so long as the harm that was done by the misuse of government authority was less damaging than the good that was done by the proper use of that authority, recognizing all the while that no perfection is attainable.

It is one thing to state some formal doctrine of just war or proper scope of government authority. It is quite a different thing to take particular instances of warfare or government's use of force in civil society, and to determine the justice or injustice of that war or civil use of force. There may be extreme instances where near-universal agreement would be found among disinterested observers. But probably in most cases there would be considerable controversy over the application of the general principles to particular cases.

As for principles of economic policy, welfare economics has developed over this century as the branch of economics that represents an effort to think systematically about those principles. It has sought to offer a handbook or a manual for the practice of economic policy. For the most part, welfare economics has developed within a general framework of economic liberalism, in that it has sought to show how and when governmental authority should be invoked to help people to achieve more fully what it is that they themselves would like to achieve. In this regard, the spirit of welfare economics is generally consistent with the liberal theme expressed in the American Declaration of Independence: that governments derive their just powers from the consent of the governed and are instituted to preserve and protect individual rights that are logically prior to government. So, too, is it generally consistent with the similar theme articulated by Abraham Lincoln, to the effect that governments should do those things that people cannot do as well on their own, acting through ordinary market processes.

In this book I seek to relate theory and practice more fully, maintaining in the process the vision of welfare economics as aspiring to offer a handbook or a manual for the practice of social agriculture in a liberal society. The central policy construction of welfare economics is that of the *corrective state*.[2] Similar to Abraham Lincoln's famous dictum, this construction has the state undertaking a range of economic activities that there is reason to presume the individual members of society would have organized on their own, except that ordinary market institutions lacked the capacity to accommodate such self-organization.

This vision of the corrective state founders on three severe problems. One is that the knowledge that is required to implement in any practical way the programmes idealized by the corrective state often does not exist. Even the best of intentions will founder on this lack of knowledge, and to the extent this happens policy measures will represent sources of state failure and not the correction of market failure.[3] Another is that the ideal of the corrective state does not deal adequately with problems created by self-interest and human willfulness. The dominant intentions of state officials might be to promote their own interests or those of their primary supporters, which can lead to policy measures far removed from the idealizations of welfare economics.[4] The final problem is that welfare economics addresses an inappropriate object for social agriculture, the formal properties of allocative outcomes, instead of the appropriate object, the constitutional framework within which government tends to its economic responsibilities.[5]

While government may represent a form of Faustian bargain, the terms of that bargain can be shaped by the constitutional framework by which a government is put together. Similar to the theory of statistics, there are two types of errors in economic policy. One error is for the state to enact a policy measure that it should not enact, which, as shall be explained below, is a policy measure that does not promote the exploitation of gains from trade among the citizenry. The other error is for the state to fail to enact a policy measure that it should enact, in which case the state fails to promote the exploitation of gains from trade among the citizenry. In the former case the state creates political failure, while in the latter case it fails to correct market failure. An affirmation of some scope for reflection and choice maintains that the terms of the Faustian bargain can be influenced by the particular way a government is constituted; alternative constitutional frameworks can yield different mixtures of the two types of errors or state failures.[6]

A theory of economic policy, accordingly, is centrally concerned with the constitutional framework within which government governs, and is only incidentally concerned with particular policy measures. A constitution is a type of filter. No filter is perfect, in that it lets through everything that is desirable and keeps out everything that is undesirable. At one extreme, a filter might possibly let everything desirable pass through, but in so doing it will also let much that is undesirable pass through. At the other extreme, a filter that manages to keep out everything that is undesirable will also keep out much that is desirable. As with statistical theory, the greater the effort made to avoid one type of error, the greater will be the errors of the other type. A constitutional filter that more tightly protects against the enactment of policy measures that should not be enacted will also more severely restrict the enactment of measures that should be enacted.

Even as the collapse of socialism in the Soviet bloc was being widely hailed, many of those same socialist forms and principles were being enacted through democratic policies in what had been the liberal West. This is quite possible when economic policy is made through democratic processes without an appropriate constitutional framework for filtering proposed state enactments. In the present age it is surely social democracy and not liberal democracy that is in the ascendancy. This is something that can happen easily through piecemeal policy, when that policy is not guided by any framework for orientation that would maintain a liberal democracy. Liberal democracy and social democracy are easy enough to distinguish in terms of principle. Liberal democracy reflects the normative orientation that people are prior to government, and that governments exist to secure those prior individual rights. Government is a reflection of people's use of their rights, and is not a source of rights. Liberal democracy adopts the orientation that people can do as they choose without requiring state permission, provided only that they do not abridge the similar rights of other people in the process.

Social democracy represents the alternative normative orientation: government is the source of rights, and people may do individually only what they are allowed to do. Under social democracy, people must seek collective, legislative approval, save for practical considerations relating to the inability of legislatures to be involved in everything. The limitations on collectivist planning, in other words, ensure some scope for individual autonomy even if the orientation of social democracy is that collective judgements trump individual rights. The lack of omniscience means that even a despotic government will allow spheres of individual autonomy to its citizens, simply because there is no alternative. A despotic state may restrict options for individual action severely, but it cannot limit those options totally. People will be able to exercise their autonomy, save to the extent that the state decides to curb that exercise. In those instances, the state's decision will override the previous exercise of individual autonomy and self-organization.

While liberal democracy and social democracy possess starkly different points of orientation, they do share a common neighbourhood that makes it easy for economic policy to head in the wrong direction. Liberal democracy does countenance limitations on individual action when such limitations are necessary to protect the rights of other people. Social democracy similarly countenances individual autonomy to the extent that such autonomy is thought to support collectively articulated interests. While the underlying normative orientations are sharply different, particular, practical cases may sometimes seem quite similar. Indeed, this similarity has been recognized in the numerous claims that the Western democracies have evolved a *mixed economy*, with the mix referring to some combination of the orientations of liberal and social democracy, or of capitalism and socialism.

To be sure, tyranny need not be experienced through being at the wrong end of rifles and bayonets. Alexis de Tocqueville, in his chapter on 'What Sort of Despotism Democratic Nations Have to Fear' in *Democracy in America*, and perhaps in anticipation of a time when the provision of 'constituent services' would become the principal activity of members of Congress, described a form of democratic tyranny that

> would be like the authority of a parent, if, like that authority, its object was to prepare men for manhood; but it seeks on the contrary to keep them in perpetual childhood: it...provides for their security, foresees and supplies their necessities, facilitates their pleasures, manages their principal concerns, directs their industry, regulates the descent of property, and subdivides their inheritances....The principle of equality has prepared men for these things: it has predisposed men to endure them, and oftentimes to look on them as benefits.
>
> After having thus successively taken each member of the community in its powerful grasp, and fashioned them at will, the supreme power then extends its arm over the whole community. It covers the surface of society with a network of small complicated rules, minute and uniform, through which the most original minds and the most energetic characters cannot penetrate....The will of man is not shattered, but softened, bent, and guided: men are seldom forced by it to act, but they are constantly restrained from acting: such a power does not destroy, but it compresses, enervates, extinguishes, and stupefies a people, til each nation is reduced to be nothing better than a flock of timid and industrious animals, of which the government is the shepherd.

It would surely be one of the terrible ironies of the coming century should some future Herodotus record that all the while the once-liberal nations were cheering the shattering of the socialist chains elsewhere, they were shackling themselves with similar chains of their own making.

The piecemeal implementation of economic policy in a democracy leaves the terms of the Faustian bargain open to the accidents of history. To secure a greater role for reflection and choice in support of a liberal society requires a constitutional orientation that involves a rejection of the *principle* of the mixed economy that has become so second-nature in the post-war period in the Western democracies.[7] That constitutional orientation recognizes that a choice must be made between *different* principles governing economic activities and relationships, with that choice implying a limitation on the particular forms of policy measures that the state can enact. This conception was central to Walter Eucken's (1952) formulation of the principles of economic policy. A liberal democracy must entail a commitment to the principles of property and contract as organizing principles that are suitable for a self-organized society whose individual members have their own purposes, and where the state itself has no purpose that does not derive from the consent of the governed within the framework of their prior rights. This constitutional commitment, in turn, provides a more adequate handbook or manual against which particular policy measures can be assessed. It does not rule out an activist government policy, but seeks only to ensure that government policy does not subvert the fundamental principles of property and contract that undergird a liberal order.

Notes

1. For a brilliant exposition of the *Federalist* as an exercise in social agriculture, see Ostrom (1987).
2. Alternatively, Buchanan (1975) distinguishes between the *protective* and the *productive* states. The protective state secures and maintains the framework within which market transactions are organized; the productive state produces those services that could not be provided through ordinary market processes, and which often are called 'public goods'.
3. This thesis is explored in Cordato (1992) and Kirzner (1992).
4. This thesis is explored lucidly in De Jasay (1985).
5. See, for instance, Buchanan and Tullock (1962), Buchanan (1967), and Buchanan (1990).
6. For emphases on the organizational framework by which a government is constituted, as contrasted with an emphasis on the language of constitutional clauses, see Ordeshook (1992) and Wagner (1993).
7. Such a rejection is articulated in Littlechild (1978).

2.   Welfare Economics, Market Failure, and the Corrective State

Welfare economics has represented a 20th-century development in economics that has sought to explore systematically the circumstances under which governmental policies and activities might improve upon the operations of a market economy.[1] That a market economy, and not some socialist economy, was generally taken as the point of departure reveals the liberal origins of welfare economics.[2] To be sure, even in the formulations of a *laissez-faire* economy, government was consigned a role through the protection of property rights and the enforcement of contracts, as envisioned by the construct of a nightwatchman or minimal state. Welfare economics has sought to explore whether something beyond a minimal state might be justified on liberal grounds.

In a society where people accept generally liberal principles to the effect that people should be free to conduct themselves as they choose, provided only that they do not infringe upon the similar liberties of other people, a market economy is the natural form of economic organization. After all, a market economy is simply the network of exchange relationships among people that arises when those relationships are governed by the principles of property, contract, and liability. One of the primary characterizations of the state in a liberal order has been that of an umpire. The state polices the participants for their adherence to the legal rules that constitute a market economy. Such policing to enforce and maintain those constitutive legal rules is a central function of government in almost everyone's judgement.

While welfare economics asks whether there is a place for the state beyond the minimal state, this enquiry does not imply that a minimal state would be a small state or a weak state. While a minimal state would surely be smaller and more focused than contemporary states, much of the apparatus of contemporary states would be found in minimal states. A minimal state would have military forces and embassies, which would be organized as bureaucracies financed by appropriations from taxpayers. The preservation of internal peace and security would similarly require police, courts, and prisons, which would similarly involve bureaucracies and budgetary appropriations. In these activities, along with the remainder of what might comprise a minimal state, points of controversy would doubtlessly arise and the Faustian dilemma would remain in force. A treatise on the minimal state would cover a lot of material.[3]

With a market economy representing simply a network of exchange relationships among people, it is reasonable to ask whether there is any sense in which the totality of the network of exchanges that take place within a market economy exploits as fully as possible the gains from trade among market participants. If exchanges are voluntary and, hence, welfare-enhancing for the participants, is there any ground for claiming that something beyond the minimal state can represent genuine improvement as evaluated by those participants? The strongest justifications for a minimal state would argue that such gains from trade are fully exploited through ordinary market processes, leaving the maintenance of the legal framework regarding property, contract, and liability the only role for the state.

To be sure, this proposition about gains from trade refers only to some *ex-ante* set of beliefs. Things do not always work out as people plan, so those initial anticipations of mutual gain may sometimes be contradicted by actual experience. An owner of a restaurant may contract with someone to expand the size of his kitchen and dining area, in the anticipation of serving an expanded clientele. Subsequent experience, however, may show that expansion to have been a bad idea. In terms of initial anticipation, the contract between the restaurant owner and the builder involved mutual gains from trade. As things turned out, there were no mutual gains, and as a result the restaurant owner was left sadder, poorer, and possibly wiser. Short of omniscience, however, cases where actual outcomes diverge from initial anticipations will be unavoidable. Market exchanges exploit *ex-ante* gains from trade, even if those gains might sometimes be revealed *ex-post* not to have been present. The voluntary character of those exchanges would surely attest to the *ex-ante* presumption that those exchanges enhance the well-being of market participants.

Welfare economics has emerged as a field of scholarship where its practitioners have sought to explore systematically the circumstances under which government authority might be used to improve upon the operation of a market economy. One of the primary propositions of welfare economics, which is sometimes called the First Theorem of welfare economics, is that in a fully competitive economy all of the gains from trade among the participants are fully exploited. In such an economy, it would be impossible for government to increase the well-being of some people without reducing it for others. There would be no scope for government to secure gains from trade for market participants that those participants could not achieve for themselves acting through market processes and institutions.

This First Theorem might seem to provide a justification for a minimal state, save for two considerations. One concerns whether actual economies conform to the conditions of a competitive economic organization required for the First Theorem to hold. The other concerns some implications and extensions of what is called the Second Theorem. The Second Theorem states that any competitive allocation can be supported by a set of lump-sum taxes and transfers. For any distribution of initial endowments, a competitive economy fully exploits the gains from trade among the participants; however, there is an indefinite number of particular competitive allocations corresponding to the indefinite number of initial endowments. Those different competitive allocations are all transformations of one another, sustained by sets of lump-sum taxes and transfers.

While the two theorems make a nice logical package, they also reflect different normative principles and point in different directions, perhaps similar to the two parabolas X^2 and $-X^2$.[4] The Second Theorem adopts an opposing point of departure from that of liberalism and the American Declaration of Independence. It does not start from individual rights and derive government from those rights, as a means of preserving and securing those rights. Rather it starts from collective ownership, and asks for some principle to justify particular patterns of individual rights or endowments. The Second Theorem converts questions of social organization into matters of collective determination. There is an indefinite number of distributions of initial endowments that are consistent with competitive outcomes, and any justification for one initial endowment over another must either be one of historical expediency, as represented by a realization that we must start from where we are, or it must be one that transforms the first question of economic organization into a collective choice of initial endowments. In this formulation, liberal principles would be allowed to operate only to the extent they were subject to some prior, collective determination that initial entitlements are just.[5]

Unlike the Second Theorem, the First Theorem is consistent with an initial acceptance of liberal principles. At the same time, it raises a number of issues regarding the meaning of a fully competitive economy. This theorem states that if an economy is fully competitive, there is nothing beyond acting as a competent nightwatchman that the state can do to make some people better off without making others worse off. There are no unexploited gains from trade that the state can help people to achieve. A declaration that a fully competitive economy is one where gains from trade will be fully exploited is one that calls for answers about what constitutes a fully competitive economy. The preponderant share of the literature on welfare economics is concerned in various ways with possible deviations from the requirement that the economy be fully competitive. One common definition requires that prices equal marginal costs in all markets, that all markets exist, and that ignorance does not exist. In turn, each such deviation from full competition is taken to represent a case of *market failure*, with 'failure' referring to a failure for market transactions fully to exploit the gains from trade among market participants. Such instances of market failure represent cases where proper government measures could potentially improve matters by undertaking the right kinds of corrective actions. While a large number of situations have been advanced as candidates for market failure, most of these are placed into one of three main categories: external diseconomies, public goods, and monopoly.

External Diseconomies and Market Failure

Externalities refer to situations where not all people who are materially affected by a trade are required to concur in the making of that trade. In consequence, social net products may diverge from private net products, as Pigou (1932) explains.[6] That divergence can be in either direction: social net product may exceed or fall short of private net product. Most of the contemporary illustrations of externalities involve settings where social net product is presumed to fall short of private net product, or, equivalently, where social cost is presumed to exceed private cost. This is the situation commonly alleged to exist with various forms of pollution.

An automobile salvage and disposal operation may harvest junked automobiles for useful parts and then dispose of what remains by incineration and burial in a landfill. Many details of the operation of the market for salvage and disposal will depend on various scarcities and relative prices. For instance, conditions are conceivable under which a competitive market would find the owners of disposal operations buying cars, just as conditions are also conceivable under which the owners of cars would pay the disposal owners to take the unwanted cars. Which form the payment would take and at what price would depend on such things as the value of the harvested parts and the cost of disposal, including landfill space.

Regardless of the particular terms of trade between salvage owners and car owners that may characterize an actual salvage market, those market transactions might impose costs on other people who do not participate in those transactions. Among other things, the scrapped automobiles will contain zinc, lead, and other minerals that might leach into water supplies. In such settings, the market exchange between car owners and salvage owners may not incorporate the interests of the users of the water supplies that now become polluted, and which may thus require costly purification treatment before usage. The trade between the owners of the incinerator and the automobile diminish the quality of the water resources available to others; only the participants in the initial trade are not required to attain the consent of those other participants.

In such cases as these, there is always a possibility that the trade between the initial participants might not have been concluded if the disposal of discarded automobiles also required the incinerator owner to indemnify, or otherwise compensate, those people who suffered a subsequent degradation in the quality of their water supplies. After all, the final disposal of the incinerated automobiles in this case does not simply require the use of land on to which the automotive remains are deposited. For with the leaching of toxic wastes into water supplies, the disposal of automotive remains also makes use of underground water supplies.

If market transactions make use of resources possessed by people who are not parties to those transactions, market failure may result, in the sense that market transactions may fail fully to exploit the gains from trade among the participants in the market economy. This situation is illustrated by Figure 2.1. There, it is assumed that disposal services would carry a positive price, indicating that the salvage value of cars is less than disposal costs. If the only participants in the market for disposal services are the owners of disposal operations and the people who are seeking to dispose of unwanted cars, the price of disposal services would be P_p and the rate at which disposal services would be supplied is D_p. In this instance, MC_p indicates the marginal cost of disposal services that is faced by the owners of disposal opera-

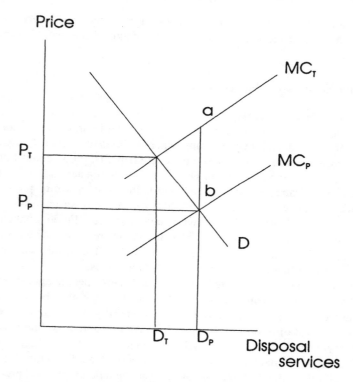

Figure 2.1   Standard analysis of external diseconomies

tions. The higher marginal cost function illustrated by MC_T illustrates the additional costs placed on users of water, who must either switch to alternative water sources or undertake costly efforts at purification and treatment.

Should these additional costs be brought to bear on the market for disposal services, the price of those services would be P_T, and only D_T of those services would be provided per time period. As illustrated by Figure 2.1, there is a failure to exploit fully the gains from trade in the supply of disposal services. At the outcome illustrated by D_p, the cost of disposal exceeds the value by ab. Alternatively, and equivalently, the value that people place on the services they must sacrifice to secure D_P of disposal exceeds by ab the value they place on those disposal services. To say that market failure *may* result, is not, however, to say that market failure must result. And even if market failure should result, it does not follow that actual state policies might correct that failure, even though an idealized policy can always be imagined that would correct that failure.

Public Goods and Market Failure

Whereas most examples of externalities involve cases where market exchanges are alleged to impose burdens on third parties, most examples of public goods involve claims where failures of markets to organize transactions involve a failure to secure benefits. Flood control provides one common illustration. The construction of a network of levies, dams, and drainage channels to control flooding in a city provides benefits to all who live in the city and who thereby suffer less flood damage than they would otherwise have suffered.[7] Flood protection cannot be withheld selectively from individual residents who do not pay through voluntary, market-like contributions. This is the essence of the market failure argument applied to public goods.

This argument is illustrated by Figure 2.2. Three people are assumed to have differing demands for flood protection, possibly because the values of their properties differ, as illustrated by d_a, d_b, and d_c. The marginal cost of flood protection is MC. As illustrated, no one person has any incentive to provide any flood protection. Yet if all three could work out a satisfactory agreement, they would all be better off by providing F of flood protection. So long as the amount of flood protection supplied is less than F, the total value that the residents place on flood protection, which is illustrated by D, exceeds the value of the services they would have to sacrifice to get added protection, MC. The rate of output illustrated by F is one where the sum of the individual payments, P, exceeds the marginal cost of flood protection. So long as output is less than F, market failure exists, as judged by the standard of the full exploitation of gains from trade.

To assert that market failure might be present does not imply that it is present. The cost of providing flood control might exceed the value that people would place upon a reduction in the risk of flooding. A failure to provide flood control in an area subject to flooding might reflect not market failure but a recognition that the cost of preventing flooding exceeds the benefit. In this case, the amount of flood protection actually provided would be characterized as being somewhere to the right of F. The state provision of a flood control project might overcome market failure, but it could also represent a form of state failure if flood control

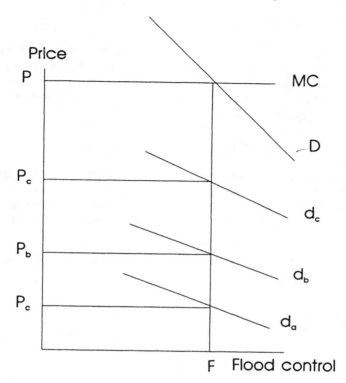

Figure 2.2   Standard analysis of public goods

is provided when costs exceed benefits. In any case, some difficult problems of knowledge arise in cases where market failure is asserted as a justification for state action. An idealized state is envisioned in the theory of public goods as a perfect substitute for those missing market transactions. However, merely to observe that the state is providing flood control is not to imply that it is overcoming market failure in the manner envisioned by the theory of public goods. It might instead be engaged in an act of state failure, either through ignorance or the force of incentive.[8] An assertion of market failure is a counterfactual assertion to the effect that there are potential transactions that could make market participants better off, but which are not made because of various limitations on market processes.

Monopoly and Market Failure

In standard economic theory, competition is a setting where the price of a product equals its marginal cost. The price of a product represents the value of a marginal unit to consumers and marginal cost represents the value of the alternative output that must be sacrificed to produce the product in question. The equivalence of price and marginal cost describes a situation where it is impossible to alter the structure of production without replacing products that consumers value more highly with products they value less highly.

Monopoly is characterized in various ways by economists. In its pure form it represents a setting where a product is produced by only a single seller. Besides this pure form, a variety of other cases are labelled as monopolistically competitive. All of these cases represent

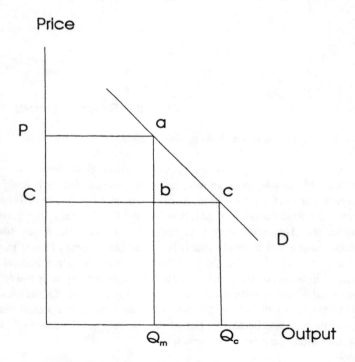

Figure 2.3   Standard analysis of competition and monopoly

situations where price exceeds marginal cost. It is this excess of price over marginal cost that represents an unexploited gain from trade, within the framework of welfare economics. Should price exceed marginal cost for some particular product, consumers value the marginal unit of that product more highly than they value the other products that they would have to sacrifice to get more of the product in question. By straightforward reasoning, illustrated by Figure 2.3, output is too low as judged by the standard of unexploited gains from trade. The monopoly price, P, exceeds the competitive price, C, and with that competitive price equalling the marginal cost of the product. One standard measure of the social loss from monopoly is the triangle abc. The monopolist captures PabC in added revenue, while consumers lose PacC in welfare. The amount abc is thus an excess burden from the monopoly.

This excess burden also indicates the unexploited gains from trade between the monopoly and its customers. At the monopoly output, the value of an additional unit to consumers exceeds the cost of producing that unit to the monopolist by the amount P–C. This excess of price over marginal cost indicates the extent to which both consumers and the monopolist could gain by instituting some programme of price discrimination, by which price is reduced below P only for units of output beyond the ordinary monopoly output, Q_m. If the existence of monopoly is accepted as legitimate, there will be gains from trade between the monopolist and its consumers, by which the consumers will accept some pattern of decreasing marginal prices that is a form of price discrimination over successive units of output. The result would be the standard competitive output, although consumers would pay more in total than they would under full competition.

To be sure, treating monopoly as legitimate leaves the owners of monopolies better off relative to consumers, as compared with what would result under full competition. Alternatively, full competition could be taken as the normative standard, which is what is typically proposed in cases of monopoly regulation, as illustrated, for instance, by the theory of natural monopoly and its regulation. In this case the monopoly price would be set at C in some manner or another. To say that the state can potentially secure gains from trade by properly restricting the exercise of monopoly power implies that the state has both the ability truly to identify monopoly power and the competence to secure the potential gains from trade for consumers. Such issues will be explored momentarily.

For monopoly, public goods, and externalities, welfare economics envisions a corrective state as acting to implement trades and transactions that ideally the participants in the market process would have brought about, but were unable to accomplish. The ideal of the corrective state, in other words, is fully compatible with a general support of economic liberalism. Welfare economics envisions the state not as replacing the market economy, but as supplementing it – as bringing about uses of resources that the participants in the market economy would have brought about themselves did they not face insuperable obstacles to those trades.[9]

Welfare economics seeks to provide a point of orientation in a liberal democracy, thereby helping to distinguish those policy measures that are compatible with the central features of liberal democracy from those measures that clash with liberal democracy. These hopes and aspirations have not been fulfilled, principally because of limitations inherent in the enterprise that welfare economics has come to represent. The conduct of actual states may diverge from that envisioned for idealized corrective states, with the result being that actual policy measures need not correct market failures, but rather may represent forms of state failure. Where an idealized corrective state secures gains from trade for market participants that those participants could not secure for themselves through ordinary market processes, in some cases the policy measures of actual states may impose networks of false trades upon market participants, which leads to a general diminution in economic well-being. The severe limitations on the capacity of welfare economics truly to serve as a handbook for social agriculture will be examined in the next three chapters.[10]

Notes

1. The relationship between welfare economics and liberalism is explored lucidly in, among other works, Baumol (1952), Little (1957), and Rowley and Peacock (1975).
2. For an explicitly socialist approach to welfare economics that acknowledges the generally liberal foundations of most of welfare economics, see Dobb (1969). Lerner (1944) has a similar collectivist point of departure, only some notion of a democratically controlled economy replaces the collectivist ideal in his formulation.
3. Adam Smith's lectures on 'Policy, Justice, Revenue, and Arms' at the University of Glasgow in the 1760s provided a framework for such a treatise, student notes from which were published by Cannan (1896). Two sets of such lectures were subsequently published by Meed, Raphael, and Stein (1978).
4. For a lucid description of the two theorems, though without any recognition of the

different normative principles they reflect, see Atkinson and Stiglitz (1980, pp. 343–50).

5. This approach of seeking to derive liberal principles from a collectivist point of departure is perhaps most closely associated with Rawls (1971, 1993).

6. The emphasis must be placed on 'may', because there is no necessity here. Externalities can exist without there being potential gains from trade among the participants, as Buchanan and Stubblebine (1962) note in their distinction between Pareto-relevant and Pareto-irrelevant externalities.

7. To be sure, they could suffer more damage in their share of the cost of providing flood protection than they would suffer from flooding. But this is a different matter.

8. Moreover, there is a greater scope for the provision of public goods through market processes than is commonly recognized in the theory of public goods, as Foldvary (1994) explains with particular reference to cities.

9. In this respect, Epstein (1985) refers to the state as engaging in 'forced transactions'.

10. For a thorough consideration of the use of welfare economics to justify state action, along with a recognition of the problems of knowledge and incentive that plagues any effort actually to do so, see the essays collected in Cowen (1988).

3. Divided Knowledge and Limited State Competence

Expositions of welfare economics typically assume that the analyst possesses knowledge that is in no one's capacity to possess. A well-intentioned administrator of a corrective state would face a vexing problem because the knowledge he would need to act responsibly and effectively does not exist in any one place, but rather is divided and dispersed among market participants.[1] Such an administrator would seek to achieve patterns of resource utilization that would reflect trades that people would have made had they been able to do so, but by assumption were prevented from making because transaction costs were too high in various ways. A corrective state that would be guided by the principles and formulations of welfare economics would be a state whose duties would exceed its cognitive capacity.

The state simply cannot obtain the knowledge that welfare economics requires it to obtain. Such an exercise as that illustrated by Figure 2.1 may have useful properties in helping to organize relevant arguments and considerations, but is of no use as an instrument of planning. For, if it were of use, planning could replace markets, which most certainly is not the case. The continual history of pathetic economic performance in the communist economies despite their general abundance of natural resources is surely compelling testimony to this point about the division of knowledge in society and the impossibility of state direction to replace market processes. Figure 2.1 gives merely a simplified representation of a far more complex reality of a real market for the disposal of unwanted automobiles.

In that real market there would be many prices and many places where disposal operations were located. In some places those operations might themselves harvest the automobiles for spare parts, while in other places the harvesting might have been done by someone other than the owner of the disposal operation. Some disposal services might pick up junked cars, while others might require those cars be delivered to the disposer's premises. Some disposal services might compact cars and then bury them, while others incinerate them before burial. And of those that use incineration, some might seek first to extract such minerals as lead and zinc before burying the remainder. Some disposal services might specialize in motor vehicles, while others accommodate a wider variety of forms of refuse.

In any case, actual markets for refuse disposal are much more complex than such constructions as Figure 2.1 would seem to suggest. It is perfectly fine to use something like Figure 2.1 as a shorthand representation of a few of the salient features of actual markets. It is not so fine, however, to seek to substitute some form of plan for the operation of actual market processes. To attempt to estimate demand and cost functions, to set price, and to assign production quotas to individual producers would create the same sort of economic mistakes and misallocations that plagued the Soviet-style economies.

This inability to substitute planning for actual market transactions extends to the development of programmes to correct alleged market failures as well. In the absence of market transactions, how is it possible to determine that market failure exists? It must be possible to determine what trades people would have made. But where would this knowledge come from? If such knowledge were available outside of market transactions, markets would be unnecessary and socialist planning could substitute perfectly for a market economy.

Market failure refers to transactions that do not occur, and with the explanation for the non-occurrence of those transactions residing in presumed limits on people's abilities to work out agreeable transactions. Market failure thus refers to something that is not directly observable. Rather, market failure is an inference that is based on certain assumptions about conditions that also themselves are not directly observable. Is a particular situation an illustration of market failure? Or is it a case where there is no problem to be overcome, because the situation represents one of ordinary scarcity? In ordinary market transactions, hypotheses about relative valuation are answered continually as resources flow into uses where people value them more highly. A plot of land might be used for raising rice or catfish. If it is presently being used to grow rice, and if someone who proposes to raise catfish is able to buy the land, the present owner of the land is agreeing that the proposed alternative use is more valuable than the present use. Market transactions reveal information about relative valuations.

Market failure can neither be verified nor falsified through observations on market transactions. From this point of departure, such scholars as Rothbard (1956) and Cordato (1992) conclude that market failure should be dismissed as a meaningful concept. There is a good deal of merit in this claim. The rate of output D_P in Figure 2.1 is said to represent market failure by comparison with D_T, because the analyst presumes to possess the relevant knowledge about transactions that would have been made in a setting of zero transaction costs. Once it is recognized that no one can possess such dispersed knowledge, it must be acknowledged that it is impossible for anyone truly to know what the D_T option would be.

It might be argued in response that policy measures that restrict output below D_P are movements in the right direction, even if they are not perfectly accurate. This response, however, cannot be asserted definitively, because without knowledge of D_T it is impossible to know whether a particular restriction of output is a movement in the right direction, from D_P toward D_T, or whether it is an excessive restriction of output to some region below D_T. In this latter case, the policy measure that restricts output may do more harm than good. In the absence of the knowledge that is in no one's capacity to possess, it is impossible truly to know whether a policy measure corrects market failure or creates state failure.

It can be granted that it is impossible to tell whether a particular policy measure truly corrects market failure, however, while still granting the usefulness of market failure as an analytical concept. It is surely reasonable to recognize the possibility that existing ownership arrangements might leave significant gains from trade unexploited, while recognizing also that those gains can be difficult to identify and easy to identify wrongly. As with the theory of statistics, two types of error are possible. A claim of market failure can be advanced when no such failure exists. Alternatively, a claim of market failure can be rejected when market failure exists.

For the most part, welfare economics is used as a means of justifying or rationalizing particular policy measures. Much of this effort goes under the heading of benefit–cost analysis. Indeed, benefit–cost analysis represents an effort to give substantive, empirical content to the formal structure of welfare economics. Every instance of alleged market failure involves a claim that the benefits of some corrective policy measure exceed the costs of that measure. In principle, it would seem possible to assess the extent to which governmental actions correct market failures by assessing the benefits and costs of those actions.

Indeed, benefit–cost analyses are conducted continually by business corporations. A brewery in considering whether to develop a new style of beer will conduct a form of benefit–cost analysis to help create an informed judgement as to whether the new beer will increase the value of the brewery. One component of benefit will be the net addition to sales that would result from the new beer, taking into account the possibly negative impact of the new beer upon sales of other beers also produced by the brewery. In any case, a projection that the new beer would be worthwhile entails a presumption that the net value to customers of the new beer exceeds the net costs of producing that beer. To be sure, anticipations may be treated harshly by reality. There is no scale of omniscience against which to compare actual choices, save that which history offers subsequently.

Just as business firms conduct benefit–cost analyses in making decisions on a wide variety of investments, so too do governments. When it comes to government, especially as characterized by the principles of welfare economics, benefit–cost analysis is conducted from the perspective of 'social profitability', as distinct from the simple profitability perspective that characterizes business firms. In the presence of externalities, choices by firms concerning the use of resources will not necessarily promote the use of resources in their most valuable employments. The social marginal cost of the generation of electricity includes the damage done by the emission of soot and sulphur dioxide, whereas the private marginal cost includes only the various resources the firm must hire to produce its output. The value people place on the marginal unit of electricity is less than the social marginal cost, which in turn implies that a change in the pattern of resource usage to one in which less electricity is produced will increase the value yielded from the same stock of resources.

So long as the output of the utility is excessive, as judged by a consideration of what would happen if the utility had to purchase the right to emit soot and sulphur dioxide, the benefit from a reduction in output will exceed the cost. An efficient curtailment of the utility's output will have taken place when the marginal benefit from that curtailment equals the marginal cost. Stated alternatively, an efficient programme of curtailment will generate the same outcome as would result if the utility made an effort to maximize its profits while counting as a cost of production the purchase of the right to emit soot and sulphur dioxide. Benefit–cost analysis thus operates within a framework of social profitability, in that it seeks to assess state programmes and policies from the perspective of the pattern of resource utilization that would have taken place under some alternative, but perhaps non-implementable pattern of ownership rights.

Any effort to assess policy options from a benefit–cost perspective inherently involves conjectures about counterfactual conditions, and hence is not amenable to empirical verification. To be sure, the same lack of empirical verifiability exists in the private sector counterpart to benefit–cost analysis. A brewery makes its choice about the introduction of a new line of beer based on judgements about future demands and conditions of production. Verification about that choice comes only later, when consumers respond to the brewery's new offering.

It is the same with government policy measures, save that there is no directly observable counterpart to a firm's measure of profitability. The standard of social profitability involves counterfactual circumstances that cannot be reduced to direct observation. If direct observation were possible, it would imply that ownership rights were differently organized, in which case market signals of profitability would be sufficient and the policy measure in question would be unnecessary.

Consider the owner of the incinerator who disposes of his wastes in a landfill, with residue from that landfill leaching into water supplies used by the brewery. In the simplest setting, either the incinerator owner would have the right to landfill his wastes as he chooses or the brewery would have a right to uncontaminated water. By the Coase theorem with well-defined, easily-enforceable property rights, which case obtained would be irrelevant for resource allocation and would affect only the distribution of wealth between the two parties. If the cost to the brewery of either purifying the water or moving to some alternative, uncontaminated location were greater than the cost to the incinerator owner of either storing his wastes elsewhere or of extracting the toxic elements in his wastes, the brewer would brew in his present location and the incinerator owner would switch to some alternative form of production. In one case the brewer would pay the incinerator owner for making the switch, while in the other case the owner would be forced to make the switch without compensation from the brewer. While the relative wealth positions of the brewer and the incinerator owner would differ between the two settings, the allocation of resources would be the same in either case.

In this simple setting, there is no need for benefit–cost analysis of any notion of social profitability, because ordinary market transactions are sufficient. In more complex settings, however, it is at least possible in principle that policy measures might correct market failures, regardless of how likely such correction might be in practice. More generally, there would be a large number of sites where wastes were deposited and there would be numerous people over a sizeable area whose water supplies might be affected by leaching of landfill contaminants into water supplies. A multiplicity of parties would be involved on both sides, and generally it would not be possible to attribute particular contamination to particular sources.

What might be at stake in this case is a proposed regulation whereby incinerator owners were required to extract such mineral residues as lead and zinc and to recycle them before depositing the remainder in landfills. The justification for this procedure might be that the reduction in contamination would be worthwhile, in that the cost of reducing the contamination through extracting and recycling the minerals would be less than the cost of doing so. Some of that benefit would inhere in the value of the extracted, recycled minerals, but the bulk of it would probably inhere in the enhanced value of the improved, less contaminated water supplies. In this case the policy measure substitutes for the market transactions that would have taken place if market processes had been relied upon exclusively. In this setting there can be no *ex-post* judgement of profitability. There is less scope for an *ex-post* assessment of policy choices than there is for business investment choices, and there may also be different patterns of incentive operating in the two settings.

As Coase (1960) explained, it is conceivable that the damage suffered by the water users was less than the gain to the incinerator owner of being able to dispose of his residues in a landfill. If the alternative to disposal in a landfill is more costly than the damage suffered by water users, the economically efficient outcome is for the incinerator owner to dispose of his residues in landfills. Coase explained that even if the users of water had enforceable rights to water free of toxic wastes from landfills, such users of the landfills as incinerator owners would be able to buy the agreement of the water users to dispose of their wastes in the landfill, despite the subsequent leaching into water supplies.

The incinerator's deposit of automotive residue in landfills clearly affects the conditions under which water is available to others. Subsequent to Coase, however, it became necessary to select between two situations, only one of which involves potential market failure. In one setting, the damage done to water users is less than the cost to the incinerator owner of some alternative form of disposal. In this case no gains from trade exist and there is no market failure. In the other setting, the damage done to water users exceeds the cost of some alternative form of disposal. In this case a market failure can be asserted, at least within the framework of welfare economics. Whether there is truly a market failure, or, indeed, whether it is possible truly to determine whether there is a market failure in any instance, is another matter.

While planning and markets may be acknowledged to represent two polar principles for social organization, it does not follow that state activity belongs exclusively to the category of planning. In idealized market situations, completely specified property rights to water would exist. A Coaseian resolution to the disposal of water would exist. Market transactions would determine such things as where landfills were located, whether they were lined, whether mineral residues were extracted and recycled after incineration, and the forms of water purification that people used.

A state planning agency clearly could not substitute for the dispersed knowledge that would be incorporated into all of these market transactions. Yet some of the information characterized by the difference between MC_T and MC_p in Figure 2.1 surely gets transmitted through political processes. Other things equal, the more severe the contamination from the leaching of toxic wastes into water supplies, the stronger will be the pressure brought through political processes to bear on the market for waste disposal. This certainly is not to say that external costs are the only source of political pressure, or even the predominate source. Yet external costs surely are a source of political pressure. The extent to which constitutional arrangements might filter through such sources of pressure while filtering out other sources shall be considered to some extent later on, though for the most part any detailed examination awaits further scholarship.

Note

1. This theme about the division of knowledge is a central feature of most of Hayek's corpus of scholarship. For a summary statement, see Hayek (1988). For a thorough treatment of the development of the Austrian tradition in economics, with which Hayek is associated, from the 1930s to the present in the United States, see Vaughn (1994).

4. Interest Groups and Biased Incentives

The mere articulation of some principle of a corrective state suggests little or no reason for the state to attempt to implement that principle. The correction of market failure envisions the state as identifying instances of market failure and then acting through a network of forced transactions to correct those failures.[1] A well-intentioned administrator of a corrective state would have a difficult problem. The knowledge that he would require to implement the missing network of exchanges would not be present. It would be necessary to use substitute sources of information. Such a benevolent authority would be optimally imperfect in bringing about a network of forced exchanges to substitute for the real exchanges whose absence was characterized by the thesis of market failure in the first place.

Why state officials should be motivated to act as well-intentioned administrators of a corrective state has rarely been addressed within welfare economics. When it has been addressed by public choice scholars, the result has been a recognition that the incentives possessed by state officials may lead them to pursue quite different policies. Actual states do not possess any selfless devotion to market correction. For the most part, actual states are dominated by the particular interests of those who occupy the principal positions of authority. The impact of these particular interests can vary greatly in their particular features. In any case the presence of such biased incentives introduces further error into the activities of the corrective state, only in this case the error operates in some systematic fashion.

Someone will knowingly locate property in a flood plain area provided that the anticipated damage due to flooding is less than the anticipated gain from location there. People can choose rationally to locate in flood plain areas and to suffer the losses from flooding when they occur, because the present value of the anticipated stream of net benefits is positive. If knowledge subsequently develops about how to reduce the severity of flood damage through the construction of dams and levies, it may be worthwhile to invest in flood control. Such investment will be worthwhile so long as the reduction in the anticipated extent of flood damage exceeds the cost of flood control. The existence of technological means for controlling flooding means that *some* investment in flood control *might* be worthwhile. It does *not*, however, mean that *any* investment in flood control *will* be worthwhile. It is quite possible that the present value of the anticipated damage done by flooding exceeds the present value of the cost of flood control. If the cost of flood control exceeds the damage done by flooding, government will not have corrected for market failure, but rather will have injected a political source of failure into the network of market transactions.

A flood control project might be provided even though the affected residents would truly evaluate the project at less than its cost, because there were particularly influential residents who did evaluate the project positively because they would receive relatively large gains and bear relatively small costs. For instance, taxes to finance a flood control project might be assessed equally against all property owners in the jurisdiction. However, only a portion of that jurisdiction might be subject to flooding. The project might well be beneficial to those particular property owners, so long as most of the cost is paid by others who do not suffer from flooding anyway. In this case the flood control project does not allow market participants to capture gains from trade, but rather transfers wealth from those taxpayers who do not suffer flooding to those whose properties are relieved from flooding.

It is well recognized by public choice scholars that democratic processes often work to concentrate benefits on beneficiaries while diffusing costs on taxpayers.[2] There might be 100,000 taxpayers, each of whom loses $10 per year to finance the flood control project. The cost of any effort to marshall opposition to the project would doubtlessly be many times greater than $10, even if it might be significantly less than $1 million. The organization of opposition would encounter the familiar free-rider problem. Successful opposition to the project would provide a public good valued at $10 for each of the 100,000 taxpayers. Any single taxpayer's contribution to the success of opposition would be small, as each taxpayer represents only 0.001 per cent of the potential opposition.

The value of the project to beneficiaries might be $600,000, concentrated on 60 landowners. With an average benefit of $10,000 and with relatively small numbers of beneficiaries, free-rider problems are more readily overcome. Hence, there is good reason to believe that democratic processes will contain incentives to enact measures that create social losses as a by-product of the private benefits they create for particular people.

Problems of biased incentive are not wholly separable from problems of incomplete knowledge. Recognition that the lack of omniscience implies a possible divergence between an *ex-ante* assessment of prospective outcomes and an *ex-post* determination of actual outcomes raises a question of fiduciary responsibility in decision making. Suppose someone thinks that a new product will make a profitable addition to a company's line because a benefit–cost analysis reveals anticipated benefits in excess of anticipated costs. This judgement is based on beliefs about the future, which cover such things as the future expenses of production and the future demands for the product. There is no way of knowing with certainty what the actual future states of these circumstances will be, so a decision must be based only on informed judgements about the future.

How knowledgeable are those judgements likely to be? Suppose the new product is, for whatever reason, a pet project of the person in charge of making the recommendation. Questions of capability aside, that person's reading of the evidence about the future may turn out naturally to be roseate. What would prevent such a reading of the evidence? For a person or for a business, the presence of a residual-claimant status creates an incentive to temper one's hopes, wishes, or prejudices because inefficient decisions will redound to the harm of the decision maker. While mistakes cannot be avoided, the system of profit and loss creates a relatively disinterested, *ex-post* check on the veracity of *ex-ante* judgements of benefit and cost.

It is different in government. The absence of price and profit information weakens the cognitive basis of a benefit–cost analysis and lessens the incentive of decision makers to pursue efficient over inefficient courses of action. There is a possible clash between the requisites for economic efficiency and the system of incentives that operates within government. While economic efficiency may result in some instances, it does not seem to be an inherent tendency within government. Business and government are similar in that the central perspective of benefit–cost analysis is equally appropriate in both settings, but they differ because of systematic differences in the information that is produced regarding the success of different choices.

Prices and profit provide information on which to base an analysis of benefits and costs in business, but this information is not available in government. Moreover, the record of actual experiences can be useful in helping to make a more informed judgement in other related instances that might arise. Additionally, the presence of an unambiguous measure of *ex-post* success (profit) serves to harness the natural tendency toward overoptimism that otherwise would almost certainly be present when someone else's money is being spent. The necessity of putting one's money on the line and of being responsible for the ultimate outcome surely has a sobering effect on the assessment of the prospects for such projects, an effect that is weakened when tax money is used in a setting where no judgement about profitability has to be faced.

If a private developer includes flood control facilities in his development, it is because he thinks it will be profitable. This judgement entails the developer's hypothesis that he thinks the benefits to consumers will exceed the costs of those facilities. If the developer is correct in his judgement, he will make a profit. With government, however, there is no direct scope for profitability to operate, so there cannot be any unambiguous judgement rendered after the fact about the value or profitability of a previous decision to commit resources to a particular use. The general usefulness of such techniques as benefit–cost analysis depends on the institutional environment within which the demand for benefit–cost analysis emerges.

In a setting in which public officials are seeking to have their agencies prosper and grow, benefit–cost analysis may well be an instrument for assisting in the selection of policies and programmes that promote that growth (Niskanen 1971). In this regard, it is perhaps curious that the application of benefit–cost analysis in government is conducted in terms of economic variables, as if the agency is seeking to maximize some indicator of social profitability or value. Votes or some other measure of political support might be a more appropriate framework around which to organize an assessment of the benefits and costs of possible programmes, at least with respect to providing information truly of interest to those responsible for making decisions. Why does benefit–cost analysis proceed within the language and categories of profit maximization when the institutional setting within which government operates is one in which the 'profits' resulting from the operation of government are non-appropriable? Perhaps projects that are shown to be inefficient by a benefit–cost analysis conducted from the perspective of social profitability would be efficient when conducted from the perspective of the interests that dominate the legislation pertaining to those programmes and projects.

Notes

1. The term 'forced transactions' is used by Epstein (1985) to convey the liberal ideal of the state acting as a reflection of individual rights to carry out transactions that those individuals would otherwise have carried out themselves, only they could not do so because of high transaction costs. To be sure, almost all of the cases that Epstein uses to illuminate his theme involve state activities that he argues violate his forced transactions ideal, and which instead represent state failure.
2. A careful textbook examination of the entire range of state activity from a public choice perspective is Blankart (1991). Olson (1987) seeks to attribute the rise and decline of nations to the degree to which they are able to withstand such processes of benefit concentration and cost dispersal.

5. Form, Substance, and Misfocused Analytics

Welfare economics seeks to offer a handbook for the systematic practice of economic policy in a liberal democracy. While this effort has generally presumed the possession of knowledge that cannot be possessed and has ignored the incentives that prevail in actual political processes, these defects are not fatal to the enterprise that welfare economics represents. There is no resolution to the knowledge problem in any exact manner, but this does not deny that some effort at approximation might be better than no effort at all. Some effort to use benefit–cost analysis to guide state policy concerning toxic wastes might be generally preferable to having no policy at all and treating water as a common property in some respects.[1]

Biased incentives may never be eliminated from politics, but agency problems also pervade the activities of market participants. The degree or extent of bias can be controlled to some extent through institutional arrangements that require some concurrence among people with differing incentives and interests, as illustrated by the principle articulated by James Madison in *Federalist*, No. 10 to the effect that no man is fit to be a judge in his own cause.

These problems of knowledge and incentive are compounded by a third, fatal problem: the inability of the formal structure of welfare economics to address the substantive issues that any handbook for the practice of economic policy must address. Welfare economics has developed purely formal categories of economic efficiency that are inadequate for the assessment of actual policy measures.[2] A market failure may be defined in terms of a divergence between price and marginal cost, but this is a purely formal definition that is not readily open to substantive implementation. An equality of price and marginal cost arises out of the logic of competitive markets, but there are no observable figures that can be examined in any particular situation to determine whether an equality of price and marginal cost actually prevails.

Among other things, cost is the evaluation that someone places on the option that must be foregone when some alternative opportunity or course of action is chosen. Price is interpersonally verifiable but cost is not.[3] Welfare economics operates with a formal logic of market failure, but it does not rely upon any substantive approach to market failure. This is shown readily by a consideration of whether the First Theorem fits modern economies reasonably well. Are modern economies reasonably fully competitive, thereby leaving relatively little scope for potential correction of market failure by government? Or do they deviate greatly from competitive standards, thereby leaving a large potential scope for the correction of market failures, even though actual governments may fail to achieve that potential?

It is not readily apparent how the formal apparatus of welfare economics can be used to address such substantive questions. To start, the goodness of fit between an analytical model and an actual situation is a judgement call that lacks a precise analytic answer. Economic models are abstract representations of some vital features of reality, they are not exact representations. Such features of the competitive model as universal price-taking behaviour are there for the sake of logic, in deriving a necessary condition for all units of output to sell at the same price. Universal price-taking is incoherent as a condition of actual economic conduct, for it would imply that prices could never change.

Such an abstract statement of necessary conditions does little to address in any substantive way whether government can improve upon market transactions as judged by the market participants themselves. There is an important difference between asserting that a model is a useful device for helping to look at reality and the quite different assertion that a model is the way reality is, or should be. The former position recognizes that models are but tools to aid in thinking about actual situations, but that those models can never apply themselves to any concrete situation. The latter position tends to confound models and reality. Price setting is a universal, inescapable feature of economic life, and yet it does not fit within the neat logic of universal price-taking. The use of a model that ignores some pivotal features of economic life to derive welfare conclusions regarding economic policy is clearly to push the use of analytical models beyond their reasonable limits.

Consider, for instance, the degree to which the full competition condition of the First Theorem fits present-day economic life. Economists have long used competition in various ways that are not easily reconcilable. Where some economists have used competition essentially as an adjective, others have used it more as a verb (McNulty 1967). Similarly, some economists have treated competition primarily as a matter of instantaneous, logical relationships while others have treated it more as a matter of historical development.

For those economists who treat competition primarily in logical fashion as an adjective, actual economies can be a long way removed from being fully competitive. For these economists, a fully competitive economy would be represented by the textbook representations in terms of there being such a large number of producers of homogeneous products that no producer could exert any influence over the price of his product by varying his production. Full or perfect competition thus becomes a polar case that has little connection with commercial life in modern society. All competition is thus imperfect in some way or another, and the potential scope for governmental action to further exploit gains from trade is wide.

With full competition taken to represent a situation where any increase in price, however slight, will lead to a full elimination of that seller's sales, imperfect competition would have to be the norm. As a purely logical matter, the conditions under which all units of a product would necessarily sell for the same price would be pretty austere, as Stigler (1957) explains. However, a formulation in terms of conditions of logical necessity need not be of overwhelming value in terms of assessing actual processes of economic organization.

An important part of competition is surely the development of new knowledge and products, and the cultivation of ways of delivering individualized and not just mass-designed products. Henry Ford has often been cited for his economical mass production by referring to how his customers could choose any colour of car they wanted so long as it was black. Automotive production today, with its incredible variety of particular offerings that entails a lot of custom-designed features tailored to the preferences of individual customers is a long way removed from the world of Henry Ford.

According to an economic theory that defines competition as an adjective and in terms of the necessary logic of price-taking, the movement from the time of Henry Ford to our present age has been one of increasing imperfection in competition. Yet consumers have never had greater ability to buy cars that fit their particular needs and desires, nor have cars ever been more reliable and dependable. There is surely something wrong with characterizing a direction of movement that everyone would surely call improvement as a movement in the direction of imperfection. And yet that is what much of welfare economics would do, in its references to deviations between price and marginal cost as representing violations of the necessary conditions for full competition. The problem in this cases lies in an inadequate conceptualization of competition in economics.[4]

These issues about the meaning of full competition create considerable controversy over the justification for various regulatory measures of government, even without considering issues of externalities and public goods. If monopoly is ubiquitous, there is much potential scope for state regulation to help people exploit gains from trade. Increasing returns present a second range of related issues. Market failure, it turns out, is a formal and not a substantive concept. It is defined conceptually as a situation where there exist unexploited gains from trade, and yet it is not clear substantively how such determinations can be made, or even whether particular policy measures would represent improvement.

For instance, arguments about increasing returns are often used to explain monopoly as a natural outcome of what might have originated as a competitive process. The welfare analytics of a comparison of competition and monopoly is a simple textbook exercise. That exercise shows the potential gains from trade from securing the competitive outcome in place of the monopoly outcome. This simple, textbook comparison, however, does not translate readily and clearly into the categories of reality. With respect to the regulation of natural monopoly, it is common to note that there are three options: leave the monopoly alone, regulate it as a public utility, or run it as a state enterprise. The latter two options are claimed to be methods for transforming the monopoly outcome into a competitive outcome, thereby securing gains from trade that would otherwise have been lost.

The world of experience, however, is not so simple as the textbook analytics would suggest. State enterprises do not seem to be paragons of enterprise and innovation. The logic of natural monopoly regulation turns out to be one where monopoly prices result anyway, as a consequence of regulatory efforts combined with rational conduct by the owners and managers of regulated enterprises (Tollison and Wagner, 1991). Among the reasons for this is that efforts to transform profits into lower prices for consumers will induce the firm's managers to develop alternative, more costly forms of production that provide benefits to managers. For instance, managers might have the firm provide ordinary $2 per pound coffee if they can take home the firm's profits, but may switch to $8 per pound coffee if regulators seek to transform profits into lower prices. Further, monopoly may often be transitory in an openly competitive market, while its demise is slowed through regulation. In other words, the First Theorem of welfare economics is a logical exercise whose applicability to reality is not easy to discern.

Notes

1. To be sure, a number of scholars would argue that the best policy is for the state to establish and maintain private ownership over the full range of water issues. As will be explained in Chapter 6, this might be the case but it is not necessarily so once it is recognized that costs are involved in any process for arranging transactions.

2. As a result, and as Streit (1992, p. 687) notes: 'there cannot exist a meaningful and operational concept of economic efficiency'. For recent efforts to incorporate more substantive concerns into welfare economics, see Prychitko (1993) and Vaughn (1995).

3. This theme is developed in Buchanan (1969) as well as in the various essays collected in Buchanan and Thirlby (1981).

4. For a careful, wide-ranging examination that points toward the construction of a more adequate conceptualization, see Kerber (1989).

6. Law and Legislation: Substitutes or Complements?

It is common to describe markets and states as representing alternative principles according to which choices regarding the use of resources are made in societies. Accordingly, economic activities can be organized either through voluntary transactions within markets or through compulsion provided by the state and its bureaucratic offices. In the case of market organization, common law rulings establish the framework of rules to which the participants adhere. When economic activities are organized through the state, the legislature is the arena within which the rules are established.

In any case, the customary emphasis is upon law and legislation, or markets and states, as substitutes for one another. The distinction between states and markets is obviously an important one, and often they do seem to represent the operation of contrasting principles governing economic conduct. However, this disjunction between states and markets may be more of a historical condition than a matter of logical necessity. Rather than representing antithetical principles of conduct, states and markets may under some conditions represent more on the order of alternative particular representations of the same consensual principle governing resource allocation.[1] This possibility shall be illustrated by two examples, one from the provision of lighthouses and one from the organization of street maintenance and refuse collection. The point of these examples is to reconsider the standard interpretation that government and the market represent alternative principles of resource allocation, with government representing the use of compulsion and the market representing voluntary organization. This reconsideration will set the stage for a rejection of the principle of the mixed economy and a policy emphasis on the constitution of economic policy in the final two chapters.

First, consider Ronald Coase's (1974) analysis of lighthouses in England. Prior to Coase, lighthouses had long served as an archetypical textbook illustration of a public good that could not be provided adequately through markets, and which led to a justification for state provision to overcome market failure. The claim of market failure was based on the argument that a lighthouse's protective beam was available to all ships that passed by and could not be withheld from those ships that would not pay for the use of that beam. Since the beam could not be withheld selectively from those ships that did not pay for their usage, the revenues a lighthouse owner could collect would be limited to voluntary contributions.

At this point, the free-rider dilemma enters. The contribution that any particular ship might make to the support of a lighthouse is a small share of the total contribution that would be required to operate the lighthouse. Regardless of whether a particular shipowner makes a contribution or fails to do so, the lighthouse's revenues will be essentially the same. With any particular contribution having an imperceptible impact on the provision of lighthouse services, people will have strong incentives to refrain from contributing to the provision of lighthouse services. As a result, lighthouses will not be supplied through ordinary market processes. To ensure that such services are provided, state provision financed through tax revenues is typically advocated.

Coase examined the actual provision of lighthouse services in the UK, and argued that, starting in the 17th century, lighthouses have been provided through market transactions and not by the state. Lighthouses were financed by tolls collected from shipowners as they brought their ships into port. Depending on the route taken by a particular ship, a number of lighthouses would have been passed. Tolls were collected based on those routes, so the amount of tolls paid by particular ships would vary directly with the amount of lighthouse services that ship was estimated to have used.

To be sure, the state had a significant presence in the supply of lighthouse services in the United Kingdom. It set the tolls and collected them from the shipowners. It also authorized the construction of lighthouses. Perhaps what the provision of lighthouses most aptly illustrates is the limited descriptive power of bifurcating forms of economic organization into states and markets. Lighthouses were provided in the UK in a market-like setting, as Coase argued. Yet the conditions and operation of that market involved the state in many ways. Lighthouses were organized as a kind of licensed and regulated public utility.

Undoubtedly, there is a general or common interest in having ships make it safely to port. No good is served by having them crash upon the rocks. An ordinary market system governed by free entry and market pricing would surely not lead to an adequate supply of lighthouse services. The method actually used in the UK placed the cost of lighthouse services upon shipowners as a form of user fee, and vested the ownership and operation of those lighthouses in private hands, though the construction of lighthouses required state permission.

An alternative form of lighthouse provision would have been direct state supply financed by taxation. Still another form would have been state supply financed by charges imposed on shipowners; this case would be closer to the system Coase described than state supply financed by taxation. There are many reasons why different particular approaches to the organization and supply of lighthouse services might have important differences, but those differences would still be rather technical and of second order significance, and certainly nothing so foundational as suggested by a dichotomy between state and market provision. Several different approaches to the supply of lighthouse services might be consistent with principles of a liberal society.

Alternatively, consider some of the changes in the methods for providing for roads and rubbish disposal in the UK starting in the 15th century.[2] Thomas (1933, pp. 40–41) reports that the Paving Act of 1431 in Northampton ordered property owners to pave and maintain the road that fronted their property. The Act provided for fines in cases where property owners failed to maintain their roads. Subsequently, this system of individual provision of roads was replaced with one of city responsibility for repairs, financed by bills sent to property owners. Rubbish disposal was handled largely by individuals contracting with suppliers to cart their rubbish to some disposal site. Eventually cities came to choose the carters to haul rubbish.

It might seem as though both paving and rubbish disposal were once organized through market arrangements, only subsequently to succumb to state provision. Such a characterization would be consistent with a principled disjunction between states and markets. That disjunction, however, does not seem to possess some logically compelling quality, no matter how strongly it might seem to apply to particular historical settings. At one time roads were maintained by individual property owners, in much the same way that property owners now maintain their lawns and driveways. There would be paving contractors on the supply side of the market, and the property owners would represent the demand side of the market for paving services. This would seem to be a privately organized market, though one where some of the rules and conditions were maintained collectively through government. People who did not maintain their portion of a road would be fined, and the money raised was used to fund road maintenance. Implicit in this process is a legal procedure by which someone files a complaint against a property owner who does not maintain his road, and in which a hearing is held and a verdict rendered. The state is intimately involved in the allocation of resources.

What about a shift to city responsibility for repairs, with bills sent to property owners? With respect to resource allocation, roads are still being repaired and with property owners paying for the repairs. There might be various reasons given for this shift in method. For one thing, there could have been a general feeling that relying upon individual complaints was costly and cumbersome for something so routine as road maintenance, and that a shift to city provision financed by property taxes would be less costly and more efficient. Alternatively, there could have been particular paving contractors who would have gained by city provision because in one way or another they wielded more political influence than other contractors. One explanation for the shift is consistent with the capture of a general efficiency advantage, while the other is consistent with rent-seeking models of market restriction. What is common to both cases, however, is a general, common interest in having roads maintained, and with there being different methods for organizing that maintenance.

It is similar for refuse disposal. In a setting where individual home-owners are responsible for taking their refuse to a disposal site, there could well be opportunities for people to specialize in carting refuse to disposal sites. In this manner the market organization of disposal services would arise. Individual residents would be on the demand side of the market, and the carters would be on the supply side. The operation of this market setting would be, and was, guided by government in many ways. For one thing, people did not have an unlimited option to let refuse pile up in their backyards. Neighbours could file complaints against people who let their refuse pile up, on the grounds of offensive odours and pests. The precedents set by such suits surely increased the demand for disposal services as the option of backyard disposal was restricted. With the growth of carters, refuse was to be disposed in approved sites and not just on the nearest vacant lot. Yet the temptation to dump rubbish on a nearby vacant lot rather than travel a longer distance to an approved site is understandable, and this clearly happened from time to time, particularly at night-time in the absence of passers-by. It is easy to imagine circumstances under which city supply of rubbish disposal might be seen as more efficient than market disposal, though it is also possible to entertain arguments about rent-seeking carters.

In either case, however, what would seem to be central was a general interest in refuse disposal, along with a recognition that there are several particular ways of accomplishing such disposal. Those ways may differ among themselves in a number of respects, and involve different types and forms of government participation, but government participation there will be in some form or another. There may be different methods adopted to handling problems of common interest. One method may be better than another for any of several reasons. But nothing cosmic is necessarily at stake in such choices regarding refuse collection and road maintenance, in that a variety of particular methods are consistent with liberal principles.

Notes

1. In this regard, see Buchanan and Tullock (1962), Backhaus (1980) and Hennipman (1982).
2. The following illustration is taken from Thomas (1933).

7.   Fallacy of the Mixed Economy

There is a sense in which the distinction between states and markets is exaggerated. This is the sense that refers to markets as representing the voluntary organization of economic activity, while states represent the organization of economic activity through force. What is exaggerated is both the voluntary component of markets and the compulsive component of states.

While a market economy does represent a network of voluntary exchanges, these exchanges are shaped and constrained by such legal rules and principles as those represented by property, contract, and liability (Eucken 1952). Not only are market exchanges constrained by legal rules, but also these rules are generally selected without the consent of market participants. For the most part those legal rules are simply accepted by market participants, who then work within those rules to conduct their economic activities. To be sure, there has been a considerable amount of scholarly controversy, of a relatively inconclusive nature, about whether common law rules might tend to promote economic efficiency.[1] Such issues need not be considered here, because all that is relevant here is a recognition that a market economy is simply an abstract noun that is used to describe economic activities that people undertake when they act within the confines of the rules of property, contract, and liability.

When it comes to democratic government, something similar would seem to exist. To be sure, government is less of an abstract noun than is a market economy, for it does represent a deliberately created organization. Yet it is a complex organization that is not subject to detailed central control, and rather represents to a large extent a network of exchange relationships within its constitutive rules (Vanberg 1992). Government is not some centrally directed entity. No one is in charge of the detailed activities that constitute the range of governmental activities. Democratic governments also possess many of the features of a spontaneous order, in that its policy measures and their implementation do not emerge so much through someone's plan or vision as through the interaction among the myriad participants whose participation is governed by the rules by which the government is constituted.[2]

Without doubt, the rules that constitute a government may be quite different from the rules of property, contract, and liability that constitute a market economy, though there is no necessity for some radical disjuncture between those sets of rules. Indeed, there is a solid tradition, much of it inspired by Wicksell (1896), in the economic analysis of state activity that seeks for some congruence between the constituting rules of market and state activity.[3]

There is also a sense in which the distinction between states and markets is underemphasized. This underemphasis is represented by facile remarks to the effect that modern economies are neither capitalist nor socialist, but are a mixture of the two. When people speak of a mixed economy, they typically have in mind an economy that operates through some mixture of two contradictory principles of operation. The market economy operates under principles of property and contract, where choices essentially represent a consensus among the informed participants.[4] In the state economy, on the other hand, compulsion and force are, or should be, the norm of operation.

The fallacy of the mixed economy (Littlechild, 1978) lies in its unstable character. Liberal principles cannot be blended with socialist principles, and the best that can be hoped for if such blending is attempted are periods of political standoff. When the state legislates according to socialist principles, it creates interest groups and incentives that operate to intensify further the pressures to undermine the liberal principles. To illustrate this theme, consider some aspects of the provision of health care in a mixed economy in relation to its provision in an economy organized under the market principles of property, contract, and liability. In a market economy people will get what they pay for, in one way or another. It would be possible to imagine a setting where all choices concerning medical matters were made within market institutions. There would, of course, be a wide variety of practices and organizations that would populate such a market. The provision of medical care would be essentially the same as the provision of any other service. A variety of insurance programmes would arise as part of the market process, as no doubt would numerous charitable organizations. People would invest in new technology, including life-extension technology, to the extent that they thought people would be willing to pay for the services offered.

Medical care would not be a 'right' of any kind. There would probably be a number of organizations that would supply medical care in a charitable manner. But the budget constraint that is inherent in life would apply as strongly to medical care as to anything else. Someone who would otherwise die without a heart transplant or without having a malignant tumour removed could have the medical procedure by having either sufficient wealth to pay the price, participation in an insurance programme (itself organized along market principles), or securing treatment from a charitable provider. To be sure, charitable providers will also face budget constraints, so there will be some limit on the number of cases they can take. Hence, there will be people who go without medical care, just as there will be people who go without drinking fine chardonnays.

In any case, life and death would be matters of personal choice and ability to pay within the framework of a market economy, as would the quality of medical care generally. Similarly, people who engage in risky occupations, dangerous leisure-time activities, or unhealthy lifestyles would bear the medical costs associated with those personal choices. If people who ride motorcycles incur higher medical costs on average than people who do not, they would bear the higher costs. If people who smoke incur higher medical costs, they would bear those costs. The provision of medical care within the framework offered by the principles of property, contract, and liability does nothing to undermine support for liberal principles.

In contrast, the collective provision of medical care in a way that violates the principles of property, contract, and liability can readily create political incentives that undermine the support for personal liberty. Consider some of the recent controversies concerning life-styles and the costs of health care, particularly those concerning the smoking of cigarettes and the drinking of alcoholic beverages. In a market economy, these life-style choices are personal matters. The actuarial evidence shows that people who smoke have lower average life expectancies than non-smokers, though there are many smokers who lead long lives and non-smokers who die early. Insurance within a market economy would charge people in different risk categories different prices that would reflect, in a competitive market, the different costs of providing service.

With collective provision, however, this changes, at least so long as collective provision does not conform to the central principles of property, contract, and liability. Suppose medical care is financed through state budgets, or, equivalently, through private insurance that is constrained by government to charge common pricing. Once this happens, a new network of interests is created. People who make relatively low use of a service form a natural interest group in opposition to those who might make relatively high use. What was once a matter of a simple toleration of different choices of life-styles under conditions where the choosers bear the costs associated with their choices, becomes a matter of political concern. In the presence of collective provision or common pricing, activities that entail above-average costs, actuarially speaking, will be shifted partially on to those whose activities entail below-average costs.

The state necessarily becomes involved as a battleground for the adjudication of disputes over personal life-styles. When economic activity was organized according to the principles of property, contract, and liability, a society could tolerate peaceably a variety of such life-styles because those who conducted more costly patterns of life would pay for them. But once the market principle of personal responsibility is abridged for some principle of collective responsibility, interest groups are automatically established that will bring personal life-styles on to the political agenda.

Capitalism, with its principle of personal responsibility, does not blend with socialism, and its principle of collective responsibility. An institutional framework represented by the principles of property, contract, and liability is a capitalistic framework for personal responsibility. Under a socialist principle, including that of contemporary social democracy, the personal responsibility represented by the principle of liability is replaced by a principle of collective responsibility. Moreover, once it is recognized that there is no such thing as a collective will and that members of a collectivity differ in many ways, to speak of collective responsibility will be always to speak of some people pursuing their interests at the expense of others.

Notes

1. A good deal of this literature is discussed in Wagner (1992).
2. Viner (1961) advances such a theme in his review of Hayek's *Constitution of Liberty*.
3. For recent efforts, see Backhaus (1992), Wagner (1988), and Backhaus and Wagner (1987).
4. Indeed, claims or hypotheses about externalities are claims that a consensus has not truly been reached because some people are having their rightful property used by others without their consent.

8. Economic Policy for a Constitution of Liberty

Returning to Hamilton's theme in *Federalist*, No. 1, the prospect for securing good government through reflection and choice requires simultaneously a normative vision about what constitutes goodness in government and a positive, explanatory understanding of the operation of political processes and institutions. The economic approach to public policy that is represented by the constructions of welfare economics represents an effort to bring reflection and choice to bear on economic policy. However, that literature ignores difficult questions of knowledge and some trying matters of political incentive that have been illuminated in recent decades by public choice scholars, and fails to address the constitutive issues of economic policy in any substantive fashion.

A market economy is not something that will form and maintain itself without some application of human intelligence. It is easy for piecemeal policy measures to generate incentives that ever more continually undermine the market economy, replacing liberty and responsibility with servility and dependence in the process. As a source of orientation for the conduct of economic policy for a liberal democracy, there is much merit to a requirement that state policy measures be congruent with the central operating features of a market economy, which entails the principles of property, contract, and liability. The point of such a constitutional orientation would be to give scope for government policy, only to do so in a way that such policy would tend to support the basic principles of a market economy, which are the principles of individual liberty, autonomy, and responsibility. The opposite principle is one that leads to differential ranks of overseers and underlings, to those who dispense noblesse oblige and those who are the recipients of that oblige.

Walter Eucken (1952) articulated a central distinction between those policy measures that conform to the central operating principles of a market economy and those measures that do not. Like many such distinctions, this one is probably easier to articulate than it is to implement. To say this, however, is not to dispute the distinction's value as a principle of economic policy. A conformable policy measure is one that is consistent with the principles of property, contract, and liability. A non-conformable policy measure is one that clashes with those principles. A policy measure that is market-compatible does not automatically create interest groups who would support a restriction of liberty. Policy measures that are incompatible with the principles of property, contract, and liability do create interest groups that would add their weight to further restrictions in liberty.[1]

By way of illustration of this distinction, Eucken (1952, pp. 267–8) offered a comparison between a tariff, which is consistent with the principles of a market economy, and a quota, which is not. To be sure, the theory of international trade postulates a central equivalence between tariffs and quotas, and in advancing that equivalence as a central point of departure the distinction between Eucken's approach and that of traditional welfare economics is rendered transparent. The first-order equivalence of tariffs and quotas follows as a straightforward blackboard exercise. In what would otherwise be an open competitive market, suppose a 50 per cent tariff is imposed on the importation of bicycles. With imported bicycles becoming more expensive after the tariff, some people will shift their purchases from imported to domestically produced bicycles.

Suppose the tariff were to reduce the sale of imported bicycles by 50 per cent. It might seem as though a quota that limited imports to 50 per cent of their pre-quota level would accomplish the same thing as the tariff. In terms of an abstract model where all units are homogenous and conditions of demand and supply are presumed to be known, this would be so under the postulated circumstances. Under real conditions the tariff and the quota would be different, not least because the tariff leaves allocative outcomes to be determined by the market principles of property, contract, and liability, while the quota uses planning principles of force and venality in the determination of allocative outcomes.

The 50 per cent tariff applies to all bicycles, as a general tax on all purchases of imported bicycles. To be sure, any tax creates incentives for avoidance and evasion whose intensity varies directly with the size of the tax. The higher the tax on imported bicycles, the stronger will be the incentive for people to smuggle bicycles and the more fully people will seek to discover and exploit such interpretative issues as what truly constitutes an imported bicycle when only part of the bicycle is foreign made. The more heavily market transactions are taxed, the more strongly people will seek to substitute transactions that bypass ordinary market channels. This is true for all taxation, and comprises the reason why smuggling and other forms of tax evasion are at least as much problems of excessively harsh taxation as problems of inadequate law enforcement.

Whatever the rate of tariff, however, ordinary market processes are used to determine particular allocative outcomes. In the absence of omniscience there is no way to know what the exact reduction will be in the coming years as a consequence of a 50 per cent tariff on bicycles. The actual amount of that reduction, as well as the way that that reduction is distributed among the various makes and brands of bicycles will be determined through the interplay of such market processes as producers deciding what to do in response to the tariff and consumers deciding individually how to react to the various producer offerings. Market outcomes are determined in an openly competitive process where buyers are able to buy the bicycles they most prefer and producers are able to choose their prices and product offerings, and with the tariff simply serving as information to inform producer choices.

In sharp contrast, a quota replaces market principles with planning principles. In the case of a quota on bicycles, a prior decision must be made to restrict the importation of bicycles to some explicit amount. It might simply be the case that total imports for the coming year are restricted to 50 per cent of what they were last year, or, alternatively, to 50 per cent of what they would otherwise have been projected to be for this coming year. In either case, or for any other method of determining quotas, market principles are expressly violated. Neither producers nor consumers are allowed to choose their best responses in light of some tax on market transactions. Rather, market processes are blocked, and a state-determined outcome is set in its place.

A quota cannot stop simply with a declaration that only a certain number of bicycles can be imported, say half of what were imported last year. This would be possible only if there was one foreign source of imported bicycles. Almost invariably there are many competitive sources of imported products. For a quota to be effective, the state must shift to a system of import licences whereby the state determines what share of a quota is granted to different foreign sellers.[2] Who produces what items for import, and in what amount, is determined not through the choices of buyers and sellers within market processes, but is determined by state officials.

With the rejection of open market processes, quotas also increase the scope for venality. Which foreign producers shall sell in the domestic market, and to what extent, do not emerge out of some decentralized market process, but are dictated by some government agency. Favourable decisions can be highly valuable, just as unfavourable decisions can be highly costly. As the economic theory of rent-seeking explains in various ways, there will tend to be an indirect market for such decisions. In some cases and places, those decisions may be made by bribery, sometimes in the open but more commonly in secret. In other cases they might be made on the basis of judgements about good character, and with the goodness of character demonstrated by such things as contributions to electoral campaigns or political action committees, through the hiring of particular legal or lobbying firms, or through the mounting of public relations campaigns. Regardless of the particular forms that arise, quotas involve the sacrifice of property and contract as allocative measures for alternative measures that violate the liberal principles of a market economy.

The distinction between conformable and non-conformable measures, if treated as a constitutional requirement for economic policy, might well serve as a kind of constitutional compass.[3] Starting from a normative affirmation of the central principles of a liberal society, such a compass would declare that a wide range of policy measures are open to the state, subject to the limitation that the particular content of those measures cannot violate the principles of property, contract, and liability. Where one state could refuse to engage in health care in any manner, another could mandate that people must participate in some programme of health insurance. The state could not, however, regulate insurance programmes so as to require some form of community rating, whereby actuarial experience is ignored and contractual principles of open competition are violated.

In this manner, such a limitation on the possible domain of policy measures would perhaps restrict some of the problems of time inconsistency and path dependency that might otherwise operate to produce a degeneration of liberal democracy through liberal democratic processes. To be sure, questions of interpretation concerning the requirement that policy measures conform to the principles of property, contract, and liability would arise. Those interpretative questions would surely be no more difficult than those that surround First or Fifth Amendment interpretation these days. Moreover, the intensity of interests in measures that are hostile to liberal principles and which are supported by policy measures that violate repeatedly the principles of property, contract, and liability will not be offset or neutralized simply through intellectual articulation. To understand how liberal democratic regimes can enact policy measures that not only violate liberal principles but also create political pressures to undermine those principles further is surely a valuable component in any arsenal of weapons for maintaining a liberal system of governance. But more than this is necessary, though to note this raises a variety of issues of constitutional order that are central to the on-going body of scholarship that constitutes constitutional political economy.[4]

Notes

1. This is not to deny the central point about the prisoner's dilemma formulation, whereby it is rational in individual cases to support market restrictions even though the general outcome may be pretty much universally harmful. Those pressures for people to seek market restrictions are always present. However, the creation of market-incompatible policy measures creates further incentives for interest group processes to operate in market-restricting fashion.
2. Alternatively, and more recently, quotas have been replaced by what are called voluntary export restraints (VERs). With VERs, the foreign government determines how a quota is to be met from among its producers.
3. That this approach to economic policy is broadly consistent with the recent literature on constitutional political economy is explained in Vanberg (1988) and Leipold (1990).
4. My own survey of this scholarship in a manner complementary with the themes explored in this essay is Wagner (1993).

References

Atkinson, A.B. and Stiglitz, J.E. (1980), *Lectures on Public Economics*, New York: McGraw-Hill.

Backhaus, J. (1980), 'The Pareto Principle', *Analyse & Kritik*, **2** (2), 146–71.

Backhaus, J. (1992), 'The State as a Club: A Perspective for Public Finance in a Prosperous Democracy', *Journal of Public Finance and Public Choice*, **10**, 3–16.

Backhaus, J. and Wagner, R.E. (1987), 'The Cameralists: A Public Choice Perspective', *Public Choice*, **53**, 3–20.

Baumol, W.J. (1952), *Welfare Economics and the Theory of the State*, London: G. Bell and Sons.

Blankart, C.B. *Öffentliche Finanzen in der Demokratie*, Munich: Franz Vahlen.

Buchanan, J.M. (1967), *Public Finance in Democratic Process*, Chapel Hill: University of North Carolina Press.

Buchanan, J.M. (1969), *Cost and Choice*, Chicago: Markham.

Buchanan, J.M. (1975), *The Limits of Liberty*, Chicago: University of Chicago Press.

Buchanan, J.M. (1990), 'The Domain of Constitutional Economics', *Constitutional Political Economy*, **1**, Winter, 1–18.

Buchanan, J.M. and Stubblebine, W.C. (1962), 'Externality', *Economica*, **29**, August, 371–84.

Buchanan, J.M. and Thirlby, G.F. (eds) (1981), *LSE Essays on Cost*, New York: New York University Press.

Buchanan, J.M. and Tullock, G. (1962), *The Calculus of Consent*, Ann Arbor: University of Michigan Press.

Cannan, E. (ed.) (1896), *Lectures on Justice, Policy, Revenue and Arms, delivered in the University of Glasgow by Adam Smith*, Oxford: Oxford University Press.

Coase, R.H. (1960), 'The Problem of Social Cost', *Journal of Law and Economics*, **3**, October, 1–44.

Coase, R.H. (1974), 'The Lighthouse in Economics', *Journal of Law and Economics*, **17**, October, 357–76.

Cordato, R.E. (1992), *Welfare Economics and Externalities in an Open Ended Universe: A Modern Austrian Perspective*, Dordrecht: Kluwer Academic Publishers.

Cowen, T. (ed.) (1988), *The Theory of Market Failure: A Critical Examination*, Fairfax, Va.: George Mason University Press.

De Jasay, A. (1985), *The State*, Oxford: Basil Blackwell.

Dobb, M. (1969), *Welfare Economics and the Economics of Socialism*, Cambridge: Cambridge University Press.

Epstein, R.A. (1985), *Takings: Private Property and the Power of Eminent Domain*, Cambridge, Mass.: Harvard University Press.

Eucken, W. (1952), *Grundsätze der Wirtschaftspolitik*, Tubingen: J.C.B. Mohr.

Foldvary, F. (1994), *Public Goods and Private Communities*, Aldershot: Edward Elgar.

Fukuyama, F. (1992), *The End of History and the Last Man*, New York: Free Press.

Hayek, F.A. (1988), *The Fatal Conceit*, Chicago: University of Chicago Press.

Hennipman, P. (1982), 'Wicksell and Pareto: Their Relationship in the Theory of Public Finance', *History of Political Economy*, **14** (1), 37–64.

Kerber, W. (1989), *Evolutionäre Marktprozesse und Nachfragemacht*, Baden-Baden: Nomos Verlagsgesellschaft.

Kirzner, I.M. (1992), 'Welfare Economics: A Modern Austrian Perspective', *The Meaning of Market Process*, London: Routledge.

Leipold, H. (1990), 'Neoliberal Ordnungstheorie and Constitutional Economics', *Constitutional Political Economy*, **1**, 47–65.

Lerner, A.P. (1944), *The Economics of Control*, New York: Macmillan.

Little, I.M.D. (1957), *A Critique of Welfare Economics*, 2nd ed., Oxford: Oxford University Press.

Littlechild, S.C. (1978), *The Fallacy of the Mixed Economy*, London: Institute of Economic Affairs.

McNulty, P.J. (1967), 'A Note on the History of Perfect Competition', *Journal of Political Economy*, **75**, August, 395–9.

Meek, R.L., Raphael, D.D., and Stein, P.G. (eds) (1978), *Adam Smith: Lectures on Jurisprudence*, Oxford: Oxford University Press.

Niskanen, W.A. (1971), *Bureaucracy and Representative Government*, Chicago: Aldine.

Olson, M. (1987), *The Rise and Decline of Nations*, New Haven, Conn.: Yale University Press.

Ordeshook, P.C. (1992), 'Constitutional Stability', *Constitutional Political Economy*, **3**, Spring, 137–75.

Ostrom, V. (1984), 'Why Governments Fail: An Inquiry into the Use of Instruments of Evil to Do Good', in J.M. Buchanan and R.D. Tollison (eds), *The Theory of Public Choice II*, Ann Arbor: University of Michigan Press.

Ostrom, V. (1987), *The Political Theory of a Compound Republic*, 2nd ed., Lincoln: University of Nebraska Press.

Pigou, A.C. (1932), *The Economics of Welfare*, 4th ed., London: Macmillan.

Prychitko, D.L. 'Formalism in Austrian-School Welfare Economics: Another Pretense of Knowledge?', *Critical Review*, **7**, Fall, 567–92.

Rawls, J. (1971), *A Theory of Justice*, Cambridge, Mass.: Harvard University Press.

Rawls, J. (1993), *Political Liberalism*, New York: Columbia University Press.

Rothbard, M.N. (1956), 'Toward a Reconstruction of Utility Theory', in Mary Sennholz (ed.), *On Freedom and Free Enterprise: Essays in Honor of Ludwig von Mises*, Princeton, NJ: Van Nostrand.

Rowley, C.K. and Peacock, A.T. (1975), *Welfare Economics: A Liberal Restatement*, Oxford: Martin Robertson.

Stigler, G.J. 'Perfect Competition, Historically Contemplated', *Journal of Political Economy*, **65**, February, 1–17.

Streit, M.E. (1992), 'Economic Order, Private Law and Public Policy: The Freiberg School of Law and Economics in Perspective', *Journal of Institutional and Theoretical Economics*, **148**, 675–704.

Thomas, J.H. (1933), *Town Government in the Sixteenth Century*, London: George Allen & Unwin.

Tollison, R.D. and Wagner, R.E. (1991), 'The Logic of Natural Monopoly Regulation', *Eastern Economic Journal*, **17** (4), 483–90.

Vanberg, V. (1988), '"Ordnungstheorie" as Constitutional Economics – The German Conception of a "Social Market Economy"', *ORDO*, **39**, 17–31.

Vanberg, V.J. (1992), 'Organizations as Constitutional Systems', *Constitutional Political Economy*, **3**, Spring, 223–53.

Vaughn, K.I. (1994), *Austrian Economics in America*, Cambridge: Cambridge University Press.

Vaughn, K.I. (1995), 'Should There Be an Austrian Welfare Economics?', in Peter Boettke and Mario J. Rizzo (eds), *Advances in Austrian Economics*, II, Greenwich, Conn.: JAI Press.

Viner, J. (1961), 'Hayek on Freedom and Coercion', *Southern Economic Journal*, 27, July, 230–36.

Wagner, R.E. (1988), 'The Calculus of Consent: A Wicksellian Retrospective', *Public Choice*, **56**, 153–66.

Wagner, R.E. (1992), 'Crafting Social Rules: Common Law vs. Statute Law, Once Again', *Constitutional Political Economy*, **3**, Fall, 381–97.

Wagner, R.E. (1993), *Parchment, Guns, and Constitutional Order*, Aldershot: Edward Elgar.

Wicksell, K. (1896), *Finanztheoretische Untersuchungen nebst Darstellung und Kritik des Stuerwesens Schwedens*, Jena: Gustav Fischer.

Index